Clickbait capitalism

Manchester University Press

Clickbait capitalism

Economies of desire in the twenty-first century

Edited by

Amin Samman and Earl Gammon

MANCHESTER UNIVERSITY PRESS

Published by Manchester University Press
Oxford Road, Manchester M13 9PL

www.manchesteruniversitypress.co.uk

British Library Cataloguing-in-Publication Data
A catalogue record for this book is available from the British
Library

ISBN 978 1 5261 6816 0 hardback
ISBN 978 1 5261 9155 7 paperback

First published 2023
Paperback published 2025

The publisher has no responsibility for the persistence or
accuracy of URLs for any external or third-party internet
websites referred to in this book, and does not guarantee
that any content on such websites is, or will remain, accurate
or appropriate.

EU authorised representative for GPSR:
Easy Access System Europe – Mustamäe tee 50,
10621 Tallinn, Estonia
gpsr.requests@easproject.com

Typeset by Newgen Publishing UK

Contents

Contributors

Cheolung Choi is Lecturer in International Cultural Studies at the Soonchunhyang University, South Korea. His research interests span cultural and political economy, critical social theory, and economic anthropology. He has published several journal articles on finance and financialisation.

Earl Gammon is Senior Lecturer in Global Political Economy at the University of Sussex, UK. His research draws on Freudian and post-Freudian depth psychology in exploring the unconscious of political-economic life. His recent work integrates insights from affective neuroscience in elucidating the role of social institutions in emotional regulation.

Sandy Brian Hager is Senior Lecturer in International Political Economy at City, University of London, UK. He is the author of *Public Debt, Inequality, and Power: The Making of a Modern Debt State* (University of California Press, 2016).

Max Haiven is Research Chair in Culture, Media, and Social Justice at Lakehead University, Canada. His books include *Revenge Capitalism* (Pluto, 2020), *Art After Money, Money After Art* (Pluto, 2018), *Crises of Imagination, Crises of Power* (Zed, 2014), and *Cultures of Financialization* (Palgrave Macmillan, 2014).

Aris Komporozos-Athanasiou is Associate Professor of Sociology at the UCL Social Research Institute, UK, where he leads the Sociology and Social Theory Research Group. He is the author of *Speculative*

Communities: Living with Uncertainty in a Financialized World (University of Chicago Press, 2022).

Lynne Layton is part-time faculty in Psychology at Harvard Medical School and a supervising psychoanalyst at the Massachusetts Institute for Psychoanalysis, USA. Her books include *Who's That Girl? Who's That Boy? Clinical Practice Meets Postmodern Gender Theory* (Routledge, 2004) and *Toward a Social Psychoanalysis: Culture, Character, and Normative Unconscious Processes* (Routledge, 2020).

Jernej Markelj is Lecturer in New Media and Digital Culture at the University of Amsterdam, the Netherlands. His research navigates the intersection of media and affect in order to investigate themes of contagion, addiction, and control. Jernej's research has been published in edited books, such as *Deleuze, Guattari and the Schizoanalysis of the Global Pandemic* (Edinburgh University Press, 2023) and in academic journals like *Convergence* and *The Journal of Media Art Study and Theory*.

Ludovico Rella is a postdoctoral researcher at the University of Durham, UK, working on the socio-political and material dimensions of contemporary digital technologies. His research has been published in the *Journal of Cultural Economy*, *Frontiers in Blockchain*, and the Second Edition of the *International Encyclopaedia of Human Geography* (2019).

Emily Rosamond is Senior Lecturer in Visual Cultures at Goldsmiths, University of London, UK. Her recent publications have appeared in *Theory, Culture & Society*, the *Journal of Cultural Economy*, the *Journal of Aesthetics & Culture*, and *Finance and Society*. Her first monograph, *Reputation Warfare: Contested Credibility in Online Platforms*, is forthcoming with Zone Books.

Amin Samman is Senior Lecturer in the Department of International Politics at City, University of London, UK, and author of *History in Financial Times* (Stanford University Press, 2019). He is co-founder and lead editor of the journal *Finance and Society*, as well as co-founder of the Finance and Society Network (FSN).

Stefano Sgambati is Senior Lecturer in International Political Economy at City, University of London, UK. His research explores the theory, history, and politics of money. He is especially interested in the study of contemporary global banking and other forms of financial leverage, and how the latter shape class and inequality.

Japhy Wilson is Lecturer in International Political Economy at the University of Manchester, UK. His research concerns the inter-twining of space, power, and ideology in the political economy of capitalist development. He has published in journals in the fields of human geography, political economy, and development studies. He is the author of *Jeffrey Sachs: The Strange Case of Dr Shock and Mr Aid* (Verso, 2014) and co-editor with Erik Swyngedouw of *The Post-Political and Its Discontents: Spaces of Depoliticisation, Spectres of Radical Politics* (Edinburgh University Press, 2014).

Noam Yuran is Senior Lecturer in the Graduate Program of Science, Technology, and Society at Bar-Ilan University, Israel. He is the author of *What Money Wants: An Economy of Desire* (Stanford University Press, 2014) and is currently working on a manuscript about the sexual economy of capitalism.

Preface

The working title for this book was *Libidinal economies of contemporary capitalism*. One of the reasons we changed it is because there is something deeply anachronistic about the term 'libidinal economy'. To anyone outside a small group of initiates, it says more about the history of capitalism than it does its cutting edge. The other reason we changed it was to capture your attention. The notion of 'clickbait' speaks directly to the intersection of money, technology, and desire, suggesting a cunning ruse to profit from unsavoury inclinations of one kind or another (outrage, voyeurism, fear of missing out, *Schadenfreude*). This kind of trick usually ends in disappointment. We hope that is not the case with this book, which is more about the economies of desire taking shape around digital technology and finance than it is about clickbait per se. The discussion of libidinal economy in the Introduction makes this clear and is intended to provide a bridge between the sets of concerns typically indicated by each term.

The book has its origins in an online workshop ('Libidinal economies of contemporary capitalism', April 15–16, 2021). Many of the chapters collected here were presented in draft form at this workshop, where they benefitted from intense but generous discussion over two days. We would like to thank everyone who attended the workshop, including Johannes Bruder, Antonia Hernández, Solange Manche, Alice Pearson, and Farwa Sial.

Pulling everything together and turning the workshop proceedings into this book was made possible by the Leverhulme Trust. Amin Samman would like to thank the trust for awarding him a research fellowship ('Economies of desire in the twenty-first century', Leverhulme Research Fellowship 2022).

We would also like to thank a number of colleagues, including Sandy Brian Hager and Stefano Sgambati, who provided much-needed encouragement during the early stages of the process, and Elke Schwarz, who offered advice and suggestions regarding the Introduction and Conclusion. Two reviewers gave crucial input for which we are grateful. We also owe a special thanks to Tom Dark, formerly of Manchester University Press, for taking on the project with such enthusiasm. The team we have since worked with have been equally great collaborators, and we wish to express our gratitude to Laura Swift and Shannon Kneis in particular.

Introduction: The desire called libidinal economy

Amin Samman

In the 2019 Netflix documentary *FYRE: The Greatest Party That Never Happened*, a wealthy New York investor reveals how far he was willing to go in order to keep the show on the road. Truckloads of Evian water had been held at customs on the island of Great Exuma in the Bahamas and, without the cash needed to pay the duty, he would prostitute himself to secure the release of the shipment in time for the arrival of the first festivalgoers. Billed as 'Woodstock for millennials', the exclusive event was promoted through state-of-the-art social media marketing, including enigmatic orange tiles posted on Instagram by celebrity supermodels and influencers, carefully designed to arouse the interest of the target market. Later, this screen would be lifted to reveal vivid footage of the models in swimsuits, glistening in the tropical sun, on yachts and pristine beaches, flirting with each other, and, at one point, cavorting with a giant hairy pig. 'We're selling a pipe dream to your average loser', said festival founder Billy McFarland as he goaded the models into the water for one more scene.[1] The event was a spectacular failure and McFarland would end up in jail on counts of wire fraud related to the festival.[2] In some ways, Fyre Festival was a classic pyramid scheme of the kind made famous in the financial sector by Charles Ponzi, as it later emerged that McFarland was paying back initial investors with the proceeds from fresh rounds of fundraising. Only, in this instance the scam was not just fuelled by greed or lust for money on the part of investors; it was also fuelled by the fantasies of thousands of aspirational twenty-somethings, fantasies of sensuous luxury, bikinis and martinis, sex on the beach. 'Blowjobs for Evian.'

A cheap trick, you might be thinking. Surely Fyre Festival is too perfect a scandal, too overtly sexualised a Ponzi scheme for this to work as a slogan for capitalism today; not everyone is in the business of prostitution. This is certainly the case, but the phrase nevertheless works as the key to a broader configuration of economy and desire. As one journalist at *The New Republic* pointed out, 'Blowjobs for Evian' was ultimately the punchline for a documentary produced by the very same media company, FuckJerry, who made the infamous promotional videos for Fyre in the first place.[3] By twisting the story of Fyre Festival around this pornographic soundbite, FuckJerry not only wrote itself out of the debacle; it also profited for a second time by trafficking in more or less thinly veiled allusions to fellatio. That it made yet more money on the way down simply means it was on the top of the pyramid, not that it was the only one who benefited. It was in fact just one of countless media, tech, and finance companies involved in the scam, which accordingly is less a 'scam' in the conventional sense than it is the signature of contemporary capitalism at its cutting edge. Fintech writer Dan Murphy put it best in a Twitter exchange with FT Alphaville's Izabella Kaminska in early 2019, coining a phrase that would eventually become the title for an ongoing FT Series: 'The entire economy is Fyre Festival'.[4]

The *Financial Times* is known for its moderate views, and its uptake of this second, more polite slogan for contemporary capitalism represents an attempt to attribute the perverse economics of the moment to the growing pains of a new 'new economy', not unlike those that characterised the birth of e-commerce in the late 1990s. But as Erik Davis already noted back in 2004, shortly after the dot-com bubble burst, the confluence of neoliberal economics with the cult of technology unleashed hectic traffic between the real and the imaginary, giving rise to a 'deregulated reality' in which fantasies are a primary fuel for the prevailing regime of economic growth, the source of its profits, rent, capital gains, and so on.[5] The bizarre has only become more routine since. Elon Musk's escapades with SpaceX and the unveiling of his Cybertruck in 2019, the cryptocurrency frenzy of 2020, the NFT craze of 2021 – these are not aberrations; they are simply the most publicly visible aspects of an otherwise overlooked, subterranean economy of desire. Elsewhere, away from the media blaze, desire does its work behind the scenes, in our everyday relation to money, to status, inequality, employment, and much, much more.

In this context, the fundamental wager of 'libidinal economy' is that contemporary capitalism can be fruitfully engaged through the lens of desire or 'libido'. This wager plays out across two related registers: the actual and the theoretical. On the side of actuality is the everyday of economic life, which, as we have just seen, increasingly appears to be organised not simply through hardnosed calculations of cost and benefit, but also via a range of unconscious processes and psychic drives. The theoretical project of libidinal economy is to bring these latter considerations to bear on economic analysis, to map 'the flows of desire, the fears and anxieties, the loves and the despairs that traverse the social field', as Foucault so memorably put it in the preface to Deleuze and Guattari's *Anti-Oedipus*.[6] It was Lyotard, however, in his book *Libidinal Economy*, who underlined the impossibility of ever completing such a process, and our ambition for this edited volume takes his point seriously. If 'every political economy is libidinal', then both the concepts and institutions of contemporary capitalism should be read as vital aspects of its psychic life.[7] Our aim is to develop such a reading from within the transits of capital today, no matter how treacherous or compromised such a task may turn out to be; to trace the psychological currents that underwrite the political and economic order of our times and to connect these, however provisionally, to capitalism's ongoing social reproduction. From online paranoia and job market nihilism to the morbid accumulation of symbolic power and the ecstatic mania of the crypto boom – these exude the unconscious of capitalism we seek to reveal, the recursive forms of psychological capture and release that keep its libidinal economies running.

By way of introduction, this chapter develops a preliminary account of the relations between libidinal economy and capitalism in three ways. First, it positions libidinal economy at the intersection of economic and psychological thought. Second, it relates the development of libidinal-economic thought to the historical development of capitalism. Third, it emphasises the role of libidinal dynamics in the social reproduction of contemporary capitalism. It concludes by briefly outlining the arguments put forward in each of the book's subsequent chapters.

Libidinal economy

What is 'libidinal economy?' A notoriously slippery couplet and much maligned too, connoting sex-obsessed psychoanalysis for some, decadent high-theory for others. Both associations are of course valid. The phrase has its origins in Freud's theory of psychical energy, or 'libido', and it underwent a decisive transformation during the mid-twentieth century as French intellectuals sought to stage an encounter between the ideas of Freud and Marx. 'Libidinal economy' might therefore be understood in modern scientific terms as marking out an intermediary space between psychoanalysis and political economy or psychology and economics. But the story of libidinal economy stretches further back than Freud, entailing a circulation of metaphors between a much wider range of discourses. The best way to approach a definition of 'libidinal economy' is through a discussion of each of these perspectives in turn.

From a scientific perspective, 'libidinal economy' is a radical hypothesis about both the human mind and the social or economic world. Benjamin Noys has recently put this in terms of the two key axioms of libidinal economy: 'one, every economy is libidinal, and two, every libido is economic'.[8] The first axiom says that economy is a matter of 'libido' or desire, rather than simply labour, production, exchange, or what have you, and that to not consider economy in terms of desire is to fail to understand economy altogether. As Noys points out, this is no longer a particularly difficult position to maintain – who does not already know, at some level, that capitalism runs on desire, not simple need or preferences? In fact, conventional economic theory has long held that we are pleasure-seeking, desiring subjects; the source of division has always been the question of from where our desires spring and with whose interest they are aligned. This brings us to the second axiom, which amounts to a much more controversial claim about the structure of the human psyche and its relation to social order. To say that 'every libido is economic' is to suggest that the mind functions as an apparatus or machine, fuelled by erotic energy ('libido') or a broader range of psychic drives (towards life, towards death, and so on). Many have disagreed with this idea, which is the hallmark of the Freudian tradition, but others – notably those influenced by Marxist thought – have instead pushed it even further.

Freud's vision is well captured by a famous passage in *The Interpretation of Dreams*, in which he draws an analogy between the psychological production of dreams and the material production of commodities.

> A daytime thought may very well play the part of *entrepreneur* for a dream; but the *entrepreneur*, who, as people say, has the idea and the initiative to carry it out, can do nothing without capital; he needs a *capitalist* who can afford the outlay, and the capitalist who provides the psychical outlay for a dream is invariably and indisputably, whatever may be the thoughts of the previous day, *a wish from the unconscious*.[9]

Here Freud suggests a number of themes that would go on to define classical psychoanalysis, including a theory of the unconscious, the concept of a mental apparatus that processes libidinal energy, and the notion that repressed desire may play out in unexpected ways (dreams, neurotic symptoms, pathological behaviour).[10] But with the analogy itself, he also reveals the centrality of an economic point of view to his vision, according to which libido is a resource that must be allocated among competing ends, sometimes 'saved' or 'spent', other times 'invested' in ideas, in group forms, or in the social body more generally.[11] Freud therefore combines energetics with economics in much the same way that captains of industry did during his time; his domestic economy of the mind mirrors a growing industrial economy of machines.

Later Marxists would of course pick up on this, taking the historical context for Freud's metaphor more seriously as a structuring force for individual and collective desire. The capitalist unconscious is the effect of a particular organisation of desire, as Deleuze and Guattari argued. Yet their concepts were no less reliant on a language of machines ('desiring-machines', 'desiring-production', 'the civilised capitalist machine', and so on). We will return to these ideas in a moment. For now, simply note how the use of figurative language calls the axiomatic perspective on libidinal economy into question. If 'libidinal economy' is a space of thought where economy appears through the lens of desire and desire through the lens of economy, then the moment of metaphor is inevitable. Indeed, the entire project of libidinal economy can be understood as a story of endless metaphorical exchange, from physics to economics, economics to psychology, psychology to political economy. David Bennett forcefully makes this point in his book *The Currency of Desire*, linking Freud's invention of psychoanalysis to prior developments in utopian socialism, sexology, thermodynamics, and neoclassical economics.[12] In this way, he argues, 'libidinal economy' is fundamentally concerned with a much deeper set of questions traditionally pursued by magic and religion, questions about what sets or keeps 'life' going. It therefore cannot ever fully divorce itself from these registers. First 'divine love' or 'mystical life-force', later 'libidinal energy' and 'desiring-production' – these enigmatic phrases are best grasped as so many attempts to name the unnameable, religious or scientific metaphors whose import is ultimately mythical in character.[13] If 'libido' brings the world into being, then 'libidinal economy' has no foundation.

And so, a fully fledged discipline of 'libidinal economy' in the strict sense is elusive for a number of reasons, and perhaps not even desirable anyway. That is why some employ the more ambiguous formulation 'libidinal economies'. The plural here could stand for a plurality of approaches, accepting one or both of the key axioms as Noys has it, with a range of different understandings of economy and desire, and therefore their relation too. As long as we speak about desire and we speak about economy, a new theoretical articulation of libidinal economy remains possible, and even if this can never be the last word on the matter, it might still offer a valuable perspective on the human condition. Another, related possibility is a libidinal economy that pushes beyond pure theory. The plural formulation could in this context suggest a shift from the abstract to the concrete, such that 'libidinal economies' becomes the name for actually existing configurations of economy and desire, for the social formations that connect the commanding heights of the global economy to the innermost reaches of subjectivity. Our aim in this book is to pursue both these routes simultaneously: to map the libidinal economies of contemporary capitalism through a wide range of concepts and theories. Any such attempt must begin by confronting the development of twentieth-century capitalism.

Libidinal economy and twentieth-century capitalism

In *The Communist Manifesto*, Marx and Engels famously wrote that capitalism had 'drowned the most heavenly ecstasies of religious fervour, of chivalrous enthusiasm, of philistine sentimentalism, in the icy water of egotistical calculation'.[14] They were only half right. Though it did put the bottom line before tradition, modern economic life was no less full of fervour or enthusiasm. Indeed, the promise of novelty was a great source of enchantment, luring the bourgeoisie into spending their money on a litany of fashions and fads. New markets for luxury goods and company shares were shot through with desire and, as these developed over time, the principle of harnessing or enhancing desire would become a cornerstone of capitalist business.[15] Libidinal economy is implicated in this story in various ways.

To begin with, the development of consumer capitalism was decisively shaped by psychoanalysis. This much is already implied by the extent to which a Freudian vocabulary persists in Western popular culture, but two key figures illustrate well how Freud's ideas enabled the rise of mass consumption. One is Edward Bernays, Freud's double nephew and the so-called father of public relations in the USA. Best-known for his 1928 classic *Propaganda*, Bernays used his uncle's theory of the unconscious to forge a powerful set of techniques for manipulating consumer as well as voter behaviour. In 1924, for example, Bernays worked with a velvet manufacturer to 'titillate the spending emotions of 3½ million women', suggestively linking the fabric to the 'sex and glamour' of New York and Paris.[16] Another industry pioneer, Ernest Dichter, trained with one of Freud's inner circle in Vienna during the 1930s before migrating to the USA in 1938, where he would go on to play a crucial role establishing the principles of advertising and branding as we know them today.[17] Like Bernays before him, Dichter took a version of the Freudian unconscious as his starting point, developing ways of identifying and catering to the psychosexual motivations of potential consumers, helping companies to sell cigarettes and cars, later Barbie and Ken dolls.[18]

These commodities are themselves suggestive of the broader transformation that psychoanalysis helped to bring about. On one

side, mechanised production processes of the kind associated with
Lucky Strikes and above all the Ford Motor car; on the other, a
new consumer subject who would buy what the factories were
pumping out, eventually idealised in purchasable figurines of
Barbie and Ken. The Fordist growth regime was in this way a
Freudian regime too, entailing not just the mass production and
mass consumption of commodities, but also something like the
mass production of subjectivity. The result was a historically
unique configuration of desire, structured by specific ideas about
its origins – as in Freud's account of the Oedipus complex – and
inscribed into subjects through prevailing political and economic
discourse. At least this was the case in the industrialised nations
of the West, where patriotic citizens were called on to work and
save, spend and consume, to repress their illicit desires during the
week, then indulge them on the weekend through the purchase of
racy commodities. Marcuse called it 'repressive desublimation'.[19]
In effect, shopping became a socially sanctioned form of transgression, a way of blowing off steam without shutting down the
libidinal-economic factory.

But it would not last long. Marcuse's attempt to fuse psychoanalysis with Marxism was part of a broader backlash against
global Fordism that repositioned libidinal economy as a disruptive
force within capitalist society. The uprisings of May 1968 were piv-
otal in this regard, reflecting the influence of Marcuse's texts on
a growing counter-culture and students' movement, while at the
same inspiring a new generation of intellectuals to pursue the politics of desire. Especially in France, the events of 1968 turned the
fate of libidinal economy into a defining concern for radical theory.
There were various important precursors to this in the French tradition, but, as Eleanor Kaufman notes, 'it seems that something
spectacular was at issue in the years following May 1968'.[20] In
a few short years, a flurry of texts on capitalism and desire were
published, chief among them being *Anti-Oedipus* in 1972 and
Libidinal Economy in 1974. Unlike the technical prose of Freud or
even Marcuse, the authors of these works adopted a frenzied style
of writing that sought to perform or enact a revolutionary politics
based on their own, much more extreme formulation of libidinal-
economic concepts.

Take the status of 'desire' itself. Though still understood in energetic or libidinal terms, the notion that desire is somehow natural is done away with completely. Instead, desire is reimagined in inhuman terms, according to which the inner world of the subject becomes the site of a desiring-logic that reflects the economic structure of society. Hence the machinic terminology employed by Deleuze and Guattari: 'desire is a machine, a synthesis of machines, a machinic arrangement – desiring machines'.[21] The consequences of this are twofold. First, the representational space associated with capitalism is called into question. Identifications, rational explanations, even critique for Lyotard – these are all so much cover for the productive power of the unconscious itself, the ability of libidinal forces to invest the social body with vivid intensities. Second, and relatedly, everything is libidinally invested, including those aspects of social life one might least suspect of being erotically charged. 'The truth', as Deleuze and Guattari put it, 'is that sexuality is everywhere: the way a bureaucrat fondles his records, a judge administers justice, a businessman causes money to circulate; the way the bourgeoisie fucks the proletariat'.[22] Even the English proletariat, according to Lyotard, enjoyed being 'fucked' by the machinery of capital during the Industrial Revolution.[23]

The upshot of all this was a form of libidinal-economic theory that valorised not just creativity and the emancipation of desire but also excess, perversity, and a certain kind of nihilistic destruction. Deleuze and Guattari wanted us to tear down the psychic walls of the Oedipus complex and unleash the flows of desire it otherwise channelled into the capitalist state, to set free the energy of social production. Meanwhile, Lyotard wanted to see what happened if we embraced the 'libidinal intensity of capitalist exchange', giving ourselves over to the 'incredible, unspeakable pulsional possibilities that it sets rolling'.[24] Either way, the invitation to psychic revolution entailed a strategy of engaging libidinal currents within capital and pushing them further, exaggerating or accelerating the process by which these remake society.

The legacy of this version of libidinal economy is decidedly ambiguous. From one vantage point, it was a complete and utter failure. The chaotic writing style, the exaltation of unchecked desire, the hope that these together would somehow subvert the functioning of capitalism – none of these were sustainable and they have not aged well either. Badiou captured the shift in mood when, in 1975, he described libidinal-economic theory as so much 'pestilential gibberish'.[25] By the 1980s, even Lyotard would renounce his 'evil book' for seeing everything only in terms of libidinal energy.[26] And yet there was something prophetic about these texts, something about the delirium they expressed that seemed to play out on the terrain of world history, albeit in unexpected ways. If *Libidinal Economy* captured the erotic nihilism that characterised a new era of never-ending financial crisis, then *Anti-Oedipus* outlined a form of nomadic, fugitive subjectivity that became the hallmark of capitalism in its post-Fordist or neoliberal phase. The result was a global libidinal economy that thrived on doing away with many of the repressive characteristics of industrial capitalism, a new configuration of economy and desire that turned freedom and flux into the latest signature of capitalist life.[27] Liberation from the family, from the factory, from lifelong careers and fixed identities – these legacies of libidinal economy also fuel the so-called desiring-machines of contemporary capitalism.

Libidinal economies of contemporary capitalism

So, what then of 'libidinal economy?' What is the currency of desire in the myriad economies of capitalism today? Such is the question that motivates this book, the pursuit of which will lead us down various pathways over the chapters that follow. But we are by no means alone in posing it. Although the post-1968 version of libidinal economy was short-lived, the notion persisted, travelled, evolved. It has fared best outside of political economy, in philosophy and the theoretical humanities, and there is by now a well-established literature in these fields that thinks capitalism in terms of its psychic life. It is even possible to speak of a renewed interested in the idea, ostensibly triggered by the breakdown of neoliberalism in the late 2000s and a related boom in radical left theory.[28] The reorientation we are proposing here can therefore be contrasted with several key intellectual developments over recent decades.

The first of these is a turn towards capitalism's sexual economy. Foucault's history of sexuality led to a proliferation of studies on sex and sex work, the politics of gender and sexuality, later the radical potential of queer desire and questions around transgender and intersex issues.[29] This strand of thought is concerned with bodies, with affect, and with the liberation of desire from the psychic repression meted out by traditional or fixed identities. Some critics have raised questions about the extent to which such a programme dovetails with the logic of neoliberalism, but many others see it as crucial to any ongoing engagement with libidinal economy.[30] The second key development is a continuation of the Deleuzian critique of capitalism, including but not limited to the Italian tradition of Autonomist Marxism associated with Hardt and Negri, Lazzarato, and others.[31] Here the emphasis on desire as a vital or productive force is coupled with a distinction, introduced in *Anti-Oedipus*, between the territorialising and deterritorialising aspects of capitalism. Accordingly, this work too oscillates between an optimistic, even messianic projection of revolutionary horizons and a bleak analysis of endless machinic enslavement. Finally, a third development is the consolidation of a particular brand of psychoanalytic critique, inspired by Lacan and popularised through Žižek's prolific output on ideology.[32] In contrast to the Deleuzian tradition, Žižek's Lacanian-Marxism posits a libidinal economy of dialectics and lack, emphasising an infernal mechanism of desire that ultimately can never deliver us over to non-alienation, transparency, or freedom from illusion. Hence the compulsive unmasking of ideology's inevitable operations – the ideology of consumer choice, of free trade and multiculturalism, of bank bailouts and austerity politics, and so on.

In this context, the latest revival of libidinal economy is organised around a coming to terms with the idea's radical promise in its post-1968 formulation. There is considerable internal variety along the lines outlined above, but throughout one encounters the notion of a lost moment to which we might return, a moment to repeat and renew the revolutionary potential of libidinal economy. Contemporary thought therefore revisits and replays many prior aspects of libidinal economy, including the signal moods attached to these. Mark Fisher's bleak vision of 'capitalist realism' is perhaps the paradigmatic statement of a depressive libidinal economy, depicting the world scene as devoid of all hope and possibility, desire fully captured by the circuits of capital. The converse would be a revamped 'accelerationism', whose manic calls to embrace technology once again hold up the idea of an unknown and radically open future.[33] Similar dynamics are evident in the concepts of 'peak libido' (a world without desire) and 'postcapitalist desire' (a world without capital), perhaps even xenofeminism (difference is freedom) and afropessimism (difference is slavery).[34] There is much to be gained from pursuing these lines of thought further. But what if there was something to be gained by reformulating the underlying coordinates of libidinal economy too?

Consider again, then, the suggestion that 'every political economy is libidinal'.[35] With this provocation, Lyotard expressed the idea that all political economies, in their different historical and theoretical guises, are fleeting efforts to foreclose the libidinal sphere. That means that not only every mode of production (feudalism, mercantilism, capitalism) but also every attempt to codify these (classical political economy, Marxist political economy, Keynesian economics) is a psychosocial configuration of desire. The desire called 'libidinal economy' wants to grapple with the libidinal dynamics of capitalism, yet it remains beholden to a very specific concept of economy derived from Marx. While no theory, according to Lyotard, is uncontaminated by desire, there is no reason to limit the economic concepts of libidinal economy to those associated with the rise of industrial capitalism. Even Deleuze and Guattari, prophetic though they were about how capitalism might 'dispatch itself straight to the moon', could not have imagined the circumstances under which Jeff Bezos and Richard Branson boarded rockets into space in 2021.[36] What is wanted, therefore, is a 'libidinal political economy' fit for the analysis of contemporary capitalism, ready to engage its latest logics and symptoms even if it remains ensnared within them.

There have been some such attempts already, mostly scattered across the fringes of the social sciences. In the field of international political economy, for example, a sustained effort has been made to articulate a version of libidinal economy that draws on the ideas of heterodox economists like Veblen and Commons.[37] Meanwhile, in recent years, a small but growing body of research has emerged that brings questions of libidinal economy onto the empirical terrain of the contemporary, providing psychoanalytically informed accounts of financial crisis, globalisation, and international development, to give just a few examples.[38] The aim of this book is to build on and contribute towards the further development of a 'libidinal political economy' along both of these lines – the theoretical and the empirical – by focusing attention on the role played by desire in capitalism's ongoing social reproduction.

In order to do this, the book brings together a motley crew of thinkers: recovering economists, geographers and development theorists, a clinical psychiatrist, various kinds of political economy scholars. The approach is informed throughout by psychoanalytic theories of desire and the unconscious, but the broader approach adopted is one of theoretical pluralism. The book therefore mobilises a range of perspectives on desire, economy, and their relation to and interplay with one another through social institutions, drawing on the ideas of Freud and Veblen, Lacan and Marx, Deleuze and Keynes, and others too. In empirical terms, the book aims to open such perspectives out onto a broader set of economic categories and themes than has been the case so far, and especially those that seem to be emerging as the leitmotifs of twenty-first-century capitalism. Whether we envisage contemporary capitalism as indebted or technologised, whether we think it in terms of assets or data, 'the economy' appears today as above all and more than ever an elaborate, recursive exercise in psychological capture and release. Tracking such dynamics in real-time requires a broad reorientation of libidinal economy towards the everyday of economic life, towards the unconscious drives that shape the practices and discourses of economy, and ultimately, towards the way these relate to the ongoing viability of capitalism as a social formation and economic system.

Structure of the book

The chapters that follow tackle this task in three phases. The first of these stages a return to the primal scenes of libidinal economy. Revisiting questions of death, money, and sex through the lens of fundamental concerns in heterodox political economy, the opening chapters foreground the role of institutions in libidinal-economic analysis. This entails revealing the unconscious desires that find oblique expression through the institutions, objects, and practices that constellate economic life. In Chapter 1, for example, Earl Gammon draws on Freud's early theory of psychical drives and Heinz Kohut's conception of narcissistic development, arguing that our efforts to attain self-cohesion through economic performativity decisively shape the evolution of capitalism. Sandy Brian Hager offers a different perspective in Chapter 2, sketching out the relation between death and economy through an engagement with the work of Georges Bataille, Norman Brown, and Jean Baudrillard. Here capitalism appears as the latest in a long series of gambits to keep mortal dread at bay. Yet, shorn of redemptive ritual, the accumulation of capital fails to alleviate guilt and anxiety, resulting in an endless thirst for ever more money, wealth, and power. Money also occupies a central place in Chapter 3, which offers a new take on the meaning and significance of distinctions between real and financial economy. Combining Freud's ideas on sex with Marshall McLuhan's understanding of technology, Noam Yuran addresses the interpenetration of eroticism and finance today. In so doing, he clarifies how a detachment from the real traverses the technological, erotic, and economic transformation involved with dating apps.

The second phase of the book puts libidinal-economic concepts into dialogue with structural features of contemporary capitalism, understood here through the broad categories of technological change and social stratification. A set of chapters is devoted to each of these, beginning with technology. Rather than analysing digital capitalism in terms of its networks, platforms, or tokens alone, these technical aspects of contemporary life are read as contentious sites of unconscious libidinal investments. Chapter 4 does so through a focus on the hostile dynamics of online communication, which Jernej Markelj links to a fragmentation of social reality set in motion by the rise of capitalism. As this is taken to new extremes by developments in digital technology, he argues, affective inclinations towards paranoia and conflict come to the fore. Hence the mindless antagonism of our moment. Emily Rosamond's analysis of social networks in Chapter 5 highlights a countervailing promise of serendipity. Social media platforms present life as a networked space of possibility, where one chance encounter with a former colleague or contact might open new opportunities and life-paths. Rosamond shows how this desire for serendipity reworks neoliberal myths of entrepreneurship while further enriching those who control the mapping of social networks. In Chapter 6, Ludovico Rella directly takes up the monetary and financial aspect of digital capitalism's libidinal economy. Comparing the ongoing boom in cryptoassets to other speculative manias in modern history, Rella argues that it represents a new and more virulent form of compounded desire bubble whose full effects remain to be seen.

Another set of chapters is devoted to issues around contemporary forms of social stratification. Again, the analysis foregrounds the role of unconscious processes in the reproduction of capitalism, here understood in connection with hierarchies of race and class. In Chapter 7, Lynne Layton focuses on the effects of social hierarchies on identity formation, tracking the rise of neoliberalism in the USA through a dynamic of unconscious group formation and reaction. America's long history of White anti-Blackness is in this way integral, she argues, to the emergence and ongoing vitality of its more openly declared commitment to neoliberal capitalism. Chapter 8 instead looks to the psychic life of global inequality, which Japhy Wilson approaches through the phenomenon of 'compassionate consumerism'. Drawing on the psychoanalytic critique of ideology, Wilson argues that explicit ethical appeals to assist those less fortunate than ourselves are underwritten by invitations to participate in a disavowed enjoyment of relations of inequality. Fantasy also figures in Cheolung Choi's account of generational inequality in Chapter 9. When global stock markets plunged during the onset of the 2020 pandemic, young South Koreans took out loans to fund risky personal investments. Choi relates the lure of speculation at work here to a fantasy of escaping the hopeless realities produced through financial capitalism, in South Korea and elsewhere.

The third and final phase of the book follows this dialectic of hope and despair onto the crossroads of political agency, offering a series of reflections on everyday responses to financial domination. These chapters trace the affective ups and downs of financialised existence from various vantage points. Chapter 10 examines a set of insider-outsider dynamics associated with debt and leverage. Using the GameStop episode as a case in point, Stefano Sgambati and I identify the emergence of a libidinal economy of leverage premised on the unending circulation of debt. Rather than the power of creditors over debtors, we argue that this economy runs on the apocalyptic nihilism of 'lesser debtors', whose very indebtedness is the source of leverage for 'greater debtors' like hedge funds. Chapter 11 then turns to the site of the neoliberal university. Here, Aris Komporozos-Athanasiou and Max Haiven explore the subterranean politics of anxiety in the student bodies of the USA, UK, and Canada. As a new generation is emerging into adulthood, for whom neoliberalism, financialisation, and its anxieties are all they have ever known, what forms of struggle, survival, and mutual aid are they inventing? Could everyday practices of student self-sabotage, they ask, become the basis for collective acts of self-sabotage aimed at the financial machinery of the contemporary university?

By way of conclusion, consider again the theoretical and historical discussion that opened this chapter. 'Libidinal economy' is an elusive proposition, more an idea than a concept or theory. It is also implicated in the historical development of capitalism in complex ways. All this means that mapping the libidinal economies of contemporary capitalism is no easy task. The organisation of the volume as a whole reflects the scope and ambition of such an enterprise, which wants to lead 'all the way from the subject to the global political economy and back', yet it also signals some of the ineradicable tensions that come along with the thought of libidinal economy today.[39] There are points of conflict, for example, between some of the chapters collected here, which veer between different conceptions of the social and the psychic, not to mention different conceptions of economy and of capital. But the point is not to somehow resolve these differences into a unified perspective. Capitalism's libidinal economies are unpredictable and unlikely to be mastered by systemic theorising. What is instead wanted is something at once both less and more, a kind of political economy that takes the desire called 'libidinal economy' seriously.

Notes

1 *FYRE: The Greatest Party That Never Happened*, dir. Chris Smith (Netflix, 2019).
2 US Attorney's Office, Southern District of New York, 'William McFarland Sentenced to 6 Years in Prison in Manhattan Federal

Court for Engaging in Multiple Fraudulent Schemes and Making False Statements to a Federal Law Enforcement Agent', Press Release Number 18–346, October 11, 2018, www.justice.gov/usao-sdny/pr/william-mcfarland-sentenced-6-years-prison-manhattan-federal-court-engaging-multiple (accessed September 6, 2022).

3 Jo Livingstone, 'Fyre Festival Was a Huge Scam – Is Netflix's Fyre Documentary a Scam, Too?' *The New Republic*, February 12, 2019, https://newrepublic.com/article/153095/fyre-festival-huge-scam-netflixs-fyre-documentary-scam-too (accessed September 6, 2022).

4 Izabella Kaminska, 'The Entire Economy is Fyre Festival', *Financial Times*, February 21, 2019, www.ft.com/content/609188e5-fc0a-38a0-9462-54c12469cb2d (accessed September 6, 2022); see also Dan Murphy, 'Fintech in Focus', Milken Institute, February 25, 2019, https://milkeninstitute.org/article/fintech-focus-february-25-2019 (accessed September 6, 2022).

5 'Reality, it seems, has been deregulated, and nothing is business as usual anymore – least of all business'. In Erik Davis, *TechGnosis: Myth, Magic and Mysticism in the Age of Information* (London: Serpents Tail, 2004), 268.

6 In Gilles Deleuze and Félix Guattari, *Anti-Oedipus: Capitalism and Schizophrenia*, trans. Robert Hurley, Mark Seem, and Helen Lane (Minneapolis: University of Minnesota Press, 1983), xviii.

7 Jean-François Lyotard, *Libidinal Economy*, trans. Iain Hamilton Grant (London: Athlone, 1993), 111.

8 Benjamin Noys, 'Axioms of Libidinal Economy', in *Libidinal Economies in Crisis Times: The Psychic Life of Contemporary Capitalism*, ed. Ben Gook (Berlin: Transcript, 2024), in press.

9 Sigmund Freud, *The Interpretation of Dreams*, trans. James Strachey (Harmondsworth: Pelican, 1976), 714, emphasis in original.

10 It is difficult to pin Freud down to one theoretical model as his thought changes over time, but the elements alluded to here are subsequently articulated in keys essays like 'Beyond the Pleasure Principle', 'The Ego and the Id', and 'Civilization and Its Discontents'. See Volumes 18, 19, and 21 respectively in *The Standard Edition of the Complete Psychological Works of Sigmund Freud*, trans. James Strachey and Anna Freud (London: Vintage, 2001).

11 On the significance of this analogy for the economics of psychoanalytic practice, see David Bennett, 'Desire as Capital: Getting a Return on the Repressed in Libidinal Economy', in *Metaphors of Economy*, ed. Nicole Bracker and Stefan Herbrechter (London: Brill, 2005), 95–109.

12 David Bennett, *The Currency of Desire: Libidinal Economy, Psychoanalysis and Sexual Revolution* (London: Lawrence & Wishart, 2016). On the prehistory of psychoanalysis, see Chapters 1 and 7 in this volume.
13 *Ibid.*, 35–43, 227–29.
14 Karl Marx and Friedrich Engels, *The Communist Manifesto: A Modern Edition*, trans. Samuel Moore (London: Verso, 1998), 37.
15 On the role of desire in early forms of 'fashionable consumption', see William Sewell Jr., 'The Empire of Fashion and the Rise of Capitalism in Eighteenth-Century France', *Past & Present* 206, no. 1 (2010): 81–120. A corresponding 'empire of finance' is depicted in Edward Chancellor, *Devil Take the Hindmost: A History of Financial Speculation* (London: Plume, 2000).
16 Quoted in William Leach, *Land of Desire: Merchants, Power, and the Rise of a New American Culture* (New York: Vintage, 1994), 321.
17 Bennett, *Currency of Desire*, 91, 95.
18 *Ibid.*, 94–104. See also Rachel Bowlby, *Shopping with Freud* (London: Routledge, 1993), chapter 7.
19 Herbert Marcuse, *One-Dimensional Man: Studies in the Ideology of Advanced Industrial Society* (Abingdon: Routledge, 2002). See also Herbert Marcuse, *Eros and Civilization: A Philosophical Inquiry into Freud* (Abingdon: Routledge, 1998).
20 Eleanor Kaufman, 'The Desire Called Mao: Badiou and the Legacy of Libidinal Economy', *Postmodern Culture* 18, no. 1 (2007), https://doi.org/10.1353/pmc.0.0008 (accessed September 6, 2022).
21 Deleuze and Guattari, *Anti-Oedipus*, 296.
22 *Ibid.*, 293.
23 Lyotard, *Libidinal Economy*, 111.
24 *Ibid.*, 109, 103.
25 Quoted in Kaufman, 'The Desire Called Mao'; the translation is Kaufman's.
26 Jean-François Lyotard, *Peregrinations: Law, Form, Event* (New York: Columbia University Press, 1988), 13.
27 Slavoj Žižek makes a version of this argument in *Organs without Bodies: On Deleuze and Consequences* (London: Routledge, 2004).
28 See Ben Gook, ed., *Libidinal Economies in Crisis Times: The Psychic Life of Contemporary Capitalism* (Berlin: Transcript, 2023).
29 Michel Foucault, *The History of Sexuality, Volume I*, trans. Robert Hurley (New York: Pantheon, 1978). For example, see Judith Butler, *Gender Trouble: Feminism and the Subversion of Identity* (London: Routledge, 1990); Lee Edelman, *No Future: Queer Theory and the Death Drive* (Durham, NC: Duke University Press, 2004);

Jules Joanne Gleeson and Elle O'Rourke, eds, *Transgender Marxism* (London: Pluto, 2021).

30 Rosi Braidotti has made this point on numerous occasions. See *Metamorphoses: Towards a Materialist Theory of Becoming* (Polity: Cambridge, 2002), chapter 1.

31 Antonio Negri and Michael Hardt, *Empire* (Cambridge, MA: Harvard University Press, 2000); Eugene Holland, *Nomad Citizenship: Free-Market Communism and the Slow-Motion General Strike* (Minneapolis: University of Minnesota Press, 2011); Maurizio Lazzarato, *Signs and Machines: Capitalism and the Production of Subjectivity*, trans. Joshua David Jordan (Los Angeles, CA: Semiotext(e), 2014).

32 Slavoj Žižek, *The Sublime Object of Ideology* (London: Verso, 1989); Jodi Dean, *Democracy and Other Neoliberal Fantasies: Communicative Capitalism and Left Politics* (Durham, NC: Duke University Press, 2009); Todd McGowan, *Capitalism and Desire: The Psychic Cost of Free Markets* (Columbia, NY: Columbia University Press, 2016); Samo Tomšič, *The Capitalist Unconscious: Marx and Lacan* (London: Verso, 2016).

33 Mark Fisher, *Capitalist Realism: Is There No Alternative?* (Winchester: Zero, 2009); Robin Mackay and Armen Avanessian, eds, *#Accelerate: The Accelerationist Reader* (Falmouth: Urbanomic, 2014).

34 The first two terms are from Dominic Pettman, *Peak Libido: Sex, Ecology, and the Collapse of Desire* (Cambridge: Polity, 2020) and Mark Fisher, *Postcapitalist Desire: The Final Lectures* (London: Repeater Books, 2020). For a broader discussion that encompasses all four terms, see the range of contributions in Gook's *Libidinal Economies in Crisis Times*.

35 Lyotard, *Libidinal Economy*, 111.

36 Deleuze and Guattari, *Anti-Oedipus*, 34.

37 Key programmatic texts within this field are Ash Amin and Ronen Palan, 'Towards a Non-Rationalist International Political Economy', *Review of International Political Economy* 8, no. 1 (2001): 559–77; Earl Gammon and Ronen Palan, 'Libidinal International Political Economy', in *International Political Economy and Poststructural Politics*, ed. Marieke De Goede (Basingstoke: Palgrave, 2006), 97–114; and Earl Gammon and Duncan Wigan, 'Libidinal Political Economy: A Psycho-Social Analysis of Financial Violence', in *Global Political Economy: Contemporary Theories*, ed. Ronen Palan (London: Routledge, 2013), 205–16.

38 David Bennett, ed., *Loaded Subjects: Psychoanalysis, Money and the Global Financial Crisis* (London: Lawrence and Wishart,

2012); Ilan Kapoor, ed., *Psychoanalysis and the Global* (Lincoln: University of Nebraska Press, 2018); Ilan Kapoor, *Confronting Desire: Psychoanalysis and International Development* (Ithaca, NY: Cornell University Press, 2020). See also Ilan Kapoor, Gavin Fridell, Maureen Sioh, and Pieter de Vries, *Global Libidinal Economy* (New York: SUNY Press, 2023).
39 Gammon and Palan, 'Libidinal International Political Economy', 111.

1

Narcissism, rage, avocado toast

Earl Gammon

On Quora, a question-and-answer website, a user asks the question: 'How is it that an avocado toast has become the symbol of recklessness and excess as [it] pertains to millennials?' Another user responds that the disdain expressed through the avocado toast stereotype reflects Baby Boomers' unwillingness to acknowledge the housing crisis afflicting millennials, as well as their implication in this crisis. They then further elaborate how Baby Boomers fail to concede that opportune postwar conditions afforded them a prosperity that neither earlier nor later generations would enjoy. The trope of the avocado toast for the Quora respondent, thus, is a type of displacement, with Baby Boomers refusing to own up to their responsibility for the current housing predicament. 'They are an entitled generation that had things handed to them by [t]he past and took from the present.'[1]

Though the use of the avocado toast cliché in such debates may be exaggerated, beliefs do prevail that young adults struggle because of profligacy and workshy attitudes. On the website of the *Daily Mail*, a British right-wing tabloid with an older readership, an article reporting that millennials have less income to spend on non-essentials is met with incredulity by several readers in the comments section. As the top-rated comment states, 'Don't believe it. Previous generations wouldn't have had the money to spend on expensive mobile phones and plans or eating out regularly.'[2] The opinion that poor spending habits are the reason for young adults' housing difficulties, though, is not held only by older generations. A whopping 48% of UK millennials agreed that a key

Clickbait capitalism

reason why young people struggle to get on the housing ladder is due to spending on small luxuries.[3]

Historical data confirms deteriorating real incomes and markedly higher housing costs for millennials compared to Baby Boomers during their twenties, inviting the question: why is there not wider acknowledgement of worsening intergenerational inequality?[4] One explanation for the persistent view of spendthrift youth is that older generations miscalculate and inflate the costs of the consumer indulgences that supposedly lead millennials astray from righteous homeownership. 'Boomer mathematics' discounts how the low-cost pleasures of millennials can be savvy economic choices, such as replacing expensive cinema outings with a Netflix subscription.[5] Another possible explanation is 'Boomer cognitive dissonance'. As one millennial poster on the forum website Reddit reflects, following some interactions with older individuals, '… it dawned on me that there is actually a wide-spread belief that millennials are spending all our money on $7 coffees and fucking Teslas, and that's why we don't have retirement accounts'.[6] Cognitive dissonance refers to Festinger's hypothesis that dissonance is psychologically uncomfortable and motivates individuals to attain consonance. It further stipulates that people actively avoid situations or information that might increase dissonance.[7] Cognitive dissonance provides some psychological insight into the disavowal of measurable generational inequalities, but it does not fully account for the complex psychological dynamics that impel individuals to seek consonance.

To better understand such forms of disavowal and their place within the ostensibly rational domain of economic life, this chapter develops a 'libidinal political economy' framework. Drawing on psychoanalysis, this approach offers a way of interpreting the dynamic formation of political-economic subjectivity, understood as the fluctuating outcome of an individual's attempts to negotiate self-coherency while immersed in the instituted practices of the market. More specifically, it looks at how we form conceptions of objects, both people and things, within our environment, in relation to the object of the self. We form objects, as will be explained, through libidinal investments that, in effect, make these objects parts of ourselves. These libidinal investments, though, are never as stable as we would wish, contributing to an unremitting tension in our relation to the outer world. Plunged into social relations that are mediated by the market in early life, we undertake forms of economic performativity to shore up the constellation of objects that define our reality. It is an onerous and incessant undertaking, but a crucial one too. The approach developed here provides a means by which to grasp the historically particular object attachments we form, and the resistances that manifest when the objects in which we libidinally invest are imperiled.

The chapter begins by sketching some core concepts for formulating a libidinal political economy framework. It outlines the dualistic schema of drives that traces back to the work of Freud. These drives, namely the life or libidinal drives and the ego or self-preservative drives, are key in understanding the intrapsychical economy of the self and the intersubjective processes of self-formation. Though there are as many ways to configure libidinal political economy as there are competing psychoanalytic approaches, I take particular inspiration from the post-Freudian self psychology of Heinz Kohut. Kohut draws on Freudian notions of narcissism to develop an account of how we forge self and object relationships to attain a sense of cohesiveness and continuity in the face of a constantly evolving external environment.

The second section brings this account of the self into conversation with notions of performativity arising out of economic sociology, revealing the motivations that drive adherence to particular forms of political-economic subjectivity. The third section then looks at the phenomenon of defensive intransigence that manifests in our economic beliefs and actions when our precarious libidinal investments are endangered. Here I argue that the disavowal of worsening intergenerational inequality is symptomatic of the defensive intransigence that occurs when sustained beliefs about oneself and one's place in the world are threatened. Finally, the chapter concludes by underlining the therapeutic potential of such a perspective. In revealing the social sources of our dangerous object attachments, a libidinal political economy promises insights into how we might defuse the defensive intransigence that leads, all too frequently, to intractable crises and entrenched social misery.

Libidinal investment and the vicissitudes of the self

There is no one way of bringing libidinal economy to bear on political economy. Among Freudian or post-Freudian contributions, including, but not limited to, Lacanianism, object relations theory, ego psychology, self psychology, and relational psychoanalysis, there is a variety of conceptual perspectives that could be fruitfully employed. So, too, works such as Deleuze and Guattari's *Anti-Oedipus* or Jean-François Lyotard's *Libidinal Economy*, psychoanalytically informed interventions that theorise the relationship between capitalism, political economy, and the libidinal economy of the self, can offer productive points of departure.[8] Here I draw on Freud's early contributions on the psychical drives and Kohut's later theorisation of the development of the self.

Despite the above variety, there are shared assumptions that give ground to a libidinal political economy. A primary assumption is that our political and economic beliefs and behaviours are shaped by unconscious motives. What we deduce as behaviour driven simply by economic imperatives are influenced by unconscious dynamics. Another assumption is that the self is fractured and fraught with internal conflicts. The self is also an intersubjective formation, with its desires shaped by the context into which it is socialised; it is not a monadical entity with an innate, preformed rationality. The development of the self is a dynamic and ceaseless process, and we never succeed in mending the fractures nor in attaining the foreclosure of the self. We are the culmination of the conflicts that we have experienced in negotiating our sense of self within the world, and the tangle of resolutions and irresolutions of these conflicts unconsciously weigh on our present beliefs and actions. Thus, there is no simple divide between rational and irrational behaviour, for the operation of unconscious processes is a-rational.[9] What is rational in the sphere of political economy is contextual, and ostensibly irrational behaviours commonly indicate a conflict between unconscious demands and what is socially expedient.

Psychoanalysis begins with an account of the psychical apparatus and its early development. In the initial stages of life, Freud theorised a state of primary narcissism, a period of life before a child becomes aware of its separation from the external world and from its primary caregiver.[10] At this stage, there are no objects conceived of as separate from a primordial self; there is no ego that yet serves as the threshold of selfhood. In a state of primary narcissism, before the frustrations of the external world are foisted upon the self, before boundaries sharpen between our inner and outer worlds, according to Freud, there exists a feeling that he describes as 'oceanic'.[11] This timeless and boundless state of primary narcissism, though, is violently interrupted by our postnatal bodily needs and the implacable constraints imposed by the external world, setting in motion the constitution of the ego as a defensive psychical formation. Through the apprehension of distinct objects, including the object of the self, the ego begins its work of minimising threats to its narcissistic integrity posed by the external world and internal somatic demands.

Though Freud's notion of primary narcissism is a longstanding source of debate in psychoanalysis, with evidence challenging the existence of an early undifferentiated stage of psychical life, it retains utility in conceptualising primordial self-formation. Early on, the notion was rejected by Melanie Klein, a founder of object relations theory who focused on child analysis, and it was later contested by infant research.[12] Rather than seen as a biological stage, it perhaps is better conceived as an Edenic myth of the self. Like Eden, the imagined stage of primary narcissism presents a paradisical state of harmony with the world. As Julie Walsh argues, there is value in preserving the notion of primary narcissism as 'a formative illusion underwritten by the fact of the infant's existence in a precarious environment'.[13] This illusion of primary narcissism taunts us with the distant hope of returning to some semblance of innocence, ignorance, and bliss, of being able to ward off the unending disturbances to the self. This reinterpreted notion of primary narcissism is akin to what Lacanians refer to as the 'Imaginary', a deception and lure that propagates illusions of wholeness, synthesis, and autonomy.[14]

The formation of the ego is a defensive reaction to the psychical tumult that the infant experiences. Buffeted by internal somatic demands and an uncompliant and threatening external world, the ego forms to avert and minimise these perturbations. Freud makes the comparison to the way that simple organisms evolved protective cortical structures to shield themselves from dangerous external stimuli.[15] The ego offers an illusion of the self and, simultaneously, a representation of the world in which it is immersed.[16]

This representation allows us to make predictions, which, coupled with the ego's executive control over motility, enables us to avoid aversive circumstances and to conciliate the body's inner demands.

To better grasp the consolidation of the ego, we need to understand the psychical drives that Freud theorises precipitate its development.[17] These drives are conceptualised by Freud as objectless (pre-representational) motor forces or internal energies that seek to overcome unpleasurable internal tensions.[18] In his earlier formulations (1910–15), Freud hypothesised two groups of primary drives: the ego or self-preservative drives, and the sexual drives. Writing about the sexual drives, Freud clarified that they are plural, and are not to be conflated with a narrower conception of genitality; they represent a much broader polyvalent sexuality that works both directly and indirectly in support of species survival and reproduction.[19] The ego or self-preservative drives seek to sustain the integrity of the ego construct against the incessant threats that life throws its way. These contrasting drives never appear in unadulterated form, but are always co-present in our object investments, which refers to the psychical energy that is mobilised and attached to salient objects, be they ideas, things, persons, parts of the body, or the self.[20]

In elaborating how the drives are invested, or cathected, in external objects, Freud compares this process to the functioning of the pseudopodia of the amoeba.[21] Pseudopodia are protrusions of the single-celled organism that allow its body to flow over and absorb external matter, like food particles. These protrusions are akin to the investment of the libidinal drives; they can be extended to encompass external objects or withdrawn back into the main body of the organism. Similarly, we can invest our libidinal drives to encompass external objects or divert the libido back into the ego itself. Though Freud later made controversial revisions to his theory of the psychical drives, namely with his introduction of the death drive, his earlier theorisation offers a useful starting point in conceptualising libidinal political economy.[22]

Heinz Kohut's contributions to Freudian thought offer a helpful conceptual framework for linking primary narcissism and object formation to political-economic life. Kohut's self psychology is an approach that 'puts the self at the center, examines the genesis and developments and its constituents, in health and in disease'.[23]

Kohut sustained that a rudimentary self-structure exists from infancy, and he envisioned self psychology as a means to discern its developmental trajectory and its strategies for averting fragmentation. Central to Kohut's work is the self's development following the early disturbance of the equilibrium of primary narcissism, and the subsequent investment in objects to support the fledgling self. Kohut coined the notion of *selfobjects*, 'objects which we experience as part of ourself'.[24] There are two main types of selfobjects in Kohut's theorisation.[25] The first, mirroring selfobjects, 'respond to and confirm the child's innate sense of vigor, greatness and perfection'. The second, idealising selfobjects, 'are those to whom a child can look up and with whom [they] can merge as an image of calmness, infallibility, and omnipotence'.[26] These selfobjects – which can be people, possessions, religious, economic, and political beliefs, forms of knowledge, rituals, and practices – are experienced as extensions of the self. Mirroring selfobjects spur desires for success, serving as sources of positive affirmation and self-esteem, while idealising selfobjects establish goals, serving as objects that one wishes to emulate, or with which one desires to merge. The relationship with our selfobjects determines the fate of the self, leading either to a cohesive and stable structure or a stunted and fragmented one. Through a Kohutian lens, political-economic life is rendered as a constellation of mirroring and idealising selfobjects, which can either be stabilising or contribute to narcissistic pathologies.

Political-economic performativity and the search for the self

When it comes to the question of rationality in political-economic life, or the lack thereof, there is little point in flogging the critique of *Homo economicus*. Behavioural economics, which applies psychological insights into decision-making to show and explain behaviour that deviates from rational expectations, has penetrated the mainstream of economics. The widely cited work of economic sociologists Michel Callon and Donald MacKenzie has compellingly argued that economic models do not merely explain but also construct the economy and format its calculative agencies. For Callon, though *Homo economicus* 'really does exist', it is, at the same time, 'pure fiction'.[27]

Clickbait capitalism

A libidinal political economy, though, does more than recognise the irrational aspects of economic behaviour, offering a
psychological uniformitarianism that permits rational and non-
rational behaviour to be explained through a singular, a-rational
framework. Though behavioural economics incorporates emotions
into models of decision-making, and proports to enhance 'the
explanatory power of economics by providing it with more realistic psychological foundations',[28] it retains the rump of a rational
actor. *Homo economicus* now appears with a dissociative personality disorder – a Jekyll and Hyde – for whom the animal spirits,
in certain circumstances, override rational economic motivations.[29]
Behavioural economics harbours the view of boundedly rational
agents, who, due to constraints on information, time and mental
capacities, satisfice rather than maximise utility.[30] This contrasts
with a-rational conceptions of the psyche in libidinal political economy, where the motivations behind both irrational and
rational behaviour are premised on the same psychical processes.
Irrationality, rather than a failure to maximise utility or to accur-
ately calculate or discriminate values, is viewed as an incoherence
or incongruency in the conception of one's self and selfobjects.[31]
Irrational behaviours are not a discrete class of behaviours, but are
driven by the same psychical processes as rational ones. In the case
of irrational behaviours, these processes have gone awry, leading to
overcompensating efforts to salvage one's narcissistic integrity. To
an outside observer, these behaviours and beliefs can appear self-
sabotaging or self-deceiving. Rational behaviour, thus, rather than
defined by effective optimisation, as with rational-choice theory,
denotes a contextual situation in which one is relatively successful
in maintaining self-coherency within their environment.

Though economic performativity studies offer valuable insights
into the constructed nature of the economy, and of how economics
formats economic agencies, the underlying motivations for the performance of the economy remain opaque. While Callon argues
that *Homo economicus* is an historical concoction, a calculative
agent formatted by economics, he does not venture into what drives
model makers or what makes agents receptive to 'performation'.
MacKenzie briefly touches on the subject of non-rational motivations. In his interviews with central actors responsible for setting
up the first exchanges for financial derivatives, he notes the lack

of rational egoism as their impetus. As Leo Melamed, a pioneer of financial futures, explains to MacKenzie, 'My father had instilled in me [the] idea that you gain immortality by tying yourself up with an idea, or a movement, or an institution that transcends mortality.' For Melamed, that idea is one of possessive individualism: 'Adam Smith taught me that you serve society best by caring for yourself.'[32]

By shedding light on motivations, libidinal political economy pushes beyond theories of economic performativity. Melamed's notion of 'gaining immortality by tying yourself up with an idea' gives apt expression to Kohut's notion of idealising selfobjects, where individuals seek to merge with objects possessing revered qualities. If we were to take as our premise the idea of 'satisficers' from behavioural economics, it is unclear why anyone would undertake such enormous personal sacrifices, like Melamed, to set up the world's first financial futures exchange. Instead, taking the premises of the illusion of primary narcissism and the drive to libidinally invest in selfobjects to maintain self-integrity, we can comprehend why non-economic motivations commonly prevail in decision-making. The loss of selfobjects used to regulate and sustain the self, as discussed in the next section, can be traumatic, and our initial reactions to selfobject threats tend to be defensive, rather than the more arduous process of self–selfobject differentiation.

A brief history of *Homo economicus* tells the story of the emergence of an idealising selfobject, one promising a cohesive and stable form of subjecthood in an uncertain world. Looking back to Hobbes' conception of the possessive individual, a prototype for *Homo economicus*, we see a selfobject that offered escape from the deep-seated anxiety that haunted him. His pessimistic view of human nature driven by self-interest and severed from empathic connections, while seemingly despondent, was an idealisation that offered safety and certainty. As Hobbes expressed, 'This perpetual fear, always accompanying mankind in the ignorance of causes, as it were in the dark, must needs have for object something.'[33] His assumptions of the brutish nature of human beings and a state of nature defined by uncertainty and mistrust made the world, and our place within it, scrutable. Adam Smith's later conception of human nature driven by self-interest, though more optimistic, also served an idealising role. As Hirschman explains, Smith takes the already simplified view that individuals are pulled in different directions by their (economic) interests and violent and tempestuous passions, and he makes the final reduction: 'noneconomic drives, powerful as they are, are all made to feed into the economic ones and do nothing but reinforce them, being thus deprived of their erstwhile independent existence'.[34] This perception of human nature governed by self-interest offered a comforting selfobject in varied ways. It alleviated individuals of guilt for pursuing their self-interest while remaining indifferent to the plight of others, and it offered the promise of a materially prosperous society. It was also an elegant solution to the age-old problem of theodicy, with self-interest aligned with a natural moral economy guided by Providence.

The idealisation of the self-regulating market in the context of the nineteenth century provided a collective selfobject with which Victorians could merge during a period of epistemological tumult. In early-nineteenth-century Britain, prevalent were beliefs in natural theology, the idea that nature operated according to a divine telos, and that within the 'book of nature' we would find confirmation of the scriptural account of the origins of humanity. Long before Darwin's revelations were the geological controversies of the 1820s and 1830s, which challenged the biblical chronology of the earth's age and the account of the great deluge in the book of Genesis. Painfully decentred from their place in the cosmos, and mourning for a lost selfobject, Victorians made a compensatory libidinal investment in the ideal of the self-regulating market. Stripped of the comforting vision of a natural economy operating according to a divinely ordained plan, the self-regulating market was idealised as a retributive mechanism for establishing and preserving social order.[35]

Idealisations of the purifying powers of the market, of its ability to cut through the emotional Gordian knot of social life, continue to allure individuals within contemporary capitalism. Cultivating an indifference to others while adhering to beliefs that individuals are politically equal, and that economic inequalities are natural and can be socially beneficial, simplifies the world. The idealisation of the market is seductive to those who find themselves in favourable socio-economic conditions, assuaging their guilt, and extricating them from messy emotional entanglements and burdensome social obligations. With beliefs in self-ownership and self-reliance, one can eschew costly empathic connections; empathy is hard work, and people engage in empathy avoidance to escape the attendant psychical toll.[36] In a group known for idealising the market's efficacy – self-identified libertarians – they show lower levels of empathic concern, reject moralities based on obligation to others, and have preference for less-binding social relations.[37]

No less important to selfhood in contemporary capitalism are the mirroring selfobjects in which we libidinally invest. Exemplifying this is the importance of home- and automobile ownership to people's identities, reflecting these possessions' role in confirming self-value and self-cohesion. In capitalism, with the widespread idealisation of self-ownership and a cultivated indifference to others, possessions and status symbols are elevated as selfobjects, substitutive of people. In Anglosphere countries, we see an obsession with homeownership, reflected in the popular genre of house buying and home renovation programmes, referred to as 'property porn'.[38] We observe how homeownership is a marker of responsible adulthood, with its attainment promising an elusive cohesion and stability. As the historian Peter Saunders writes of Britain, 'Financial gain is not the only reason why home ownership has become so popular, for many people also find in home ownership a means for expressing and realising values of autonomy, personal independence and emotional security.' He adds, 'it fosters a stronger sense of belonging and personal achievement'.[39] Psychologist Mihaly Csikszentmihalyi gives apt expression to the mirroring role of our possessions: 'A person who owns a nice home, a new car, good furniture, the latest appliances, is recognised by others as having passed the test of personhood in our society.' He continues, 'they tell us things about ourselves that we need to hear in order to keep our selves from falling apart'.[40]

Thus, with political economy viewed through a Kohutian lens, *Homo economicus* is replaced with *Homo narcissus*, a subject beset by illusions of narcissistic wholeness, and who libidinally invests in selfobjects to shore up their self-integrity. From the perspective of self psychology, we all live in 'a matrix of selfobjects from birth to death'. We need these 'selfobjects for [our] psychological survival, just as [we] need oxygen in [our] environment throughout life for physiological survival'.[41] We do not just flit between selfobject investments, and threats to these objects can endanger our very self-constitution. We pour enormous energy into these investments, which, in the sphere of political economy, explains recalcitrant behaviours that appear irrational. We are far from the hedonistic conception of individuals that Veblen rebuked, the view of the individual as 'a lightning calculator of pleasures and pains, who oscillates like a homogeneous globule of desire of happiness under the impulse of stimuli that shift [them] about the area but leave [them] intact'.[42]

Narcissistic injury and pathological political economies

For Kohut, the focus of his approach was on the psychology of what he termed 'Tragic Man', a person who constantly strives to give expression to their nuclear self, but whose failures overshadow their successes.[43] This was in contrast to the focus of earlier psychoanalysis on 'Guilty Man', the individual riven by internal conflicts arising from repressed unconscious desires, and who lives in perpetual fear of punishment. The debilitated image of the tragic person gives expression to the fact that, despite our greatest efforts, our selfobject investments commonly fail to maintain the delicate state of self-cohesion.

The plight of the tragic person's fraught efforts to attain self-cohesion plays out in the evolution of capitalism. Throughout its history, different permutations of selfhood have been collectively idealised, tempting with the illusion of narcissistic fulfilment. In the late Victorian era, widely popular author Samuel Smiles, the father of self-help, sold to working-class men an ideal of personal independence attained through frugality and industry. He professed, 'Economising for the purpose of being independent is one of the soundest indications of manly character.'[44] This idealisation befit an era dominated by what regulation theorists term the 'regime of extensive accumulation', lasting from the mid-nineteenth century until World War I.[45] The idealised selfhood portrayed by Smiles aligned with this era of capitalism, characterised by expanding markets to new areas with prices determined by uncoordinated autonomous agents, and it resonated with ideologies of settler colonialism, like the 'frontier spirit'. In the postwar era, which saw an 'intensive regime of capitalist accumulation' based on the mass consumption of standardised goods, collective bargaining, social welfare, and Keynesian demand management, there arose another idealised selfhood. In this period, the Fordist era, lasting up until the 1970s, the idealisation of selfhood was distinct from previous iterations. This one saw an idealisation of conformism in consumption, the white patriarchal nuclear family, and loyalty to company and country. The ascendance of neoliberalism in the 1970s, though, saw another shift in the idealisation of selfhood. Now emphasis was on a strict ethos of self-reliance and self-responsibility, self-expression through consumerism, commitment to maximum economic freedom, and an entrepreneurial disposition. The transitions in forms of selfhood corresponded with their diminishing capacities to adequately fulfil idealising needs and to thwart narcissistic injury.

Threats to or the loss of selfobjects are challenging and painful, and in particular circumstances precipitate strong defensive reactions. With the deprivation or diminishment of our selfobjects, we undergo a process of mourning and a withdraw of our libidinal investments. This can be a positive step in our psychical maturation. Kohut referred to a process of 'transmuting internalisation', which entails de-idealising the selfobject in which we have invested.[46] We come to recognise the imperfection and limitations of the selfobject, but we can re-internalise aspects of it in a more nuanced manner. We recognise its shortcomings while retaining its positive qualities and functions as part of our self. Exemplifying this is the way a child relinquishes an idealised view of its parents, recognising their faults, but it then integrates the parents' positive qualities as part of its self-structure. Through de-idealisation and differentiating from the selfobject, the structure of the psyche is strengthened. A vital requirement for the success of transmuting internalisation, though, is an empathic environment. Others, who are able to recognise the nature of our frustrations and disappointments with our selfobjects, can provide support in redirecting our libidinal investments.[47]

Lacking an empathic environment, and beset by selfobject failures, the reaction can be one that Kohut termed narcissistic rage, characterised by the unleashing of destructive aggression. Narcissistic rage is '[t]he need for revenge, for righting a wrong, for undoing a hurt by whatever means, and a deeply anchored, unrelenting compulsion in the pursuit of all these aims'.[48] Narcissistic rage is not just aggression employed to satisfy a limited objective.

It arises from a narcissistically injured individual who 'cannot rest until [they have] blotted out a vaguely experienced offender who dared to oppose [them], to disagree with [them], or to outshine [them]'.[49] This rage can manifest in acute outbursts, or in a more chronic manner, taking the form of a grudge, expressed as a passive aggression which indirectly works to undermine the offending object.[50] In addition to being targeted externally, this rage can be directed towards the self, contributing to depressive states and self-sabotaging behaviour.

With the failure of collective selfobjects in capitalism, we have seen manifestations of narcissistic rage. The aggression displayed in the nationalistic wars of the first half of the twentieth century links to the shortcomings and frustrations with the idealised visions of selfhood promoted during the extensive phase of capitalist accumulation. Nationalistic fervour was a compensatory idealisation, replacing that of rugged individualism. Kohut explains, 'At certain historical moments there exists a widespread painful awareness of narcissistic imbalance in large segments of a country's population.' He continues, 'Shame propensity and readiness for rage are ubiquitous. Individuals seek to melt into the body of a powerful nation.'[51] At the end of the Fordist era, the idealisation of White working-class selfhood, as I have argued elsewhere, was unsettled by the civil and equal rights movements. This precipitated the punitive use of intensified market competition and selective state retrenchment against those who narcissistically wounded Fordist man.[52]

In the contemporary epoch, neoliberal selfhood, while enduring, is a failed selfobject, which by promoting disempathy and discompassion creates conditions conducive to chronic narcissistic rage. It celebrates meritocracy, offering countless examples of those who, because of grit and resourcefulness, have 'made good', earning what they deserve. But like a lottery, the myth of meritocracy relies on possibilistic thinking, though the odds of winning are improbable. The evidence, though, shows that the needle's-eye passage to economic success has winnowed in the neoliberal era. The Organisation for Economic Co-operation and Development (OECD) reports that the social elevator is broken, and that, on average, within member states, it would take 4.5 generations for those in low-income families to approach the mean income.[53] Lauren Berlant describes the phenomenon of 'cruel optimism' that has taken hold since the 1980s, whereby we make problematic investments in objects, objects that betray us, but still manage to keep us entranced.[54] Despite the growing intergenerational inequality, many young people are taken in by what is known as 'hustle culture', a performative workaholism that glorifies relentless toil and long work hours.[55]

Returning to the disavowal of intergenerational inequality, and the defensive intransigence that manifests in the face of clear evidence, it is symptomatic of a chronic form of narcissistic rage. To those who fared well under neoliberalism, who experienced upward mobility, and whose conception of the self is enmeshed with ideals of self-made individuality, the suggestion that they were historically fortunate is an existential provocation. The implication that their relative success is conjunctural and contingent – that, among other things, they benefitted from asset price inflation in housing – represents a narcissistic affront. Chronic narcissistic rage is exhibited in the persistent refusal to acknowledge the deteriorating economic conditions for younger generations, and in passive aggression through the support for politics that obstruct efforts to redress and rebalance the stark inequalities.

Conclusion

Libidinal political economy should aim to do more than simply explain the psychic life of capitalism. In these times of war, simmering ethnonationalism, gross inequalities, and, not least, climate crisis, the approach needs to be directed towards overcoming the dangerous attachments that obstruct the development of healthy self-structures. A libidinal political economy needs to be therapeutic. In the current conjuncture, the idealisation of neoliberal selfhood fuels a vicious circle by promoting indifference and empathy avoidance, which in turn reinforce pathological selfobject constellations. Without a more empathic social environment, there is little prospect of transmuting internalisations to transform problematic selfobject relationships and to redirect narcissistic needs towards prosocial ends.

Promoting empathy is a daunting undertaking. In a period that Kohut would likely characterise as one of widespread narcissistic imbalance, marked by defensive intransigence and chronic rage, there are severe impediments to empathy. Everywhere individuals have cultivated defences against empathy that forestall identification with others. In some cases, the barriers to empathy are likely insurmountable, especially when the idealisations that individuals have integrated as part of their self-structures are based on notions of racial, gender, and class superiority. It is vital, though, to stress that empathy – or 'vicarious introspection' – is not sympathy.[56] We can have empathy for others without liking them. By understanding the narcissistic needs that compel us, by appreciating the selfobject failures that we all experience, we can conceive practicable strategies for disarming the defensive intransigence that politically paralyses us in the face of crisis.

Notes

1 Kerri Copeland, 'How Is It That an Avocado Toast Has Become the Symbol of Recklessness and Excess as Pertains to Millennials?', Quora, August 14, 2019, www.quora.com/How-is-it-that-an-avocado-toast-has-become-the-symbol-of-recklessness-and-excess-as-pertains-to-millennials/answer/Kerri-Muir-4 (accessed September 2, 2022).
2 George Martin, 'Millennials Have Less to Spend on Non-Essentials than Older Generations Had at the Same Age, Study Shows', Mail Online, June 20, 2019, www.dailymail.co.uk/news/article-7160963/Millennials-spend-non-essentials-older-generations.html#comments (accessed September 2, 2022).
3 The Policy Institute and the Institute of Gerontology, *Housing, Hard Work and Identity: Generational Experiences and Attitudes* (London: King's College London, 2022).
4 In the OECD the middle-income group has grown smaller with each successive generation, with 60% of Millennials part of the middle class, compared to 70% of Baby Boomers when they were in their twenties. The rise in housing costs is notable, having grown three times faster than household median income over the 2000s and 2010s. OECD, *Under Pressure: The Squeezed Middle Class* (Paris: OECD, 2019), 15, 24.
5 Sarah Manavis, 'Boomer Mathematics: Why Older Generations Insist that Millennials are Financially Inept', *The New Statesman*, February 8, 2022, www.newstatesman.com/society/2022/02/boomer-mathematics-why-older-generations-cant-understand-the-millennial-struggle-to-buy-a-house (accessed September 2, 2022).

6 u/Earlgrey02, 'I've Finally Realized the depth of Boomer Cognitive Dissonance and It's Pissing Me Off', Reddit, September 13, 2020, www.reddit.com/r/offmychest/comments/irt9g6/ive_finally_realized_the_depth_of_boomer/ (accessed September 2, 2022).

7 Leon Festinger, *A Theory of Cognitive Dissonance* (Stanford, CA: Stanford University Press, 1957), 3.

8 Gilles Deleuze and Félix Guattari, *Anti-Oedipus: Capitalism and Schizophrenia*, trans. Robert Hurley, Mark Seem, and Helen Lane (London: Athlone, 1984); Jean-François Lyotard, *Libidinal Economy*, trans. Iain Hamilton Grant (Bloomington: Indiana University Press, 1993).

9 Linda Brakel and Howard Shevrin, 'Freud's Dual Process Theory and the Place of The A-Rational', *The Behavioral and Brain Sciences* 26, no. 4 (2003): 527–28.

10 Sigmund Freud, 'On Narcissism: An Introduction', in *The Standard Edition of the Complete Psychological Works of Sigmund Freud*, vol. 14, ed. James Strachey (London: Hogarth, 1957), 67–102.

11 Sigmund Freud, 'Civilization and Its Discontents', in *The Standard Edition of the Complete Psychological Works of Sigmund Freud*, vol. 21, ed. James Strachey (London: Hogarth, 1961), 59–145, at 68.

12 Donald L. Carveth, *Psychoanalytic Thinking: A Dialectical Critique of Contemporary Theory and Practice* (London: Routledge, 2018), 101.

13 Julie Walsh, *Narcissism and Its Discontents* (Basingstoke: Palgrave Macmillan, 2015), 9.

14 Dylan Evans, *An Introductory Dictionary of Lacanian Psychoanalysis* (London: Brunner-Routledge, 1996), 82.

15 Sigmund Freud, 'Beyond the Pleasure Principle', in *The Standard Edition of the Complete Psychological Works of Sigmund Freud*, vol. 18, ed. James Strachey (London: Hogarth, 1955), 1–64, at 58.

16 Sigmund Freud, 'The Ego and the Id', in *The Standard Edition of the Complete Psychological Works of Sigmund Freud*, vol. 19, ed. James Strachey (London: Hogarth, 1961), 1–66, at 25.

17 One of the sins committed by Freud's English translators was their rendering of the German *Trieb*, meaning drive or motor force, as 'instinct'. Edward R. Clemmens, 'An Analyst Looks at Languages, Cultures, and Translations', *The American Journal of Psychoanalysis* 45, no. 4 (1985): 310–21. Arguably the use of the more biological 'instinct' was employed to lend Freud's work a more scientific intonation, though it distorted the intended meaning. Thus, it is common within post-Freudian work to see 'drive' used instead of the word 'instinct' that appears in the *Standard Edition* of Freud's oeuvre.

18 Freud, 'The Ego and the Id', 47.

19 Sigmund Freud, 'Instincts and Their Vicissitudes', in *The Standard Edition of the Complete Psychological Works of Sigmund Freud*, vol. 14, ed. James Strachey (London: Hogarth, 1961), 109–40, at 138.
20 Jean Laplanche and J. B. Pontalis, *The Language of Psycho-Analysis* (London: Karnac Books, 1988), 62.
21 Sigmund Freud, 'Introductory Lectures on Psycho-Analysis, Part III', in *The Standard Edition of the Complete Psychological Works of Sigmund Freud*, vol. 16, ed. James Strachey (London: Hogarth, 1963), 243–463, at 416.
22 Freud, 'The Ego and the Id', 40.
23 Heinz Kohut, *The Restoration of the Self* (New York: International Universities Press, 1977), xv.
24 Heinz Kohut and Ernest Wolf, 'The Disorders of the Self and Their Treatment: An Outline', in *The Search for the Self: Selected Writings of Heinz Kohut: 1978–1981*, vol. 3, ed. Paul Ornstein (London: Karnac, 2011), 361. This chapter employs the concept of selfobject without a hyphen, as Kohut dispensed with it in his later work to emphasise that 'the function-providing object is not experienced as separate from the self'. Allen M. Siegel, *Heinz Kohut and the Psychology of the Self* (Routledge: London, 1996), 72.
25 Kohut introduces a third type, twinship selfobjects, but the concept is not as fully developed. Heinz Kohut, *The Analysis of the Self: A Systematic Approach to the Psychoanalytic Treatment of Narcissistic Personality Disorders* (London: Hogarth Press, 1971), 115.
26 Kohut and Wolf, 'The Disorders of the Self and Their Treatment: An Outline', 361–62.
27 Michel Callon, 'Introduction: The Embeddedness of Economic Markets in Economics', in *The Laws of the Markets*, ed. Michel Callon (Oxford: Blackwell, 1998), 1–57, at 51; Donald MacKenzie, *An Engine Not a Camera: How Financial Models Shape Markets* (Cambridge, MA: The MIT Press, 2006).
28 Colin Camerer and George Loewenstein, 'Behavioral Economics: Past, Present, Future', in *Advances in Behavioral Economics*, ed. Colin Camerer, George Loewenstein, and Matthew Rabin (New York: Russel Sage Foundation, 2004), 3.
29 George Akerlof and Robert Shiller, *Animal Spirits: How Human Psychology Drives the Economy, and Why It Matters for Global Capitalism* (Princeton, NJ: Princeton University Press, 2009).
30 Herbert A. Simon, 'Rational Choice and the Structure of the Environment', *Psychological Review* 62, no. 2 (1956): 129–38.
31 Sebastian Gardner, *Irrationality and the Philosophy of Psychoanalysis* (Cambridge: Cambridge University Press, 1993).

32 C. B. Macpherson, *The Political Theory of Possessive Individualism: Hobbes to Locke* (Oxford: Oxford University Press, 1990); MacKenzie, *An Engine Not a Camera*, 152.

33 Cited in Jan H. Blits, 'Hobbesian Fear', *Political Theory* 17, no. 3 (1989): 417–31, at 425.

34 Albert O. Hirschman, *The Passions and the Interests: Political Arguments for Capitalism before Its Triumph* (Princeton, NJ: Princeton University Press, 1977), 109.

35 For a fuller account, see Earl Gammon, 'Affect and the Rise of the Self-Regulating Market', *Millennium: Journal of International Studies* 37, no. 2 (2008): 251–78.

36 Cameron Daryl, Cendri Hutcherson, Amanda Ferguson, Julian Scheffer, Eliana Hadjiandreou, and Michael Inzlicht, 'Empathy is Hard Work: People Choose to Avoid Empathy Because of Its Cognitive Costs', *Journal of Experimental Psychology: General* 148, no. 6 (2019): 962–76.

37 Ravi Iyer, Spassena Koleva, Jesse Graham, Peter Ditto, and Jonathan Haidt, 'Understanding Libertarian Morality: The Psychological Dispositions of Self-Identified Libertarians', *PLOS One* 7, no. 8 (2012): e42366.

38 Fiona Allon, *Renovation Nation: Our Obsession with Home* (Sydney: University of New South Wales Press, 2008).

39 Peter Saunders, *A Nation of Home Owners* (London: Unwin Hyman, 1990), 314.

40 Cited in Russell W. Belk, 'Possessions and the Extended Self', *The Journal of Consumer Research* 15, no. 2 (1988): 139–68, at 148.

41 Heinz Kohut, 'Reflections on Advances in Self Psychology', in *The Search for the Self: Selected Writings of Heinz Kohut, 1978–1981*, vol. 3, ed. Paul Ornstein (London: Karnac, 2011), 261–357, at 306.

42 Thorstein Veblen, 'Why is Economics Not an Evolutionary Science?', *The Quarterly Journal of Economics* 12, no. 4 (1898): 373–97, at 389.

43 Kohut, *The Restoration of the Self*, 133.

44 Samuel Smiles, *Self-Help: With Illustrations of Character and Conduct* (London: John Murray, 1859), 285.

45 Alain Lipietz, *Mirages and Miracles: The Crises of Global Fordism*, trans. David Macey (London: Verso, 1987).

46 Kohut, *The Analysis of the Self*, 49–50.

47 *Ibid.*, 41.

48 Heinz Kohut, *Self Psychology and the Humanities: Reflections on a New Psychoanalytic Approach*, ed. Charles Strozier (London: W.W. Norton, 1985), 143.

49 *Ibid.*, 148.
50 *Ibid.*, 157.
51 *Ibid.*, 57.
52 Earl Gammon, 'The Psycho- and Sociogenesis of Neoliberalism', *Critical Sociology* 39, no. 4 (2013): 511–28.
53 OECD, *A Broken Social Elevator? How to Promote Social Mobility* (Paris: OECD, 2018).
54 Lauren Berlant, *Cruel Optimism* (Durham, NC: Duke University Press, 2011).
55 Erin Griffith, 'Why Are Young People Pretending to Love Work?', *The New York Times*, January 26, 2019, www.nytimes.com/2019/01/26/business/against-hustle-culture-rise-and-grind-tgim.html (accessed September 2, 2022).
56 Kohut, *The Restoration of the Self*, 306.

2

Capital as death denial

Sandy Brian Hager

How does money affect emotional state? A study conducted in Poland in the early 2010s developed a clever way of exploring this question.[1] As part of the experiment, 120 adults were divided into three groups: a treatment group counting the overall value of a stack of real bank notes, another treatment group counting the same overall value of a stack of play money (identical to the real thing but with one side blank), and a control group counting the same numbers (in non-monetary terms) on white pieces of paper the same size as the real and fake notes. All three groups then completed a fear-of-death questionnaire, consisting of 'yes' or 'no' responses to short statements about death anxiety (e.g., 'I am very much afraid to die'). The result? Participants in the treatment groups that counted money, no matter whether it was real or fake, reported significantly lower fear of death than those in the control group that counted numbers on white pieces of paper.

According to the researchers that conducted this study, the findings provide affirmation for 'terror management theory' (TMT), an approach within social psychology that has amassed a remarkable body of experimental evidence to show how unconscious fears about death shape our behaviour in often disturbing and destructive ways.[2] Building on the work of Ernest Becker, the core theoretical claim of TMT is that human activity, including all forms of culture, is '… designed largely to avoid the fatality of death, to overcome it by denying in some way that it is the final destiny of man'.[3] TMT argues that money, as part of the cultural scheme of things, serves as an 'existential anxiety buffer' that soothes anxieties about our finite existence. Money plays this role by helping its possessor to attain literal and symbolic immortality. Literally, because money buys cutting-edge technologies aimed not only at extending human life spans but which also bear the promise of one day eliminating 'natural' death altogether. Symbolically, because money leaves a legacy; it buys seemingly timeless monuments and can be left as inheritance and endowments to heirs and benefactors.

TMT regards death denial as a universal human experience, and this emphasis on universality makes it difficult if not impossible for the approach, especially given its experimental research design, to say anything about what is unique in the way capitalism denies death. Striving for immortality through acquisition and consumption is as old as hierarchical civilisation itself. But as the protracted debates about the origins of capitalism make clear, the mere hoarding of wealth tells us very little about the historical specificity of capitalism as a political economic regime.[4] One thing we can learn from these debates is that capitalism is unlike anything that preceded it, and this novelty stems from a specific behaviour among capitalists that leads to sustained growth: the routine reinvestment of profits in the anticipation of future profitability. What might this novel feature of capitalism have to do with death denial? What kind of phenomenological specificity is bound up with this historical specificity?

My aim in this chapter is to tackle these questions, primarily through a comparison between the role of death in capitalism and the archaic gift economy. This path was, admittedly, already well-trodden in the post-World War II period by thinkers directly and indirectly associated with libidinal economy. Georges Bataille's *The Accursed Share*, Norman O. Brown's *Life Against Death*, and Jean Baudrillard's *Symbolic Exchange and Death* all sought to uncover the psychological dimensions of capitalism via comparison with the archaic.[5] What is the point, then, of journeying down this path again? One reason is that recent literature ignores the most crucial insights of the postwar thinkers and, as a result, draws misleading parallels between capitalist and archaic practices. Another reason is that these postwar insights were developed during the industrial era. Since the 1970s, the global economy has undergone structural transformations associated with technological change, globalisation, neoliberalism, and financialisation, and it remains to be seen whether these transformations have any implications for the death-denying properties of capitalism.

To determine whether there is anything unique about the way capitalism denies death, we first need to have a clear understanding of what we mean by 'denial'. In the existing literature, denial has been conceived of in different ways by different people, creating all sorts of confusion.[6] Furthermore, unless we are clear in defining death denial, we risk reproducing the conceits of modernity, projecting a distinctly modern attitude towards death back in time, proclaiming it to be universal, and thereby robbing our analysis of historical and cultural nuance.[7] With these potential pitfalls in mind, I take on board the assumption that fear of death is an 'organising force' common to all societies, but recognise that the way this fear is managed varies across time and space.[8] For the purposes of this essay, management is the same as denial and denial is used interchangeably with various other terms (defence, repression, sublimation).

Conceptualising death denial in broad terms is, I think, necessary and consistent with the way it is conceived in TMT and the other strands of thought mentioned above. Death denial, as Becker argued, primarily involves the construction of cultural symbols intended to outlast the physical body. A society without death denial would be a society without culture, and society without culture is no society at all. Other animals may grieve but feel no compulsion to actively manage the fear of death; that part is handled by biological instincts. It is humans that cannot accept death, at least not at *face value*. To say that denial of death varies is to place it on a continuum. At one end of this continuum is low denial, a culture where death and the dead are omnipresent, playing a social role equal to life and the living. At the other end is high denial, a culture where death and the dead are entirely excluded from social life.[9]

My argument can be summarised as follows. First, I place the archaic gift economy, organised around the redistribution and destruction of surplus, on the low end of the death denial continuum. Archaic economic activity is collective and sacred, actively involving the dead and death in order to make payable the existential debts that haunt us from the moment of biological birth. Cyclical time and periodic redemptive ritual are purposefully designed to prevent accumulation of anything, whether it be wealth, power, time, anxiety, or guilt. Second, I place the capitalist economy, organised around the routine reinvestment of surplus for profit, on the high end of the death denial continuum. With capitalism, economic activity is individualised and de-sacralised and the dead and death are banished, resulting in unpayable debts. Capital accumulation is the primary psychological defence mechanism, a power intended to stave off mortal dread. But because accumulation rests on linear time and is shorn of redemptive and sacrificial ritual, guilt and anxiety also start to accumulate. The system is driven by an endless and increasing neurotic charge. Third, I claim that since the 1970s, capitalist death denial has intensified. Structural transformations in the so-called 'advanced' economies over the past few decades have dissolved the remaining vestiges of collectivism in economic life and shattered any shared vision of social progress. The result is a disintegration of the remaining collective outlets needed to share, expiate, and, to some extent, relieve the cumulative guilt and anxiety of capitalist life. Intensified death denial in the contemporary era finds its most spectacular manifestation in Silicon Valley's quest for literal immortality. This privatised immortality project is a morbid escapism intended to hive the ruling class off from the irredeemable masses.

In what follows, I develop these arguments systematically, moving from the gift economy to capitalism to financialised capitalism, then concluding with some brief thoughts on possible alternatives to capitalist death denial. But before getting to my own analysis, I want to set the scene by discussing the limitations of some current thinking on the relationship between capitalism and death.

Modern mana?

TMT draws attention to the role of money, wealth, possession, and consumption as existential anxiety buffers, but has little to say about capitalism and even less to say about its central process of capital accumulation. The same cannot be said of some of the recent work of one of the leading lights of contemporary philosophy: Byung-Chul Han. In a collection of essays entitled *Capitalism and the Death Drive*, Han explicitly addresses the question of how mortal fear shapes modern economic life.[10]

Han draws on a longer lineage that interprets Freud's 'death instinct' not as an innate desire to die, but instead as a neurotic human incapacity to accept the reality of death.[11] In this way, Han claims that humans are haunted by an unconscious fear of death and that the repression of this fear is what drives human aggression and destructiveness. He argues that in capitalist societies, the primary way in which this fear gets repressed is through the accumulation of capital. The logical sequence of Han's argument runs as follows: more capital means more power and more power means less death. There is also a temporal aspect to the argument: time is money (capital), and 'infinite amounts of capital create the illusion of an infinite amount of time'.[12] Fear of death, along with our efforts to repel it, drive capitalism's irrational affinity for limitless production and growth, a compulsion that spells both ecological and mental catastrophe.

Han sees this destructive pattern running throughout history. In archaic societies, he argues, fear of death also spurs accumulation; what gets accumulated, however, is not capital but killing capacity in the form of sacrificial animals, slain enemies, their dried severed hands, skulls, and so on.[13] Here violence substitutes for capital as the basis for social power. In the archaic world, the exertion of more violence means more power and more power means protection against death. Han claims that the origins of money can be traced to its use as a medium of exchange for the purchase of sacrificial animals. Those with money thus acquire a divine right to kill. From the Mohawk warrior to the Japanese day trader, a shared psychic impulse is at play.

> The hoarded money gives its owner the status of a predator. It immunizes him against death. At the level of depth psychology, this archaic belief continues to operate in the idea that accumulated killing capacity, and accumulated capital assets, will ward off death. Capital's logic of accumulation corresponds exactly to the archaic economy of violence. Capital behaves like a modern version of mana. Mana is the name of that powerful, mysterious substance that one acquires through the act of killing. One accumulates it in order to create a feeling of power and invulnerability.[14]

What are we to make of Han's equation of capital with mana? Though the imagery is seductive, it is also misleading and contradictory. If we take seriously the baseline definition of accumulation as routine reinvestment for profit, then it is difficult to see any resemblance between capital and archaic killing capacity. For the logic of capital accumulation to 'correspond exactly' to the archaic economy of violence, an enterprising warrior would have to take the body parts of slain enemies, sell them on the market, and then re-invest the proceeds to expand their killing apparatus in the hopes of obtaining more body parts for ever-greater profits in an endless cycle of expansion. Ritual sacrifice lays bare the absurdity of Han's analogy even more starkly. At its core, sacrifice entails the lavish squandering of surplus, not its profit-seeking reinvestment, thus putting paid to the idea that sacrificial animals could ever be accumulated, at least in any meaningful sense of the term.

Even if we could conceive of war trophies and sacrificial animals in terms of accumulation, there would still be insurmountable problems with Han's formulation. As Han himself appears to acknowledge, the compulsion to grow is what accounts for the peculiarity of human destructiveness under capitalism. But then if all societies accumulate, they grow. And if all societies experience growth, then there is nothing distinct about capitalism's destructiveness. This may sound like a critique built on a mere technicality, but it strikes at the heart of how we think about the relationship between capitalism and death. Han may be correct in identifying capital accumulation as a defense against death, but it is a novel form of defense unlike anything that preceded it.

Sacred gifts

If we want to capture what is unique about capitalism's revolt against death, we need to take a different approach. Rather than emphasise continuity, we should instead take seriously the idea that capitalism is a fundamental break with the past. This line of inquiry leads us to the ideas of postwar thinkers like Bataille, Brown, and Baudrillard. Each of these thinkers approaches the psychological dimensions of capitalism with their own unique style and nuance. Yet what unites them is a method of uncovering the distinctiveness of capitalism by juxtaposing it with the archaic. What also unites them is an understanding of the archaic gift economy through engagement with the work of Marcel Mauss.[15]

Mauss' famous essay on archaic gift economies makes clear their stark differences with capitalism. In archaic societies, production and distribution are governed by principles of giving and sharing rather than taking and accumulating. Similarly, power, prestige, and rank in archaic societies, which Han discusses under the rubric of 'mana', derive not from accumulating a surplus but from giving it away. The complex systems of reciprocity that underpin the gift economy have two main defining features. The first is that exchange is only rarely between individuals and is almost always collective, involving all members of the clan, tribe, or family. Crucially, the members of this collective include not only the living but also ancestors, spirits, and gods, who actively participate in gift exchange, often through their masked representative, the shaman. To involve the dead in exchange is to render it sacred, and this sacred nature of the archaic gift economy is its second defining feature. Even the things exchanged are sacred in that they possess their own living soul or spiritual power (referred to as 'hau' in Māori culture). In giving a gift, the giver offers a piece of their own soul, and holding on to that spiritually charged object represents a grave danger for the beneficiary, who risks coming under its magical control.

Though the return of a gift is technically voluntary, it is in fact obligatory to prevent social disorder. What is the psychology of this obligation to give and to receive, to match gifts with counter-gifts? Most importantly, what compels someone to give in the first place when the best they can hope for is to break even (i.e., receive a counter-gift) and never to gain in any lasting way from an act of exchange? In answering these questions, we must abandon all of the rationalist, utilitarian assumptions that underpin modern economic theory. The gift, Brown argues, is a form of self-sacrifice that addresses the universal human need to expiate the burden of guilt. Brown takes as his point of departure the arguments of Nietzsche in *The Genealogy of Morals* regarding the relationship between debt and guilt.[16] Finding lingering traces of Smithian utilitarianism in Nietzsche's claim that conscience (guilt) derives from a universal propensity to trade, Brown reverses the argument, deriving trade from conscience (i.e., from guilt).

For Brown, it is the later work of Freud, rather than Nietzsche, that provides the better starting point for thinking through the universal human experience of guilt and its relationship to the archaic gift economy. This sense of guilt can be traced back to earliest childhood. In the womb, a child experiences what Freud describes as the 'oceanic feeling', a non-dualistic state of oneness, the unadulterated pleasure principle.[17] Birth is therefore an act of separation from this state of oneness and the child experiences separation as a death of the mother. In a condition of primary narcissism and a feeling of omnipotence, the child denies this separation and seeks to regain the unity found in the womb. Subjective omnipotence (the pleasure principle) confronts objective dependence and the need for parental support and authority (the reality principle). These early experiences are anxiety-inducing, painful, and traumatic, and the child is forced to repress their desire for reunion. The child's self-repression sets in motion feelings of frustration and aggression towards the object of love. And as Brown observes, aggression against those simultaneously loved results in feelings of guilt.[18]

Put another way, from a state of primal unity in the womb, birth entails a splitting of life from death. Life is the traumatic realisation of human limits and the most fundamental of these limits is the limit on lifespan, our own and of those we love. The anxiety-inducing realisation of human limits leads to a denial of such limits. In its human form, the death instinct is simply our incapacity to accept death. Anxiety leads to denial, denial works as repression, and repression leads to guilt. The need to expiate guilt and alleviate death anxiety are therefore two sides of the same coin.

Ritual rebirth

How then does reciprocal giving expiate guilt? Gift exchange does not eliminate guilt but it does create a form of social organisation that allows people to share, and therefore mitigate, its burden. In archaic societies, gods and ancestors are present in exchange to make debts payable and therefore to expiate the guilt that comes with existence. At the heart of archaic cosmology is cyclical time, which prevents the accumulation of anything, whether it be wealth, power, time, anxiety, or guilt. In the words of Becker,

> [p]rimitive man lived in a world devoid of clocks, progressive calendars, once-only numbered years. Nature was seen in her imagined purity of endless cycles of sun risings and sun settings,

moon waxings and wanings, seasons changing, animals dying and being born, etc. This kind of cosmology is not favourable to the accumulation of either guilt or property, since everything is wiped away with the gifts and nature is renewed with the help of ritual ceremonies of regeneration. Man did not feel that he had to pile things up.[19]

The archaic economy is sacred, which is another way of saying that it is embedded in religion. As we have seen, the archaic gift economy is sacred because it involves living and dead members of the community as well as the exchange of spiritually charged objects. But there is another vital way in which the gift economy is sacred. It is not only an exchange between the living and dead, but also an exchange of life and death itself.

The centrality of life and death to the archaic economy can be seen in initiation rituals. Initiation can involve the sacrifice of humans, animals, and other precious goods, or auto-sacrifice through circumcision, the knocking out of teeth, the amputation of fingers, bloodletting, scarification, and so on. In ritual sacrifice, death is given to the gods, spirits, and ancestors, either literally through killing or symbolically through mutilation. Counter-gifts are then received from the gods in the form of blessings, protection, secret vocabularies, or new names, all of which signify a new life, a ritual rebirth in which the initiate becomes a complete member of a community.

Mircea Eliade gives a rather stark example to illustrate this exchange of life and death in the 'being born again' ceremonies of the Bantu people of sub-Saharan Africa.[20] During the ceremony, a father sacrifices a ram and wraps his son in the animal's stomach membrane and skin. Just before entering the ram skin, the boy gets into bed and cries like an infant. After three days in this symbolic womb, the son emerges, is circumcised, and undergoes a ritual rebirth. Eliade also mentions how the Bantu people will place their dead in the fetal position and bury them in the skin of a sacrificed ram. Through initiation, death is transformed into a rite of passage; it marks the death of a profane life and the rebirth to a 'new spiritual existence'.[21]

Baudrillard assesses the underlying meaning of this symbolic trading of life and death.[22] The archaic gift economy, which Baudrillard refers to as a system of 'symbolic exchange', does not conjure away death but instead articulates it socially through

collective ritual. Most importantly, the involvement of the dead
and death in symbolic forms of exchange prevents the splitting
of life from death that Brown and Freud argue haunts human
existence from the very moment of (biological) birth. According
to Baudrillard, unless this split is prevented through collective
and sacred exchange resulting in social rebirth, life itself becomes
a fatality, a biological irreversibility, an absurd physical destiny, a
condemnation to inevitably decline and decay with the body.[23]

Unpayable deaths

What changes with capitalism? In place of the principles of giving
and sharing that govern the archaic gift economy, capitalism
substitutes taking and possessing. With this shift, power, prestige,
and rank are no longer derived from destroying or redistributing
surplus to other members of the community (living and dead), but
from accumulation, defined earlier as the routine reinvestment of
profits in the anticipation of future profitability. Collective ritual
gives way to individual contract. The sacred becomes profane
insofar as the dead and death are thrown out of economic activity
and exiled to the margins of social life. That which is exchanged
no longer embodies the soul of the giver, now a seller, and thus
the beneficiary, now a buyer, need no longer worry about coming
under its magical control. This, however, is a process of pseudo-
secularisation; the power and magic are still there, it is just that the
key institution of exchange, money, no longer acts as a stand-in or
representation of the sacred; it is itself sacred. As Bataille makes
clear, the precapitalist pursuit of wealth is a means towards an end
of unproductive religious consumption, while capitalism makes the
pursuit of wealth an end in itself.[24]

   What relationship does this regime of accumulation have to the
universal human experience of guilt? Recall that the gift economy
alleviates guilt through sacrifice. The gods and ancestors exist in
order to make the debts that start accruing from the moment of birth
payable, and the cyclical time of archaic cosmology means periodic
redemption and the wiping clean of the slate of guilt through regen-
erative ceremony. Archaic exchange with the dead (and of death)
prevents the splitting of life and death that accompanies biological

birth, a technique for openly and collectively managing the guilt and anxiety that accompany the human incapacity to come to terms with death. But in capitalism, the gods retreat from economic life, resulting in unpayable debts. The individual alone is meant to shoulder the existential burden, as death is de-socialised and displaced to the unconscious. Time becomes linear, guilt and anxiety become cumulative, and the burden of existence can no longer be periodically alleviated through collective ritual. Instead, the economic system is fuelled by the psychic charge of guilt and anxiety.

So how is one to cope with the bleakness of capitalism? In short, by denying guilt and anxiety and accumulating capital as a psychological defence mechanism. Capital is a form of power, one that is accumulated as a way of denying death, of sublimating the mortal dread that characterises human existence. Thus Han is largely correct in identifying capital with power and death denial, even though his analysis is full of obfuscation, and even though he was by no means the first to make the connection. Where Han errs, however, is in conflating capital with precapitalist forms of wealth. Whether it was squandered in the potlatch or used to construct medieval cathedrals, wealth has throughout history served as a form of immortality power. Precapitalist wealth was a means to a religious end, which meant that to unlock its immortal power it had to be given up. Freed from these divine limits, the immortality power of capital derives not from giving it up, and not even from holding on to it, but instead from investing it with the aim of making more of it. Capitalist wealth can be distinguished from precapitalist forms of wealth in that it *breeds*.[25] Capitalism's freeing of the economy from divine limits also means that the future no longer rests on the whims of the gods and becomes quantifiable and manageable, even if still fundamentally unknowable.[26] With this forward-looking orientation, capitalist immortality power is exercised not only in the here and now, but also over the future.

What makes capitalism distinct is its sustained growth dynamic, which enables unprecedented material wealth and spectacular technological advancement. Yet for all its dynamism, capitalism is also much more wasteful than precapitalist societies predicated on unproductive consumption. Waste and inefficiency amid growth and innovation. This paradox results in what Brown, in his poetic reflections on Bataille, refers to as a 'schizophrenic symbiosis of spendthrift symbolic projects with a mainline dynamic of thrifty accumulation'.[27] But the main point is that neither the spendthrift nor the thrifty are truly redemptive because they are not truly sacrificial. Without redemptive ritual, life and death are split. Life is governed by the accumulation of dead things. Life in service of the death instinct.

Free-floating

The way that capitalism manages death anxiety is historically unique. On the continuum of death denial, capitalist society scores high relative to the archaic gift economy. But what can we say about death denial in different periods of capitalist development? More specifically, what are the implications of global economic changes since the 1970s for the death-denying properties of capitalism? Do the structural shifts associated with technological change, global-isation, neoliberalism, and financialisation constitute a radical rup-ture in capitalism's relationship with death?

Of the postwar thinkers engaged with in this chapter, Baudrillard is perhaps best equipped to help us navigate these questions. While Bataille and Brown penned their definitive works in the early postwar era, Baudrillard's *Symbolic Exchange and Death* was published amid the disintegration of the postwar order in the mid-1970s. In the book, Baudrillard is trying to come to terms with some of the dramatic transformations in the West that, at the time, were only beginning to unfold: deindustrialisation, automation, digitalisation, the rise of the service economy, the waning influence of trade unions, the proliferation of financial instruments and cross-border capital flows, rampant inflation, and the collapse of the gold standard.

According to Baudrillard, these shifts are all manifestations of a revolution in the law of value in capitalist economies, from the commodity law of the industrial era to the structural law of what we might now refer to as the financialised era. The monetary signs of the financial sphere no longer have any meaningful relationship with the 'real' sphere of material production.[28] Money becomes an 'autonomous simulacrum', a 'floating and indeterminate' signifier emancipated from constraints and opened to infinite speculation.[29]

With this revolutionary break, political economy itself, predicated on the commodity law of value, is robbed of any determinacy. Floating theories and floating money, both searching in vain for a corresponding 'reality'.

Baudrillard is an unruly thinker, and one of the frustrating aspects of *Symbolic Exchange and Death* is that its arguments about the transformation of contemporary capitalism are not systematically integrated into its analysis of the political economy of death. The book does nonetheless leave some clues on how to connect them. In addition to money and theories that freely float, the structural revolution of value also creates free-floating humans. In Baudrillard's effusive prose, 'Today, individuals, disinvested as subjects and robbed of their fixed relations, are drifting in relation to one another, into an incessant mode of transferential fluctuations: flows, connections, disconnections, transference/counter-transference.'[30]

It is this growing atomisation of society, this free-floating of humanity, that I argue distinguishes death denial in the contemporary era from earlier phases of capitalist development. In the industrial era, which found its apogee in the 'advanced' economies of the postwar period, the individual was expected to bear the existential burden, but some vestiges of collectivism in economic life remained. Though riven with class conflict, as well as racialised and gendered forms of exclusion, the Keynesian consensus meant that the captain of industry, the repressed financier, the factory worker, and the activist state official all bought into a shared aim of achieving macroeconomic stability and widespread prosperity. Accumulation was the sacred end of economic activity, but this was accompanied by a widespread belief that the pursuit of that sacred end would result in social progress. Capitalists and workers alike embraced a productivist, state-led utopia of unlimited material wealth, scientific advancement, and the perfectibility of humanity – they just disagreed on how the growing output should be controlled and distributed. We can therefore see the postwar order as a shared project of symbolic immortality, an inter-class endeavour striving towards something more enduring and larger than oneself. Not exactly the communal ecstasy of archaic ritual, but nonetheless a shared vision and sense of purpose for containing mortal dread.

Since the 1970s, the remaining vestiges of collectivism in economic life have more or less vanished. The Keynesian consensus has broken down. The capitalist class has become fractured, workers have been dispersed, and the solidaristic ethos of the welfare state has been shattered.[31] Accumulation remains sacred. Yet with stagnation, rising inequality, and ecological breakdown, no one seriously believes that it will bring about social progress. The dissolution of social bonds and the disillusionment with societal improvement mark a disintegration of the remaining collective outlets needed to share and expiate the cumulative guilt and anxiety of capitalist life. The project of immortality becomes fractured, individualised, and privatised, and the result is intensifying death denial.

Valley of death

The privatisation of immortality finds its most spectacular expression in Silicon Valley's recent investments in innovations aimed at cheating death. As mentioned earlier, money can buy literal immortality by vastly extending life in the hope of someday eliminating 'natural' death. The deeper one digs into Silicon Valley's real-life quest for immortality, the more difficult it becomes to distinguish it from the darkest, most dystopian phantasms of science fiction.

Take, for instance, the start-up Ambrosia that has been linked with billionaire venture capitalist Peter Thiel. Until it was shut down by the US Food and Drug Administration in 2019, the company had been charging customers aged thirty-five and older $8,000 for a purportedly age-reversing transfusion of blood from donors aged twenty-five or younger. It seems Marx's famed description of capital as a vampire sucking the blood of living labour is no longer a mere metaphor.[32] Or consider the non-profit Alcor, which specialises in cryonics, a procedure that preserves the body at ultra-low temperatures in the hope that future medical advancements will allow the person to be revived. Counting Thiel among its customers, Alcor outlines its transparent pricing structure on its website: $200,000 for full-body cryopreservation, a fee that drops to $80,000 for neuro cryopreservation (i.e., deep-freezing the head only). But for true tech fantasists, the most promising cryonic pathway to immortality may lie in digital consciousness. In experiments with rabbits, another start-up called Nectome has developed a way of preserving the brain with the promise of one day being able to upload its contents to the cloud. The company made headlines in 2018 for securing a $10,000 deposit from angel investor Sam Altman to join its waiting list. Luckily for Altman, the deposit is refundable, but there are other costs attached to Nectome's digital immortality package – to have their brain preserved, customers must literally be euthanised. Altos Labs, backed by Jeff Bezos, and California Life Company (Calico), a subsidiary of Alphabet, are exploring cell and tissue reprogramming to fight disease, extend life, and, ultimately, 'solve death'.[33] Though cellular reprogramming is considered on the cutting edge of anti-ageing science, the mice on which it has been tested so far have developed teratomas: rare 'monstrous' tumours (from the Greek for monster, 'teras') containing a mix of hair, muscle, teeth, and bone tissues.[34]

Having washed their hands of social compromise and shared notions of progress, dominant capital now resorts to the most elaborate forms of escapism. Remote private islands, phallus-shaped space rockets, and life-extension technologies are being secured as part of a wider strategy by the chosen few to hive themselves off from the irredeemable masses. The ruling-class pursuit of literal immortality has a long history, from Chinese emperors in the third century BCE guzzling purportedly life-preserving potions made of mercury to Slovakian countesses in the seventeenth century bathing in the blood of virgins.[35] What distinguishes the ruling class of today is that it possesses the financial and technological power to make its pursuit scientifically plausible. The current mood is captured by Daniel Ives, founder of Shift Bioscience, a UK anti-ageing start-up.

> The individuals contributing this wealth [to anti-ageing research] don't have anywhere else left to go. The funders have got everything – the high life and more profit than they can dream of. The only thing left to do is to change reality. This really feels like a new frontier because we've never been able to stand on the precipice of resetting our biology and having a second life. It's going to be a long, difficult road but it's not going to peter out – there's too many people piling in and too much promising data for it to go back to zero. But it would be such a shame if we dragged our feet and didn't quite get there. We would end up being the last generation who suffered the tragedy of age-related diseases.[36]

Paradoxically, this drive to eliminate death is itself morbid. It is morbid not only because of its gruesome failures to date. It is morbid not only because it is unsustainable to try to support ageless billionaires with extreme carbon footprints on a dying planet. Setting aside all this, the whole enterprise would still be a morbidity because death and finite existence are what give vitality and meaning to life. Without death, life itself becomes sterile and lifeless.

In the archaic gift economy, the wisdom of this paradox was embodied in collective rituals for preventing the splitting of life and death. With the rise of capitalism, this wisdom was largely forgotten. In the industrial era, the dead and death were banished from economic life, but the living could still partially contain cumulative guilt and anxiety through a shared immortality project. Now with free-floating financialised capitalism, the split between life and death has widened to a point where it becomes almost impossible to find existential relief. But the crucial takeaway from this timeless paradox is that as much as capitalist societies try to bury death, it will always come bubbling to the surface.

Losing ourselves

If capitalist immortality is a dead end, then what is the way out? There are no easy answers, but simply acknowledging that unconscious fears about death shape our destructive behaviours seems like an important first step. Only when we make these unconscious fears conscious can we begin the work of envisioning less destructive ways of managing that fear, of channelling it into more creative and humane ways of living.

As Brown suggests, examining the role of death in economic life offers a simple but profound insight for political economy: we do not live by bread alone.[37] Economic activity, from the gift economy to financialised capitalism, is as much about the spirit as it is about the stomach. Today we see this search for spiritual connection all around us, and it is easy to be cynical about it. But some alternative modes of consciousness – indigenous, Eastern, psychedelic – contain the promise of truly revolutionary ways of living and dying. Politically, the challenge is to connect these alternative modes of consciousness to radical new forms of economic organisation.

Letting go of the fear of death involves loosening the grip of the ego, and that seems like a useful, maybe even a necessary, psychological accompaniment to any collective project based on democratic ownership, mutual care, and ecological restoration. Without an unwavering commitment to integrate the psychic and the economic, the former is too easily absorbed by the logic of capital, appropriated and coopted, individualised and privatised, drained of its radical potential.

Maybe Marx and Engels were right.[38] Maybe we really do have nothing to lose but our chains. Only, losing those chains might mean something more like what Brown had in mind: losing ourselves.

Notes

1 Tomasz Zaleskiewicz, Agata Gasiorowska, Pelin Kesebir, Aleksandra Luszczynska, and Tom Pyszczynski, 'Money and the Fear of Death: The Symbolic Power of Money as an Existential Anxiety Buffer', *Journal of Economic Psychology* 36 (2013): 55–67.

2 For an overview of TMT research, see Tom Pyszczynski, Sheldon Solomon, and Jeff Greenberg, 'Thirty Years of Terror Management Theory: From Genesis to Revelation', *Advances in Experimental Social Psychology* 52 (2015): 1–70. For applications beyond social psychology, see Lindsey A. Harvell and Gwendelyn S. Nisbett, eds, *Denying Death: An Interdisciplinary Approach to Terror Management Theory* (New York: Routledge, 2016).

3 Ernest Becker, *The Denial of Death* (London: The Free Press, 1973), xvii.

4 Ellen Meiksins Wood, *The Origins of Capitalism: A Longer View* (London: Verso, 2017).

5 Georges Bataille, *The Accursed Share: An Essay on General Economy, Volume I*, trans. Robert Hurley (New York: Zone Books, 1991); Norman O. Brown, *Life Against Death: The Psychoanalytical Meaning of History* (Middletown, CT: Wesleyan University Press, 1959); Jean Baudrillard, *Symbolic Exchange and Death*, trans. Iain Hamilton Grant (London: Sage, 2017).

6 Laura Tradii and Martin Robert, 'Do We Deny Death? II. Critique of the Death-Denial Thesis', *Mortality* 24, no. 4 (2019): 377–88.

7 Ai-Ling Lai, 'The "Mortal Coil" and the Political Economy of Death', in *Death in a Consumer Culture*, ed. Susan Dobscha (London: Routledge, 2016), 261.

8 Calvin Conzelus Moore and John Williamson, 'The Universal Fear of Death and the Cultural Response', in *Handbook of Death and Dying, Volume I*, ed. Clifton Bryant (Thousand Oaks, CA: Sage, 2003), 4.

9 Another modernist conceit I want to avoid: conflating low and high death denial with low and high culture. Baseline culture stems from death denial, but cultures with low death denial are every bit and oftentimes even more symbolically complex and sophisticated as those with high death denial.

10 Byung-Chul Han, *Capitalism and the Death Drive*, trans. Daniel Steuer (Cambridge: Polity Press, 2021).

11 Freud was not entirely consistent in his thinking on the death instinct. See, for example, the discussions in Victor Blüml, Liana Giorgi, and Daru Huppert, eds, *Contemporary Perspectives on the Freudian Death Drive: In Theory, Clinical Practice and Culture* (London: Routledge, 2019). The main dividing line in the subsequent literature is between those who interpret the death instinct as fear of death and those who interpret it as enjoyment of death. Han associates the reworking of the death instinct as death fear with Baudrillard, but its essential contours were already laid out by Otto Rank, one-time protégé of Freud and a major inspiration for Becker and TMT. See Otto Rank, *Will Therapy and Truth and Reality* (New York: Alfred A. Knopf, 1945), 114–18. One of the most prominent examples of the death instinct as enjoyment (or *jouissance*) can be found in the work of Jacques Lacan. For example, see Jacques Lacan, *Écrits: The First Complete Edition in English* (New York: W.W. Norton & Co., 1966). It is worth noting that whether one interprets the death instinct as death fear or death enjoyment, the consequences associated with it are largely the same: aggressive and destructive behaviour towards the self, other humans, and more-than-human nature.

12 Han, *Capitalism and the Death Drive*, 6.

13 Han seems to pivot between two different definitions of the archaic, one as ancient civilisation and one as traditional or, in outdated language, 'primitive' societies. In this chapter I stick to the latter understanding of the archaic and, to minimise sweeping generalisations about archaic societies in general, focus on the gift economy.

14 Han, *Capitalism and the Death Drive*, 7.

15 Marcel Mauss, *The Gift: The Form and Reason for Exchange in Archaic Societies*, trans. W. D. Halls (London: Routledge, 2002).

16 Friedrich Nietzsche, *On the Genealogy of Morals: A Polemic*, trans. Michael A. Scarpitti (London: Penguin, 2013). See also Amin Samman and Stefano Sgambati, 'Financialising the eschaton', Chapter 10 in this volume.

17 Sigmund Freud, *Civilization and Its Discontents*, trans. David McLintock (London: Penguin, 2004), 2.

18 Brown, *Life Against Death*, 268.

19 Ernest Becker, *Escape From Evil* (New York: The Free Press, 1973), 87.

20 Mircea Eliade, *The Sacred and the Profane: The Nature of Religion*, trans. Willard R. Trask (New York: Harvest, 1989), 190–92.

21 *Ibid.*, 196.

22 Baudrillard, *Symbolic Exchange and Death*.

23 *Ibid.*, 153.

24 Bataille, *The Accursed Share*.

25 Brown, *Life Against Death*.

26 Peter L. Bernstein, *Against the Gods: The Remarkable Story of Risk* (New York: John Wiley & Sons, 1996); Shimshon Bichler and Jonathan Nitzan, 'The Capitalist Degree of Immortality', *Working Papers on Capital as Power*, December 23, 2021, https://capitalaspower. com/2021/12/2021-06-bichler-nitzan-the-capitalist-degree-of-immortality/ (accessed September 2, 2022).

27 Norman O. Brown, *Apocalypse and/or Metamorphosis* (Berkeley, CA: University of California Press, 1990), 189.

28 Though space constraints prevent me from exploring the point further, it is worth noting that there are compelling reasons to question whether the financial sphere ever had any meaningful relationship with the 'real' sphere of material production in the first place. See Jonathan Nitzan and Shimshon Bichler, *Capital as Power: A Study of Order and Creorder* (London: Routledge, 2009).

29 Baudrillard, *Symbolic Exchange and Death*, 24 and 44.

30 *Ibid.*, 45.

31 Mark S. Mizruchi, *The Fracturing of the American Corporate Elite* (Cambridge, MA: Harvard University Press, 2013).

32 Karl Marx, *Capital: Critique of Political Economy, Volume I*, trans. Ben Fowkes (London: Penguin, 1990), 342.

33 Harry McCracken and Lev Grossman, 'Google vs. Death', *Time*, September 30, 2013, https://time.com/574/google-vs-death/ (accessed September 2, 2022).

34 Anjana Ahuja, 'Silicon Valley's Billionaires Want to Hack the Ageing Process', *Financial Times*, September 7, 2021, www.ft.com/content/24849908-ac4a-4a7d-b53c-847963ac1228 (accessed September 2, 2022).

35 Theo Zenou, 'The Long and Gruesome History of People Trying to Live Forever', *The Washington Post*, May 1, 2022, www.washingtonpost. com/history/2022/05/01/immortality-gilgamesh-bezos-thiel/ (accessed September 2, 2022).

36 Quoted in Anjana Ahuja, 'Can We Defeat Death?' *Financial Times*, October 29, 2021, www.ft.com/content/60d9271c-ae0a-4d44-8b11-956cd2e484a9 (accessed September 2, 2022).
37 Brown, *Life Against Death*, 17.
38 Karl Marx and Friedrich Engels, *The Communist Manifesto*, trans. Samuel Moore (London: Penguin, 2015), 258.

3

The eroticism of technology and finance

Noam Yuran

The second use of technology is erotic. One can come up with some familiar historical examples for this rule of thumb: the relatively short lapse of time between the invention of photography and the first nude photographs; the emergence of alt.sex usenet groups after establishing the Internet as a computer network immune to nuclear attacks; dickpics sent from smartphones. This speculative proposal, however, pertains to more than temporal ordering. It is not simply that erotic uses of technology come second. Rather, they are erotic because they are second in relation to the uses for which the technology was originally designed. With every technological innovation, the erotic poses a tantalising answer to the inevitable question: 'What else can we can do with this?' The most famous cinematic depiction of the industrial assembly line, in Charlie Chaplin's *Modern Times*, demonstrates the eroticism of technology's second use. Chaplin is swallowed by the machine and then emerges from it changed: a human extension of the machine, robotically repeating his mindless task, applying it to the wrong objects. First, he annoys his coworkers with his tools, but then immediately turns to an erotic aim, chasing women whose dress buttons he mistakes for screws that need tightening. Going into the machine: the wrong, improper use of technology reveals what technology is in itself, manifested in an erotic form. Freud's view of sexuality and Marshall McLuhan's view of technology converge at this point. For Freud, sexuality has to do with repetition beyond aim: thumb-sucking is the paradigmatic example of infantile sexuality, because it simulates the activity of nourishment without actual nourishment.[1] For McLuhan, the significance of technology lies beyond its instrumental use. What we do with machines, which McLuhan defines as their content, typically obfuscates their message, which refers to what they do to us as societies and living beings.[2]

Chaplin's scene can also be read in economic terms. Repetition that has become an aim can articulate an internal difference between financial and real economy, understood not as two distinct domains of economic activity, but as two partially overlapping perspectives on the economy. Such a conceptualisation is folded into Wesley Mitchell's view of the economy as encompassing both the art of making goods and the art of making money.[3] From this perspective, grounded in a Veblenian framework, capitalism can be defined as an economy where the art of making money governs the art of making goods. The proper use of technology in the assembly line represents the real economy as the art of making things. The improper use signals a shift of perspective which highlights how the process assumes the form of aimless repetition. In this use things are immaterial, a pretext for repetition itself. It embodies a financial perspective on the economy, where things are placeholders in a circulation of endlessly increasing value. Diving into the machine to re-emerge in non-human form, Chaplin articulates the familiar image of finance as parasite, both external and internal to productive capital. Marx formulated a theoretical ground for this image. The financial circulation M-M' is external to the production process (it draws on surplus value produced somewhere outside it), but it is at the same time an internal principle of productive capital, designated by M-C-M', where the production of things is organised in order to accumulate value.

This chapter examines a configuration of technology, economy, and sexuality typical of capitalism. It is grounded on a homology between three conceptual couplets in the three respective fields: the content and message of technology, real and financial economy, and sex and eroticism. Each couplet implies a detachment from aim or substitution of means for ends. The message of technology transcends its content, financial economy transcends the aim of making things, and eroticism transcends the sexual aim of reproduction. Yet more than a homology is at stake here. The configuration of these couplets in capitalism relies on an interplay between them. A technological approach to sex inscribes on it a financial logic and a technological approach to money eroticises it. The chapter explores this triple knot through some contemporary cultural representations of technology and eroticism; it proceeds to present the mutual infiltration of eroticism and finance at the dawn of the twentieth-century sexual revolution, and concludes with a quick glance at dating apps and contemporary hook-up culture.

Technology as a form of desire

Neil Strauss' misogynistic bestseller *The Game* is a blatant example of eroticism permeated by a capitalist logic. The book recounts Strauss' initiation into a 'secret society' of pick-up artists and his ascent within their circles. This informal community is founded on the idea of developing and sharing techniques for seducing women. Its ulterior motivation, however, has more to do with male camaraderie and competition than with sex. Sexual success grants members a higher status within the community, sometimes described as 'legendary'. Alongside this competitive drive a strong sense of camaraderie pervades the community: pick-up artists embark on seduction expeditions in bars together; they are committed to sharing knowledge and techniques. They also have their own lingo abounding with acronyms (LMR – last-minute resistance; SHB – super-hot babe; AFC – average frustrated chump). These serve a double purpose, conferring a technical semblance on their methods and maintaining the notion of clandestine knowledge as a means of male bonding. Indeed, Strauss sometimes refers to their activities in terms of a collective amateur scientific project. Readers unacquainted with this subculture might be misled by the air of sophistication conveyed by such terminology. In truth, a distinct sense of masculine infantilism pervades the book. One of Strauss' favorite techniques is the ESP trick: ask a woman in a bar to think of a number, then impress her by guessing 'seven'.

Nonetheless, the pick-up artists are emotionally invested in their technical lingo and seem to derive pleasure from its use. Sometimes they even refer to their shared knowledge as 'technology'.[4] What does this term mean, granted that no real sense of technology is entailed in their activities? *Technology is the form of their desire.* They desire women technologically. Two aspects are significant in this respect. First, the imaginary notion of technology renders the pick-up artists' search for sex a mirror image of the capitalist spirit.

As Max Weber defines it, the capitalist spirit is not identical with the desire for riches, but aims at the systematic, rational production of profit.[5] Similarly, it is not simply sex that the pick-up artists want. What they seek is a *method*: an impersonal technique of getting as many women as possible to have sex with them. In economic terms, technology signals a shift of perspective from the real to the financial. A success is unimportant in itself, as a sexual pleasure, and matters only when counted as an accumulation of some kind of abstract value. Second, the notion of technology expresses a desire, prevalent in pornography, for turning women into mechanisms, finding a way to activate them, or making them lose their conscious self-control.

An objectification of women is obviously implied in these two aspects of technological desire. It is important to stress, however, that objectification is not an answer to the question of why a cap-italist logic pervades eroticism. It is, rather, a reformulation of the question. Pick-up artists objectify women, yet their desire is not aimed at objects. Had they wanted sexual gratification through objects, there are enough of these today to easily satisfy their desires. Objectification as a process that is never consummated is the grammar of their desire. A transformation between subject and object moves their desire. Or, better yet, one can ask: what kind of objects do they want when they objectify women? It is a peculiar kind: an object that wants; a woman given to desire she can no longer control. Of one of the legendary pick-up artists, it is told that his techniques are so powerful that he makes women pay to give him blowjobs.[6] What a legend! It is futile to ask whether it is the money or the blowjob that he wants, for it is the combination that moves his desire. It is a tensed combination articulating sex as a form of control in a paradoxical way. The price delegates desire to the women; it is they who want it, while he only acquiesces. At the same time, the price also serves as a defence mechanism. The technological-erotic fantasy revolves not only around the woman as an object that wants, but as an object that knows no limits to desire. The price neutralises the horrifying kernel of this fantasy. There is only so much she can afford.

What kind of an object informs this objectification of women? A possible answer is capital, an economic object which also traverses the line separating objects and subjects. According to

Marx, the existence of capital entails the same interplay between controlling and being controlled. Capital entails a limitless drive to accumulate, but this drive can take effect only insofar as a capitalist surrenders his own desires to the drive of capital. Capital exists insofar as a capitalist makes 'the objective content of the circulation', namely the limitless drive of accumulation, 'his subjective purpose'.[7] It exists insofar as the capitalist acts as if he obeys the drive of capital itself to accumulate. Quoting Goethe's *Faust*, Marx offers a description of capital which bears uncanny resemblance to the women in the pick-up artists' fantasies: 'an animated monster which begins to "work," "as if its body were by love possessed"'.[8]

In *The Game*, technology is but a lewd fantasy structuring desire, yet a similar fantasy accompanies some mainstream depictions of real technology. It is clearly echoed in David Fincher's movie *The Social Network*. The misogyny of *The Game* is encoded in the film in a myth-like narrative of how Facebook emerged from the revenge of one angry man on the whole of the female gender. At the beginning of the movie, after being humiliatingly dumped by his girlfriend, Mark Zuckerberg publishes acerbic remarks about her on his blog, but as these do not quench his thirst for revenge, he tries something bigger. He hacks into Harvard's computers, downloads the photos of all female students, and sets up a website that rates them in order of attraction; users receive pairs of photos and decide which one is hotter, then an algorithm weighs all individual decisions into a collective male judgement. Another improper use of technology. During the night, Harvard's computer system crashes due to the rating craze. The key elements of the same fantasy are realigned here: female eroticism rendered in the abstract language of value, competition, and collective erotic male activity. Zuckerberg did in fact create the rating site FaceMash, but the revenge motive is an artistic licence Fincher took to frame the narrative (in the final scene, Zuckerberg sits alone in a litigation room after betraying all his business partners, obsessively refreshing the Facebook page of the girlfriend who dumped him). This theme, however, provides an essential link to *The Game*. It underlines the meaning of grading photos of women as a substitute form of acting on them, doing something to them, a way of applying power from a distance. It presents again the complexity of the entanglement of sex with technology: a technological mediation of sexuality is at the same time an erotic relation to technology.

Financialisation of eroticism and eroticisation of finance

Technology, real or imagined, articulates sex and economy. It gives expression to a capitalist or financial logic permeating eroticism. Two texts from the 1930s may shed light on this link. In his *General Theory*, Keynes famously compared financial speculation to a beauty contest. A year later, Willard Waller published a study of the dating scene in American colleges, describing a financial erotic economy underlying it. Technology in the ordinary sense of the word is less prominent in the two texts. They present, however, a double movement of infiltration: eroticism is financialised while finance is eroticised. The timing of publication of these two texts at an initial stage of the twentieth-century sexual revolution is most important. It suggests that the explanation for this double movement goes against some familiar intuitions about the entanglement of sex and economy.

A basic critical approach to economy and sex relies on a notion of expansion: with the progress of capitalism, market relations continually expand and eventually encompass our emotional life and intimate relationships. The timing of publication of Keynes' and Waller's texts suggests the opposite: financial language permeates eroticism when sex is partially *excluded* from the economy. From a real economy perspective, the sexual revolution marks a growing distance between sex and economy. In the precapitalist patriarchal tradition, sex was directly included in the economy. Ideally regulated through matrimony, sex was confined to the household, which was an important locus of economic life. In that tradition, marriage in the propertied classes was arranged according to economic considerations in the broad sense of the term, aiming at the ongoing prosperity of the household. Today, marriage is still an important economic institution, being the main locus of consumption and the transfer of wealth, but with two significant differences from the precapitalist patriarchal tradition. First, it is not usually conceived in economic terms (and when it is, it colours marriage with an obscene undertone). Second, sex is no longer regulated exclusively through matrimony. The sexual revolution brought about a new domain of eroticism, centred on sexuality external to the real economy, as represented by the household. The paradoxical point that a reading of Keynes and Waller suggests is that with the partial detachment of sex from the real economy, some forms of eroticism manifest a financial logic.

Willard Waller's classic study of the 'rating and dating complex' in American colleges in the 1930s demonstrates precisely this point. Waller contrasts dating to traditional forms of courtship still customary at the time. The latter were an efficient social mechanism for producing a high rate of marriage, while protecting individuals from possible traumatic experiences involved in the process. Their core was a procedure in which 'every step in the courtship process has a customary meaning and constitutes a powerful pressure toward taking the next step – is in fact a sort of implied commitment to take the next step'.[9] Eroticism may have had a place in traditional courtship, but it was subordinated to the goal of matrimony. Dating liberated intimate relations from their subordination to a goal. It allowed, in Waller's words, 'thrill-seeking' activity conducted for its own sake, in a whole range of new legitimate practices: dancing, petting, necking, the automobile, the amusement park, and more.[10] It gave rise to a certain form of eroticism as an articulation of sexuality outside the goal of marriage and reproduction. The crucial point, however, is that the detachment of eroticism from marriage did not result in its liberation from the economy but in a new form of economy, defined precisely by the absence of a definite aim. Economy is at the core of Waller's study, which focuses on the notion of differential values of men and women as dates, values which may be termed *erotic values*. These erotic values are public and to some extent collectively constituted. For men, for example, belonging to a better fraternity is essential to their rating as 'class A' dates. Among the factors that determine value some are real and objective (for men, supply of spending money, access to a car, nice clothes). Others are performative and subjective in nature (dancing well, having a 'good line').[11] The intriguing point, however, is that the erotic value of women follows the economic pattern of speculative values. The most important factor determining a woman's erotic value is her popularity as a date, the perception that everybody wants to date her. This perception can be intentionally cultivated but might also be undermined by mistakes. To cultivate reputation, a female student should not date too often the same student. Girls 'must be seen when they go out, and therefore must go to the popular (and expensive) meeting places'.[12] Mistakes such as accepting last-minute invitations might, on the other hand, impair a girl's reputation and diminish her erotic value.

The erotic value of female students as distinct from that of men follows the pattern of capital: 'here as nowhere else nothing succeeds like success.'[13] The parallel is the notion of financial capital which appears as money that begets money. The erotic value of women recapitulates Marx's definition of capital as 'self-valorising value'.

Eroticism is permeated by a financial logic when it is detached from marriage and traditional courtship. In a more speculative part of the study, however, Waller suggests that marriage too may go through a change as dating becomes a new form of courtship. In contrast to traditional courting, dating as courting involves 'falling in love', a process which typically occurs 'with a certain unwillingness'.[14] It displays some further aspects of a financial logic, evident in a dynamic of signs and their relation to reality. Like traditional courtship, falling in love is driven by reciprocal signs, but their nature is different. They are inflated signs. The young man tries to convince the young woman that he has already fallen seriously in love with her, 'a sort of exaggeration, sometimes a burlesque, of coquetry'. Furthermore, just as financial values are affected by expectations, and as promises of future value can materialise in the present, falling in love involves sentiments that are formed through pretending: 'each encourages the other to fall in love by pretending that he has already done so'.[15] As in financial assets, the slippage between expectations and reality is prone to crisis; in some cases, falling in love is facilitated by a series of 'periodic crises' which redefine the relationship on deeper levels of involvement. Lovers' quarrels are fuelled by the ambivalent status of speech in the context of dating. A form of erotic technique is involved. Waller stresses the role of 'the conventionalized "line"' in dating, noting how this form of erotic speech facilitates a sort of 'pluralistic ignorance' because it obscures the real state of mind of the interlocuters. It gives rise to the suspicion that one's partner does not experience a growth of feeling parallel to one's own.

The process as a whole displays a dynamic of self-inflating values and detachment from reality.

> A idealizes B, and presents to her that side of his personality which is consistent with his idealized conception of her; B idealizes A, and governs her behavior toward him in accordance with her false notions of his nature; the process of idealization is mutually re-enforced in such a way that it must necessarily lead to an increasing divorce from reality ... one falls in love when he reaches the point where sentiment-formation overcomes objectivity.[16]

Traditional courting and falling in love are distinguished by different economies of signs. Both are driven by performative signs: signs as implied commitments in the traditional form as against signs of love in the newer form. Yet the status of performativity is different and can be described in terms of a contrast between positive and negative performativity. In the traditional form, signs ideally create a solid commitment. As performative signs, they produce a new situation, but they do so by attesting to something that is really there. They are signs that have a 'cash value', so to speak. Falling in love, by contrast, is governed by signs of the nature of masquerade. They perform something which is not there yet but can sometimes materialise through its signalling. One cannot escape the formal parallel of this contrast to the distinction between the commodity theory of money and the credit theory of money. In the commodity theory, money is a thing, a piece of gold, and when signs, such as paper notes, are circulated as money, it is because they can be converted into the money-thing. In the credit theory, which according to Geoffrey Ingham captures the uniqueness of the capitalist form of money, signs do not refer to things but to no-thing: debt. Its creation involved an intricate institutional apparatus which transformed promises to pay into money.[17] Promises referred to a money-thing but became themselves means of payment and of settling accounts.

The parallel is important because the contrast between commodity theory and credit theory is in truth not exclusive. There is no clear dividing line between commodity money and credit money. Originally, debt bills could circulate as money because they were in principle convertible to gold, and the last ties between the international monetary system and gold were severed as late as the Nixon

Shock in 1971. Similarly, even if the credit theory is proper to capitalist money, it would be wrong to conclude that the commodity
theory is simply a mistake. For a very long time it was, rather, a
necessary illusion, essential for maintaining a system of credit-based
money. Returning to the speculative proposal presented at the beginning of this chapter, eroticism may be inscribed in the foundations
of credit money. It is a second, improper use of technology, of what
Ingham calls the social technology of money.[18] Better yet, credit
money is entangled with the implicit understanding that money is
indeed a technology. Commodity theory could refer to money as
an inert object, whereas the credit theory presents it as an intricate
mechanism coordinating social action through objects. In the credit
theory, money is defined by indefinite deferral and the removal of a
final aim, or by repetition beyond aim. Like Freud's thumb-sucking,
it simulates the activity of nourishment (receiving 'real' payment)
without actual nourishment. In the beginning of the credit-money
system in the eighteenth century, when credit still appeared to be
a different kind of thing than money proper, Defoe articulated this
erotic potential explicitly, writing that 'Credit is, or ought to be,
the tradesman's *mistress*.' The unspoken supplement to the analogy is that money is the tradesman's wife. Defoe also describes the
seduction technique necessary to secure credit, not unfamiliar to
pick-up artists. The tradesman must 'play hard to get'; to get credit
he should behave as if he does not need credit. 'If you court her, she
is gone; if you manage so wisely as to make her believe you really
do not want her, she follows and courts you.'[19]

The same contrast between marriage and eroticism is the metaphor Keynes also chose to express his suspicion of economic speculation. In a famous passage in the *General Theory*, Keynes explicates
the mechanism of financial speculation with a comparison to a
beauty contest in a newspaper. With some important distinctions,
it foretells Zuckerberg's FaceMash, with men collectively rating the
beauty of women.

> [P]rofessional investment may be likened to those newspaper
> competitions in which the competitors have to pick out the six
> prettiest faces from a hundred photographs, the prize being awarded
> to the competitor whose choice most nearly corresponds to the
> average preferences of the competitors as a whole; so that each com-
> petitor has to pick, not those faces which he himself finds prettiest,

but those which he thinks likeliest to catch the fancy of the other competitors, all of whom are looking at the problem from the same point of view.[20]

The erotic metaphor expresses a concern over the disrupting power of financial markets. As in Waller's study of dating, eroticism marks here a divorce between short-term expectations and long-term considerations, a situation where expectations of quick profits follow their own dynamics, which may be opposed to healthy long-term investment considerations. Furthermore, Keynes's erotic metaphor expresses a detachment from reality: a collective opinion materially created by people trying to guess the collective opinion.

It is no wonder, then, that Keynes finds in matrimony a metaphor for healthier investment mechanisms: 'The spectacle of modern investment markets has sometimes moved me towards the conclusion that to make the purchase of an investment permanent and indissoluble, like marriage, except by reason of death or other grave cause, might be a useful remedy for our contemporary evils.'[21] The unstable distinction between real and financial economy is mapped onto the distinction between marriage and eroticism. This mapping frames his argument as a nostalgic reaction to anxiety over the domination of financial markets in the economy. The nostalgic overtone is manifest in the multiplicity of ways his argument appears quaint. The idea of enforcing lifelong investment commitments was probably an impossible fantasy already at the time of writing. From our perspective, the form of the beauty contest Keynes invokes would also appear quaint. It expresses the distinction between real and financial economy by distinguishing between real, individual attraction and social conventions. The speculator is compared to a newspaper reader who suppresses his own erotic tastes to guess the popular taste. Moreover, popular taste is fashioned when all participants suppress their own tastes. Setting aside the question of financial markets, such a beauty contest would appear today awkwardly outdated. It runs against the basic premise of media obsession with female eroticism, namely that there is no distinction between a woman being a representative of collective male desire and her being desirable in herself. A contemporary parallel to Keynes' beauty contest is the media theme of 'hottest' bachelorettes lists. The women in such lists are directly desirable as women desired by 'everybody'. As the captions in such a list on

MSN declare: 'Every guy wants to date her, and every girl wants to friend her', 'Who wouldn't want such a catch on their arm?', 'X's svelte body has put her on everybody's radar again'.[22] These clickbait headlines are obviously performative rather than factual; they drive mediatised eroticism rather than report some statistical findings about desire. The ubiquity of this format should not blind us to the enigmatic form of desire it represents. It is not simply that media technology intervenes with our intimate fantasies, but it does so as a stand-in for society, interposing an anonymous 'everybody' between us and the object of our desire.

The most perverse aspect of this media theme lies in the form of the rated list. As this rating cannot but be arbitrary, a question arises: if magazines wish to publish photographs of beautiful young women, why do they not do just that? Why should the women be ranked from one to ten? The format of a rated list is not a simple pretext, conferring on the collection of photographs the form of information and a measure of legitimacy that comes with it. The list is also an ulterior form of desire. It is one further example of the technological and financial form of erotic desire. The women in the list are desired as embodiments of erotic values. Their erotic value follows the inherent instability of value that Marx attributed to financial capital as a 'value which is greater than itself'.[23] They are not really the 'hottest'; they are 'hot' (desired by the presumed reader) because they are presented as 'hottest'.

As a metaphor for financial markets, hottest-women lists would have provided a different view on finance than Keynes' awkward beauty contest. The latter served him to portray finance as an external threat to the real economy, substituting social conventions for real values. Hottest-women lists, by contrast, assume an identity between personal and conventional desire. Their economic counterpart would be the shareholder value theory, grounded on renouncing the distinction between real and financial values.

Does the erotic metaphor express an eroticisation of finance? A partial answer is found in Marx. Just as eroticism wears a financial form once sex is excluded from the realm of real economy, for Marx, money assumes the form of capital because it is excluded from the world of commodities. In the first chapter of *Capital*, Marx repeats this idea in several formulations: an object becomes money when it is excluded 'from the whole world of commodities'.[24]

Exclusion marks the way money embodies value not as a positive property, but through what it lacks, namely use value, which makes ordinary commodities qualitatively different and thus precludes the possibility of their quantitative comparison. The full meaning of this exclusion, however, unfolds in the concept of capital, where the lack of use value assumes a positive role. Because of this lack of qualities, the circulation of capital, which begins and ends with money, M-C-M', implies a limitless drive of quantitative increase.

Marx also uses some erotic metaphors to describe the relation between money and commodities: 'commodities are in love with money', prices are 'wooing glances cast at money by commodities', and the use value of commodities 'attracts the gold'.[25] These metaphors are important because they highlight a conceptual claim that Marx makes to distinguish his thought from the work of economists. The latter hold a narrow perspective on exchange, focusing solely on what he calls its 'physical aspect', where one object is given in return for another. This focus obscures the real riddle, which, according to Marx, is what happens to the form of the commodity in exchange. Marx uses a host of terms to refer to this other aspect of exchange: 'a change of form', 'metamorphosis of commodities', 'conversion', even 'transubstantiation'. Exchange involves two types of relations; in one, objects change hands, in the other, they change form – money becomes a commodity, and a commodity becomes money.[26] These two relations overlap the distinction between real and financial perspectives on the economy. In the first, objects are simply what they are. In the second, they are stand-ins for the movements of abstract value.

For that reason, Marx's erotic metaphor – like most of his metaphors – can be read literally. What distinguishes his theory is a potential libidinal view of the economy inscribed in its foundations. While for mainstream economics, things are what they are as physical objects, for Marx, they are also constantly transforming carriers of value. That is precisely the difference that in psychoanalysis defines libido in its distinction from hunger. Lacan makes this point clearly: 'the fact that a man may ejaculate upon seeing a slipper does not surprise us ... But surely no one imagines that a slipper can serve to abate an individual's hunger pangs'. This susceptibility to transformations of objects is what renders a behaviour sexual: 'The element of displacement is an essential mainspring of the set of behaviors related to sexuality.'[27] While the mainstream economic outlook is oriented towards needs and their respective objects, Marx's theory encompasses alongside needs an economy of desire, defined by the lack of a constant object. An obvious form of this desire is capital, whose movement is aimed neither at goods nor at money but driven by the constant changes of forms between them. Inadvertently, Marx also diagnosed how eroticism pervades consumption. Consider the lascivious overtone typical of luxury commercials. Is it not a visualisation of the commodities 'in love with money'? Luxury goods are eroticised when they are not simply physical objects but also represent expensiveness.

Promiscuous puritanism and online hook-up culture

Waller's study is still relevant today, after almost a century of continuing sexual liberation. A quick look at dating apps and hook-up culture suggests that promiscuous sex does not mark a liberation from the last remnants of puritanism. On closer examination it emerges, paradoxically, as a lewd version of the puritanical framework of traditional patriarchy. In her provocative argument about sexual paranoia on American campuses, Laura Kipnis shows how the institutional handling of sexual harassment rests on retrogressive assumptions about women's lack of sexual agency, 'recycling the most conventional versions of feminine virtue and delicacy'.[28] This puritan framework ostensibly runs counter to the libertine spirit of the hook-up scene, but Kipnis argues that the latter is in fact a symptom of the same spirit. The heavy use of alcohol in this scene serves students to shed inhibitions, revealing the age-old gender stereotypes lurking behind a superficial mask of gender progress, with bombed students 'acting out the respective gender extremes: men as aggressors, as predators; women as passive, as objects'.[29]

Kathleen Bogle's study of the hook-up scene shows how it resonates with the patriarchal economy of sex. Ostensibly, the hook-up scene manifests a further detachment of sex from the economy. It typically takes place in parties and bars which students attend in peer groups, and where some couples are formed for a short-term sexual encounter. The perennial economic questions that accompanied dating, 'Who pays for what?' and its obscene undertone, 'To what does payment entitle one?', have lost their meaning. Yet an economic aspect informs sex itself: it is still what men get and women give. Moreover, men are expected to get as much of it as they can – those who excel in it are recurrently referred to as 'deal closers' – while women are expected to be careful in allocating it. We are far removed from traditional societies where sex was regulated within a private property regime and wives were the property of husbands. Yet the logic of property informs sex in the hook-up scene as apparent in the significance imputed to male exclusivity in sexual access to women. It is a grave mistake for a woman to hook up with a friend of someone she has formerly hooked up with, and it is worse still to hook up with two men from the same fraternity. In one of the fraternities studied, such women were nicknamed with the breathtakingly vulgar pejorative 'house rats'. One of the students interviewed explains: 'How do you expect these people not to talk [when] they're friends? ... She would have to realise that these guys are close buddies and of course they are going to know. I'd almost say that would be her fault.'[30]

The Victorian double standard is clearly at work here, only now it wears a more public form. In the nineteenth century, John Stuart Mill attributed the resilience of women's subjugation to its unique locus in the privacy of the household, where the female subject of male power 'lives under the very eye ... of one of the masters – in closer intimacy with him than with any of her fellow-subjects; with no means of combining against him'.[31] In the hook-up scene, the forces that support the new Victorian double standard are straightforwardly collective. The matching takes place in public, and everybody knows, immediately or after the fact, who hooked up with whom.

Dating apps point at a further technological-financial aspect of the economy of sex. The hallmark of the dating apps social world is the feature of swiping, introduced by Tinder in 2012. This feature, where users approve or dismiss connections proposed by the application by swiping photos either left or right, contributed to the company's climb to a dominant position and was quickly adopted by its competitors. Some commentators note that the feature confers a sense of efficiency on date searching – sifting through candidates with a twitch of a thumb.[32] Others point out that swiping makes choosing prospective partners similar to choosing products.[33]

Efficiency and choice – that is how the language of economy pervades online dating. A crucial clarification is required, however. Swiping photos of people arouses an obscene thrill because of a certain 'as if' that accompanies it. Men swipe photos of women *as if* they are products, and the erotic thrill has to do with the awareness that they are *not* products. In other words, economic terminology permeates dating with a shift in its meaning. It is not real efficiency and choice that Tinder provides but a conscious simulation of them.

Simulation in fact signals a triple shift in the conjunction of technology, economy, and eroticism. First, technology is eroticised. Swiping is a technological relation to women, and at the same time an erotic relation to technology. This double movement puts in question the notion of efficiency. As sociologist Holly Wood notes, for many users, especially males, dating apps have effectively replaced dating. People she interviewed complained about the poor results they get from apps, saying, 'I'm on Tinder for hours every day.'[34] They do so precisely because swiping is itself erotic. As one young man told *The Atlantic*: 'I kinda use it now just for entertainment when I'm bored or standing in lines.'[35]

Second, the meaning of the economic terminology of choice and efficiency changes with the 'as if' appended to it. An obscene economy is brought to the fore. The subject matter of this economy is not efficiency and choice of objects but domination over people: the shadow of power and control over women. Swiping is an erotic technology because it invokes a sense of exerting power over women. In relation to economy, this 'as if' is in truth a moment of demasking. Mainstream economics may give the impression that the economy consists of objects, but heterodox perspectives, from Mandeville, through Marx to Veblen, share the view that the real substance of economy is the antagonistic relations between people mediated through objects.

Third, in dating apps, eroticism wears a financial form. A smartphone with Tinder stands for an indefinite potential of dates. As Julie Beck writes, 'Perhaps the apps' actual function is less important than what they signify as a totem: A pocket full of maybe that you can carry around to ward off despair.'[36] The notion of an object as an actual embodiment of potential lies at the root of an ethical injunction fuelling financial activity. That is how Weber defined the capitalist spirit in his reading of Franklin's corny financial advice.

Money stands for all the possibilities of its use, and thus forgoing an opportunity of profit should really be counted as an actual loss. Spending time idly, one should count as a loss not only the money he has spent, but also the money he could have earned. In Weber, this conjunction of actuality and potentiality explains how profit-seeking assumes the form of an austere ethic: 'a duty of the individual toward the increase of his capital, which is assumed as an end in itself'.[37] In relation to Tinder, this ethic is echoed in titles of stories in *The Atlantic*, one asking, 'Why is dating in the apps era such hard work?', and another diagnosing a 'dating app-fatigue'.[38] Potentiality explains how the language of value, competition, and achievement informs dating. In a *Vanity Fair* story foretelling a 'dating apocalypse', men, in contrast to female users, constantly talk in numbers. 'Guys view everything as a competition', one says, 'Who's slept with the best, hottest girls?'[39]

Though formally symmetrical in relation to gender, the Tinder scene is also obviously permeated by a modern version of the Victorian double standard. Monogamous marriage still informs the workings of this standard. As in the familiar form of the double standard, women who follow typical male sexual behaviour in the new dating scene are deemed unfit for marrying.[40] Interestingly, however, a *renunciation* of marriage has created a new version of the double standard. In this version, women who inquire after the status of an ongoing sexual relationship might face the accusation of being uptight, fishing for a husband.[41] Ostensibly that is the opposite of the Victorian double standard – a renunciation of marriage for the sake of liberated sexuality. Yet, like the double standard, it orients the sexual field around male desire for emotionless sex, free of commitments. Alana Massey describes this mechanism as the 'chill' attitude to sex: 'It is as if I've broken some unwritten law when I ask what they are looking for and am dissatisfied with the answer "I don't really like to put labels on things." ' Despite its air of relaxed freedom, Massey describes chill as one further stage in the tradition of power mechanisms addressed at women: 'Chill is a sinister refashioning of "Calm down!" from an enraging and highly gendered command into an admirable attitude.'[42]

This new form has an economic subtext. In its original form, the Victorian double standard articulated in sexual terms the meaning of marriage as male ownership over a woman at a time when this meaning was formally waning. Today, it is also a renunciation of the institution of marriage that tilts the sexual field around male sexual orientation. It is now oriented towards male desire to *not own* a woman in order to amass sexual experience. It expresses a change in the status of women from property to capital. The protagonist of Sarah Dunn's *Big Love*, looking back at the frustrations of her search for a relationship, dedicates her newspaper column to 'Romantic Market Value'. Her theory is somewhat of a cliché, but it spells out explicitly an asymmetry in the erotic field: 'men and women's Romantic Market Value is based on different things; women are valued for youth and beauty, men for wealth and power'. Insofar as there is an economy to eroticism, the value of men refers to what they *have*, while the value of women to what they *are*.

A detachment from the real traverses the technological, erotic, and economic transformation involved with dating apps. Tinder's founders conceived of the app in terms of a game, modelled on a deck of cards. That is how the idea of swiping came about.[43] In swiping, digital images become quasi-tangible things, objects that one can drag and move about. Swiping substitutes relations to people with relations to digital things. A detachment from the real defines the financial perspective on the economy but also informs its eroticisation. In parallel, the detachment of sex from its embeddedness in the real economy informs the way financial language infiltrates eroticism in the early stages of dating. Dating apps redouble this detachment in an eroticisation of technology and a technologisation of eroticism.

Notes

1 Sigmund Freud, 'Three Essays on the Theory of Sexuality [1905]', in *The Standard Edition of the Complete Psychological Works of Sigmund Freud*, vol. 7, ed. James Strachey (London: Hogarth Press, 1981), 179–80.
2 Marshall McLuhan, *Understanding the Media: The Extensions of Man* (Cambridge, MA: The MIT Press, 1994), 7–21.
3 Wesley Mitchell, 'Making Goods and Making Money', in *The Backward Art of Spending Money* (New York: McGraw-Hill, 1937).

4 Neil Strauss, *The Game: Penetrating the Secret Society of Pick-Up Artists* (New York: Harper Collins, 2005), 39.
5 Max Weber, *The Protestant Ethic and the Spirit of Capitalism* (London: Routledge, 1992), 22.
6 *Ibid.*, 12.
7 Karl Marx, *Capital: A Critique of Political Economy*, vol. 1, trans. Ben Fowkes (London: Penguin, 1976), 254.
8 *Ibid.*, 303.
9 Willard Waller, 'The Rating and Dating Complex', *American Sociological Review* 2, no. 5 (1937): 727–34, 728.
10 *Ibid.*
11 *Ibid.*, 730.
12 *Ibid.*
13 *Ibid.*
14 *Ibid.*, 733.
15 *Ibid.*
16 *Ibid.*, 734.
17 Geoffrey Ingham, *The Nature of Money* (Cambridge: Polity, 2004), 114.
18 *Ibid.*, 3.
19 Daniel Defoe, *The Complete English Tradesman* (Gloucester: Alan Sutton, 1987), 233.
20 John Maynard Keynes, *The General Theory of Employment, Interest and Money* (Basingstoke: Palgrave Macmillan, 2018), 137.
21 *Ibid.*, 140.
22 MSN, '50 Hottest Hollywood Bachelorettes', MSN News, December 12, 2018, www.msn.com/en-nz/news/other/50-hottest-hollywood-bachelorettes/ss-BBuFFsP, (accessed March 20, 2021). Mysteriously, the article is no longer available on the MSN website.
23 Marx, *Capital*, 258.
24 *Ibid.*, 159.
25 *Ibid.*, 202, 205, 203.
26 *Ibid.*, 200.
27 Jacques Lacan, 'The Symbolic, the Imaginary and the Real', *On the Names-of-the-Father*, trans. Bruce Fink (Cambridge: Polity, 2013), 13, 12.
28 Laura Kipnis, *Unwanted Advances: Sexual Paranoia Comes to Campus* (New York: Harper, 2017), 19.
29 *Ibid.*, 193.
30 Kathleen Bogle, *Hooking Up: Sex, Dating, and Relationships on Campus* (New York: New York University Press, 2008), 108.

31 John Stuart Mill, *The Subjection of Women* (Auckland: The Floating Press, 2009), 21.
32 Julie Beck, 'The Rise of Dating-App Fatigue', *The Atlantic*, October 25, 2016, www.theatlantic.com/health/archive/2016/10/the-unbearable-exhaustion-of-dating-apps/505184/ (accessed September 2, 2022).
33 Nancy Jo Sales, 'Tinder and the Dawn of the "Dating Apocalypse"', *Vanity Fair*, August 6, 2015, www.vanityfair.com/culture/2015/08/tinder-hook-up-culture-end-of-dating/ (accessed September 2, 2022).
34 Quoted in Beck, 'The Rise of Dating-App Fatigue'.
35 *Ibid.*
36 *Ibid.*
37 Weber, *The Protestant Ethic*, 14, 17.
38 Judith Shulevitz, 'Why Is Dating in the App Era Such Hard Work?', *The Atlantic*, November 2016, www.theatlantic.com/magazine/archive/2016/11/dating-disrupted/501119/ (accessed September 2, 2022).
39 Nancy Jo Sales, 'Dating Apocalypse'.
40 *Ibid.*
41 *Ibid.*
42 Alana Massey, 'Against Chill', Medium, April 1, 2015, https://medium.com/matter/against-chill-930dfb60a577 (accessed September 2, 2022).
43 Laura Stampler, 'Inside Tinder: Meet the Guys Who Turned Dating Into an Addiction', *Time*, February 6, 2014, https://time.com/4837/tinder-meet-the-guys-who-turned-dating-into-an-addiction/ (accessed September 2, 2022).

4

Digital paranoia in a post-truth world

Jernej Markelj

Perhaps the cultural text that most aptly sums up the mood of the digital political sphere in recent years is the internet meme called 'Ficki Fiona'. The meme is based around the image of a very angry woman with short hair and glasses (referred to by some as an 'Angry feminist') being confronted by a Trump supporter. The image is often captioned with the word 'triggered', which originally denoted the reactivation of a traumatic experience with war veterans but has since come to mean a strong emotional reaction to a disagreeable political position. While the term is mainly used on the right (often to discredit or dismiss the supposedly exaggerated reactions of the liberal left), strong antagonistic emotions are equally present on the other side of the political spectrum. Antagonistic affectivity of this kind within the political sphere is itself nothing new, but the complex set of specifics introduced into it by networked technologies have yet to be fully grasped.

This chapter examines these antagonistic affective structures in relation to socio-cultural fragmentation and the resulting disappearance of a common frame of reference – a development which has been associated with the emergence of a 'post-truth' universe. Building on Gilles Deleuze and Félix Guattari's analysis of the dynamic of capitalism, I explain how our social existence is becoming increasingly fragmented – or 'schizophrenised' – by the disruptive forces of global capitalism and digital technologies. This crumbling of society manifests itself not only in the crisis of various governmental organisations across different scales, but also in the proliferation of political echo-chambers, isolated online milieus, musical and artistic microscenes, and other similar phenomena. My contention is that such cultural fragmentation incites a propagation of affective tendencies that Deleuze and Guattari understand as paranoid. In their view, paranoiac tendencies seek to enforce a particular order of things and police the conceptual and physical borders that define it. Under conditions of fragmentation, paranoia invests increasingly dissimilar social realities, leading to polarisation and conflict, attempts at censuring, and, ultimately, the impossibility of emphatic communication.

In addition to Deleuze and Guattari's conception of paranoia, I draw on Benedict Spinoza's conception of ambition, which describes an unconscious striving that compels every human being to seek 'that everyone should love what he loves and hate what he hates'.[1] Like paranoia, ambition seeks to impose one's own organisation of affects onto others, but also strives to preserve its own affective organisation. To be able to conserve our affective disposition, our instinctive defence mechanisms block out and repress any affections that are incompatible with it (dissenting opinions and other disagreeable stimuli). This suggests that emerging social antagonisms should be examined from the perspective of their underlying affective mechanisms. Following Beth Lord and Alexander Douglas, I propose that the idea of 'cancel culture' and movements like 'no-platforming' tend to be less driven 'by a rational consideration of potential harm' engendered by certain views than they are by a visceral resistance to opinions of others experienced as intolerable.[2]

The chapter is divided into three parts. In the first, I explain Deleuze and Guattari's conception of capitalist social formation and its innate disruptiveness. Here I draw on *Anti-Oedipus* to spell out how capitalism provokes social fragmentation and instigates paranoid tendencies. After this, I analyse how such fragmentation is intensified by networked technologies, which cause disorientation by demolishing a common frame of reference, and thus bring about what is often referred to as the post-truth condition. Finally, I use Deleuze and Guattari's concept of paranoia and Benedict Spinoza's concept of ambition to examine the antagonism and polarisation that take shape under contemporary conditions of fragmentation. Here I specifically consider hostile dynamics from the perspective of the affective inclinations that motivate them, speculating how these inclinations play themselves out in the context of movements such as 'no-platforming'.

Capitalism and schizophrenisation of culture

To theorise antagonistic affectivity via Deleuze and Guattari and situate it within the fragmented social reality of capitalism, we need to begin with the model of the unconscious that underlies it. According to Deleuze and Guattari, the unconscious should be understood in terms of 'desiring-production'.[3] They see unconscious desire as a productive force that has no predetermined aims or objectives, but only seeks its own proliferation. In their anti-anthropocentric view, it is precisely this productive desire – and not an autonomous subject – that is the true motor of all activity and thus the agent of history. Since desire, in its unrestrained form, indiscriminately forms connections with whatever is conductive to its production, constantly switching between different energy sources, Deleuze and Guattari equate it with schizophrenia. Instead of seeing this as a clinical condition, for them, schizophrenia amounts to uninhibited vital energy, a pure process.

Deleuze and Guattari illustrate the productivity of this vital process by drawing on Henri Michaux's account of a 'table' built by a schizophrenic. Michaux describes the table as an 'overstuffed ... table of additions', which was finished:

> only in so far as there was no way of adding anything more to it, the table having become more and more an accumulation, less and less a table ... Its top surface, the useful part of the table, having been gradually reduced ... the thing did not strike one as a table, but as some freak piece of furniture, an unfamiliar instrument ... for which there was no purpose.[4]

The construction of this schizophrenic table allows us to understand the way unrestrained desire produces. Like desiring-production, which has no set objects, the table is fabricated without a plan or blueprint. Instead, the schizophrenic produces it almost unthinkingly and in a bricolage manner, through the indiscriminate and contingent additions of whatever is at hand. Insofar as the connections between added elements are productive, the schizophrenic is indifferent to what he adds to his table. Such a table, as a hodgepodge accumulation of elements, has little social use or value. The only 'value' that guides this schizophrenic production is the joy of production itself. So, while a schizophrenic would enjoy producing such a table, not many people could find use, or appreciation, for it.

Deleuze and Guattari claim that organising a society is precisely a matter of regulating this chaotic productive energy. For them, a 'society is only afraid of one thing: *the deluge of this energy*', which is the enemy of all forms of organisation.[5] To maintain a social order and avoid being engulfed by unrestrained desire, each social formation must put on its productive activity a set of restrictions, which guarantee that production occurs in a certain way. To turn a person into a diligent worker, for example, one has to organise her desire so that she is not inclined to get drunk, have sex, or plan an insurgence, but instead invests her energy into performing the required labour. Paranoia is an unconscious tendency that arises when desire invests a set of prescribed restrictions and becomes, as Foucault puts it, 'enamoured with power' that exploits us.[6] As a result of investing these restrictions, paranoid desire starts to regulate *itself* and police *its own* productive connection. An investment of borders that, for example, defines a reliable employee results in an instinctive suppression of every attachment that could render them as lazy or untrustworthy. Additionally, paranoid tendencies seek to impose the same restrictions *on others*. Paranoia, then, invests a particular order of things, enforces the borders that define it, and guards it against change and interruption.

For Deleuze and Guattari, capitalism has a very different way of dealing with the deluge of desire than precapitalist social formations. The despotic state, for example, uses a variety of intimidation techniques and displays of violence to channel desiring-production into the domain of obligatory labour and away from rebellion.[7] Straitjacketing of desire is here achieved through a more or less unchanging constellation of symbolic codes, which prescribe what should be done *today, tomorrow, and forever*. Capitalism, on the other hand, is the first social organisation that functions by constantly rearranging its social order and disrupting the hierarchies that ground it. To organise production and realise profit, capital needs to recurrently assemble labouring bodies, raw materials, machines, and know-how.

These resources are extracted from their social context on the basis of cost-effectiveness, which is a criterion that trumps religious, moral, and political codes. Once they are no longer profitable, they are abandoned as capital is reinvested elsewhere. Marx and Engels, consequently, suggest that 'constant revolutionising of production, uninterrupted disturbance of all social conditions, everlasting uncertainty and agitation' melt 'all that is solid ... into air', eroding all fixed relations and traditions.[8] In addition to production, consumption, too, is ceaselessly revolutionised as the management of consumer tastes constantly refreshes demand for ever-new products and services.[9]

These increasingly disruptive rhythms of production and consumption destabilise the restrictions imposed by tradition, thus unleashing the schizophrenic indeterminacy of desire, the deluge of its flows. Yet, in order for capitalism not to undermine its own foundations, it has to recapture and coopt the unleashed desire. This is done by means of state institutions, corporate bureaucracies, advertising, and other antiquated ideologies, which engender paranoid investments and thus reconstitute subjects as workers, consumers, and law-abiding citizens. According to Deleuze and Guattari, all our unconscious investments fall between these two poles of desire: the unrestrained, schizophrenic pole and the repressive, paranoid one. Insofar as our subjectivities are stable, they are inevitably grounded in durable investments in a particular order of things, and are thus to a certain extent paranoid.[10]

Yet, it should be noted that under the conditions of fragmentation brought about by the escalating spiral of capital, paranoid tendencies unfold differently than in precapitalist societies. The despotic social machine, for instance, could persist only by enforcing absolute systems of belief, which are permanently applicable to the entire social field. The despot, who is the supreme figure of paranoia, upholds a single standard of value, one that judges as good only that activity that brings him glory. Under capitalism, however, such distinct consensus reality is increasingly eroded by the economic operations organised by the market, a mechanism that assigns value in an impersonal manner. In the absence of a coherent ideology, meaningless calculus of the market is complemented with fragmented, often archaic beliefs that are established ad-hoc. 'Everything returns or recurs: States, nations, families', note Deleuze and Guattari. That is what makes the ideology of capitalism 'a motley painting of everything that has ever been believed'.[11]

Cultural fragmentation and digital technologies

While capitalism should thus be seen as the underlying condition of what we might call the *schizophrenisation* of culture, this cultural fragmentation has crossed another threshold due to the effects of technologies developed by capitalist production.[12] My contention is that the disintegration of our shared social world can be largely attributed to the effects of digital networks, which have profoundly disrupted our ways of thinking and acting. As it has provided channels for a decentralised dissemination of information, Nick Land claims that our 'epistemological authorities have been blasted apart by the internet'.[13] In his view,

> [w]hether it's the university system, the media, financial authorities, the publishing industry, all the basic gatekeepers and crediting agencies and systems that have maintained the epistemological hierarchies of the modern world are just coming to pieces at a speed that no one had imagined was possible.[14]

While Land's position might sound somewhat exaggerated, it is hard to deny that what we might refer to as consensus reality is getting increasingly destabilised. This destabilisation, or even disappearance, of a common frame of reference, is what is often referred to as the 'post-truth' condition.[15] A prominent manifestation of this condition is the effectiveness of 'alternative facts' disseminated during the 2016 US presidential campaign and election of Donald Trump, but also the traction gained by alternative accounts related to the existence of global warming, the efficacy of vaccination, or even the shape of our planet.

The post-truth condition is thus, I argue, a matter of fragmentation of the common frame of reference by an information overload. The main contours of this condition can be instructively examined through the case of the music scene observed by the critic Simon Reynolds. Reviewing the lists ranking the best records of the 2000s, Reynolds claims that in (the second half of) this decade, 'it grew harder and harder for people to reach consensus about ... what albums are important'.[16] According to him, this period felt 'diasporic, scenes splintering into sub-scenes, taste bunkers forming', such that the question ' "Have you heard X?" [was] increasingly likely to meet a shake of the head or a look of incomprehension'.[17]

Reynolds sees this fragmentation as an effect of the stark increase in music production, which took place due to the cheapness of home audio workstations, combined with the affordances of digital media. The latter opened new distribution channels and enabled immediate access to the entire history of music. 'The result of all this over-production was that "we" were spread thin across a vast terrain of sound', writes Reynolds, which is why 'if you look at the ... end-of-decade polls across the gamut of music magazines, there's so little overlap'.[18] Building on his analysis, he speculates that 'the culture-wide slide into entropy is speeding up'.[19]

This cultural entropy corresponds to what Slavoj Žižek refers to as the decline of symbolic efficiency. 'If the efficiency of a symbol designates its mobility, its ability to transmit significance ... from one setting to another', sums up Jodi Dean, 'the decline of symbolic efficiency points to an immobility or failure of transmission'.[20] This immobility of meanings is glaringly obvious when one tries to move between different online environments. As each of them has its own rules, terms, and styles of expression, it becomes impossible to always discern irony from sincerity, humour from seriousness. This uncertainty is perfectly illustrated by Poe's law, an internet proverb which states that 'it is impossible to create a parody of extreme views so obviously exaggerated that it cannot be mistaken by some readers for a sincere expression of the views being parodied'.[21] Similarly to Reynolds, Dean also relates the decline of symbolic efficiency to the inexhaustibility of online information. The latter, in her view, precludes any possibility for fully anchoring a meaning. Since 'there's always another option, link, opinion, nuance, or con-tingency that we haven't taken into account', she claims, 'final assessment [or complete understanding] of any statement becomes effectively impossible'.[22]

The collapse of a common frame of reference coincides with the proliferation of fragmented networked publics. According to Wendy Chun, this segmentation is algorithmically assisted.[23] Chun claims that the feeds of information that articulate these online milieus are governed by algorithms, which function by sectioning people into closed segments based on personal interests, political views, sexual orientations, and so on. This algorithmic segmentation takes place in accordance with the well-known 'if you liked that, you might also like this' principle, that is, by offering the same suggestions to users with a similar digital footprint.[24] In this way, algorithms help arrange the vast online infoscape into microenvironments and echo-chambers, which are, on the one hand, becoming increasingly homogeneous and, on the other, increasingly unlike one another. As they are exposed to radically diverse media ecologies, these fragmented networked publics tend to become ever more polarised and antagonistic.

Social fragmentation and affective antagonism

To theorise affective antagonism, let us begin with a vivid illustration of the experience of polarisation provided by the Chilean philosopher and neurobiologist Francisco Varela. Varela characterises the polarisation that led to the 1973 Chilean civil war in a way that many of us will find relatable.

> You could go to the newsstands in the morning and one newspaper would say 'It's raining', the other would say 'It's not raining'. 'A is a son of a bitch'; 'A is the king of the universe'. It was literally like that. And you know, three years before these two were reasonable newspapers, who agreed that a table is a table, and that blue is blue. But by 1973 this was not possible anymore. They couldn't literally agree on anything, the time of the day or the colour of the sky. The polarity created a continual exaggeration of the sense of boundary and territoriality: 'This is ours; get out of here'.[25]

Polarisation thus manifests in a radical divergence of experienced social realities. The concepts of boundary (or limit) and territoriality evoked by Varela bring us back to Deleuze and Guattari's notion of paranoia, which allows me to conduct this analysis at the level of unconscious investments. For David Lapoujade, a Deleuzian scholar, the boundaries that mark out the identity of an individual are precisely what the paranoid tendencies cling on to.

> 'From now on, it's my home, it's mine ...' [Paranoid investment] makes the limit a jealously guarded, in principle impassable, frontier. Is the paranoid even interested in anything else? The limit must preserve an identity of unalloyed purity, protect its territorialities from foreign infiltrations or invisible spies; it must shield a healthy body from microbes and filth. The paranoid is the guardian of limits.[26]

Paranoiac tendencies seek to protect or enforce the order of things that validates the invested identity, be it that of a diligent worker or a political militant. To achieve this, these unconscious investments seek to regulate their own organisation of desire (by instinctively repelling all unwanted connections). In addition to that, paranoid investments seek to control the behaviour of others, who might disrupt the invested state of things.

This antagonistic paranoid dynamic can be further examined through Arlie Hochschild's idea of 'feeling rules', which concerns the rules that prescribe a particular organisation of one's affective register. For Hochschild, feeling rules are a matter of what 'do people *want to feel*, what do they think they *should or shouldn't* feel, and what *do they feel* about a range of issues?'[27] She adds that 'when we listen to a political leader, we don't simply hear words; we listen predisposed to want to feel certain things'.[28] Examining the antagonism between left- and right-wing feeling rules in the USA, Hochschild suggests that:

> the right seeks release from liberal notions of what they *should feel* – happy for the gay newlywed, sad at the plight of the Syrian refugee, unresentful about paying taxes. The left sees prejudice. Such rules challenge the emotional core of right-wing belief. And it is to this core that a freewheeling [Republican] candidate such as the billionaire entrepreneur Donald Trump ... can appeal, saying, as he gazes upon throngs of supporters, 'See all the *passion*'.[29]

To consider feeling rules from Deleuze and Guattari's perspective is, first of all, to acknowledge that they are underlain by a set of paranoid investments organising one's affective disposition. The republican affective organisation is predisposed to productively link up with discourse about family values, the free market, and deregulation, which shores up their investments. Conversely, preserving the invested identity in the face of democratic pleas to have more empathy for underprivileged minorities requires mobilisation of a defence mechanism.

For Deleuze and Guattari, this instinctive mechanism amounts to the forces of repulsion, which block out desiring connections with whatever threatens to alter our affective disposition. Even though this experience of a refusal is not always consciously acknowledged and, in fact, regularly goes unnoticed, it occurs frequently. It takes place at a higher level of intensity whenever we are confronted with a thought or assertion that is so utterly incompatible with our affective organisation that the latter rejects it. If, for example, someone who has spent years studying political theory is being told in all sincerity that 'cultural Marxism is the root of all evil', he will be left feeling bewildered. He can clearly comprehend the meaning of this statement, but it will still strike him as a kind of madness. This statement is so alien to his disposition that it gets instinctively rejected as delirious. Its refusal is not a question of a failure in rationality or signification but is rather a matter of affect.

This experience of a visceral rejection of a disagreeable view is common under the conditions of antagonistic polarisation. An instructive example of this took place in the Slovenian parliament at the beginning of 2021.[30] There, the Slovenian prime minister and an MP, each belonging to an opposite side of the political spectrum, told one another that they should be taken to a psychiatric ward. Leaving the insensitivity of their remarks aside, I suggest that they in fact adequately gloss how they experience each other's positions. This can be put into perspective by Deleuze and Guattari's claim that psychosis is in essence nothing but a misapprehension. In their view, the statement of Judge Schreber, the famous psychotic patient whose memoirs Freud analysed, 'I have sunbeams coming out of my ass' seems to a normalised subjectivity delirious in exactly the same way as the leftist insistence that 'we desperately need a welfare state' seems to a Tea Party Republican. In both cases, we are dealing with an encounter between two radically different organisations of desire. These affective dispositions are separated by what Hochschild refers to as the 'empathy wall', 'an obstacle to deep understanding of another person'.[31] Hochschild suggests that an empathy wall 'can make us feel indifferent or even hostile to those who hold different beliefs or whose childhood is rooted in different circumstances'.[32]

We can add further nuance to our consideration of affective antagonism by examining it from the perspective of Spinoza's philosophy of affect. The latter can be, with the help of Deleuze's rendition of Spinoza, read alongside Deleuze and Guattari.[33] According to Spinoza, our actions and thoughts are directed by an unconscious effort, a capacity to act and produce, which strives to seek out what enhances this capacity and avoid that which decreases it.[34] In line with Deleuze and Guattari, he thus assumes that our power of acting is dependent on empowering or inhibiting affective relations (or desiring-connections) that our productive unconscious is susceptible to. All our emotions and desires are produced within the coordinates of this affective relationality.

Our engagement with social media is affectively motivated in exactly the same way. Susanna Paasonen, who works within a similar theoretical framework, suggests that 'affective intensities both drive online exchanges and attach people to particular platforms, threads, and groups'.[35] In her view, it is the positive (enhancements) and negative affective intensities (inhibitions) that direct our use of social media (towards certain platforms and apps, and away from others), but also produce our attachments to certain platforms and apps. This stickiness, which results from accumulative association of positive and negative affective value with objects and people, is what animates users to stay and revisit these sites, apps, and discussions.[36]

Yet, Paasonen also suggests that the affective stickiness of online interactions draws boundaries between different groups. Analysing a heated online debate regarding an episode at a dance event, she observes how affective intensities of the exchange articulate hierarchical divisions between 'us' and 'them', 'between queer and non-queer club participants; between heteronormative and nonheteronormative ones; between queer people sensing injustice in the incident discussed and those failing to do so; [and so on]'.[37] By repeatedly associating one side with enhancing intensities and the other with inhibiting ones, online interactions reinforce boundaries between territorialities related to gender, class, race, party politics, cultural capital, and so on, and thereby contribute to cultivating polarised affective dispositions.

To investigate the encounter between such affective dispositions, let us now consider Spinoza's account of ambition. In his peculiar understanding, ambition is an effort 'to bring it about that everyone should approve of' the ideas or objects that increase our capacity to act and disapprove of those that diminish it.[38] If we are, for example, enthusiastic about a film, a book, or a song, ambition will drive us to provoke the same kind of enthusiasm for it in others. For Spinoza, ambition arises due to the innate human tendency to imitate what we imagine others feel and desire. As imagining that others admire what we approve of will additionally enhance our sources of empowerment, we consequently seek to convince them to do so. Since we all strive to cause others to think and feel as we do, and thus try to make others adopt our attitude to life, Spinoza claims humans are often strenuous to one another and tend to 'provoke mutual dislike'.[39]

This mutual distaste is, naturally, intensified in the encounter of antagonistic affective dispositions. Yet, since attempts to change the mind of an opponent under conditions of extreme polarisation are met with forceful resistance, ambition here manifests itself differently. Beth Lord and Alex Douglas suggest that in this case ambition becomes 'the desire to "avert from ourselves" those who cannot be convinced to [think and feel as we do] – for those dissenters diminish our sense of self-worth'.[40] From Spinoza's perspective, having to listen to something we disagree with produces negative affective intensities and inhibits our capacities (both directly and via the imitative loop), which is reflected in our self-image. As a result, our capacity to act instinctively seeks to remove this source of inhibition, which can result in hostile, exclusionary behaviour.[41]

Lord and Douglas speculate that what has been contentiously called 'cancel culture' might be at times motivated by ambition. Attempts at 'de-platforming' individuals are usually justified in terms of the denial of freedom of speech on account of its potentially harmful effects. Even though most of us tend to agree that the latter can constitute legitimate reasons for limiting one's freedom of speech, these harmful consequences are, as Lord and Douglas rightly suggest, generally hard to predict and estimate. Still, in their view, the context of such attempts at censure sometimes suggest that they are not based on a rational consideration of harm, but instead are driven by ambition.

The (admittedly offline) examples that Lord and Douglas provide to support their claim are the 2020 no-platforming cases of historian Selina Todd and former Conservative MP Amber Rudd.[42] Both Rudd and Todd had their invited lectures cancelled by the organisers on account of their alleged trans-exclusionary feminist views. Yet, refusal to provide them with a platform and engage with their argument can hardly be seen as reducing the harmful effects of their views. Lord and Douglas rightly point out that 'Todd and Rudd are prominent people in positions of authority – so cancelling their events, while causing a public splash, is unlikely to dent their freedom to speak on these or other issues at other times and in different forums.'[43]

As cancelling their lectures did not restrict their ability to communicate with the public, attempts to silence them might be understood as driven by a desire to avoid being exposed to dissenting views. In striving to avert the threat of affective inhibition, ambition, therefore, precludes the possibility of a rational debate. It is safe to say that, from the perspective of Spinoza, who sees rationality as a collaborative project, such isolationist refusal to engage has thus little to do with reason. Similarly, Paasonen observes that rational negotiation is anything but common on social platforms. In dialogue with Zizi Papacharissi, she claims that 'the Habermasian ideal of the public sphere as one of critical rational exchange can be mapped onto emotionally wired online discussions only with some difficulty', and reiterates that 'online exchanges, once heated up, are animated by a search for affective intensity rather than rational argumentation'.[44]

Lord and Douglas go on to suggest that no-platforming is in fact a part of our everyday experience. For them, 'refusing to hear an argument and seeking to silence it is a mild form of no-platforming motivated by ambition'.[45] Online this refusal manifests itself in simply hitting the mute, unfollow, or block button. Even though Spinoza warns us of the dangers of ambitious desire and its divisiveness, we should not assume that his ethics entails simply exposing oneself to every opinion that one finds intolerable. Giving the benefit of the doubt and suspending judgement, as F. Scott Fitzgerald warns, 'open[s] up many curious natures to [us]', but can also make us 'the victim of not a few veteran bores'.[46] Instead, I suggest that the ethical orientation for our polarised times is to be found with Spinoza's injunction 'not to deride, bewail, or execrate human actions, but to understand them'.[47] Being able to formulate such understanding is for Spinoza, who puts conceptualisation of human actions and emotions at the core of his project, empowering in itself as it enhances our thinking capacities. It is also a step in the direction of breaking down the empathy walls that, with increasing cultural fragmentation, more and more divide us from one another. Cultivating such understanding might indeed be infinitely difficult. Still, if we agree with Spinoza that other people are, to the extent that they are rational, the most powerful source of enhancement available to us, it is perhaps ultimately worth it.

Notes

1 Benedictus de Spinoza, *Ethics*, in *The Complete Works*, ed. Michael Morgan, trans. Samuel Shirley (Indianapolis, IN: Hackett, 2002), 213–382, at 339.
2 Beth Lord and Alexander Douglas, 'Spinoza and "No Platforming": Enlightenment Thinker Would Have Seen It as Motivated by Ambition Rather than Fear', *The Conversation*, March 11, 2021, https://theconversation.com/spinoza-and-no-platforming-enlightenment-thinker-would-have-seen-it-as-motivated-by-ambition-rather-than-fear-133379 (accessed September 8, 2022).
3 Gilles Deleuze and Félix Guattari, *Anti-Oedipus: Capitalism and Schizophrenia*, trans. Robert Hurley, Mark Seem, and Helen Lane (Minneapolis: University of Minnesota Press, 1983), 1–9.
4 *Ibid.*, 6.
5 Gilles Deleuze, 'Capitalism, Flows, the Decoding of Flows, Capitalism and Schizophrenia, Psychoanalysis, Spinoza', Lectures by Gilles Deleuze, February 2007, http://deleuzelectures.blogspot.com/2007/02/capitalism-flows-decoding-of-flows.html (accessed September 8, 2022).
6 Michel Foucault, 'Preface', in Deleuze and Guattari, *Anti-Oedipus*, xi–xiv, at xiv.
7 If the despotic state is incapable of containing the flows of desire, it simply annihilates them.
8 Karl Marx and Friedrich Engels, *Manifesto of the Communist Party*, on Marxists Internet Archive, www.marxists.org/archive/marx/works/1848/communist-manifesto/ch01.htm (accessed September 8, 2022).
9 Similar disruptions can be caused by financial operations, which are able to inflate or destroy assets based on rumour alone.
10 When Deleuze and Guattari speak of paranoia, they do not necessarily mean clinical paranoia, the pathologically active sense of being in danger or conspired against, which corresponds only to the extreme end of the paranoid spectrum. Paranoiac investment for them simply denotes any stable unconscious investment, and a degree of stability or structure is necessary even for the most chaotic of ethical or political projects.
11 Deleuze and Guattari, *Anti-Oedipus*, 267.
12 Deleuze and Guattari insist that 'it is not machines that have created capitalism, but capitalism that creates machines' (*Anti-Oedipus*, 233). In their view, it is the realisation of profit that drives technological innovation, which disrupts established ways of acting and thinking.

13 Marko Bauer and Andrej Tomažin, 'The Only Thing I Would Impose is Fragmentation: An Interview with Nick Land', Synthetic Zero, June 19, 2017, https://syntheticzero.net/2017/06/19/the-only-thing-i-would-impose-is-fragmentation-an-interview-with-nick-land (accessed September 8, 2022).
14 *Ibid.*
15 For example, see Steve Fuller, *Post-Truth: Knowledge as Power Game* (London: Anthem Press, 2018) and Lee McIntyre, *Post-Truth* (Cambridge, MA: The MIT Press, 2018).
16 Simon Reynolds, 'Notes on the Naughties: The Musically Fragmented Decade', *The Guardian*, December 7, 2009, www.theguardian.com/music/musicblog/2009/dec/07/musically-fragmented-decade (accessed September 8, 2022).
17 *Ibid.*
18 *Ibid.*
19 *Ibid.*
20 Jodi Dean, *Blog Theory: Feedback and Capture in the Circuits of Drive* (Cambridge: Polity, 2010), 5.
21 Emma Grey Ellis, 'Poe's Law: Troll Culture's Central Rule', *Wired*, June 5, 2017, www.wired.com/2017/06/poes-law-troll-cultures-central-rule (accessed September 8, 2022).
22 Dean, *Blog Theory*, 5.
23 See Wendy Hui Kyong Chun, 'Queerying Homophily', in *Pattern Discrimination*, ed. Clemens Apprich, Wendy Hui Kyong Chun, Florian Cramer, and Hito Steyerl (Lüneburg: Meson Press, 2018), 59–99.
24 According to Hito Steyerl, Chun's claim about social networks like Facebook is that they algorithmically generate their recommendations based on 'the idea that you like what you like, and that you will like the things that people who are like you like' (Hito Steyerl, 'A Sea of Data: Pattern Recognition and Corporate Animism [Forked Version]', in *Pattern Discrimination*, 1–22, at 13). In Chun's view, these recommendation systems thus take into account your likes and dislikes and suggest what others with similar (dis)likes are interested in. In this way, these algorithmic operations actively propagate segmentation with regard to these preferences.
25 Francisco Varela, 'Reflections on The Chilean Civil War', *Lindisfarne Newsletter* 8 (1979): 13–20, at 15.
26 David Lapoujade, *Aberrant Movements: The Philosophy of Gilles Deleuze*, trans. Joshua David Jordan (Los Angeles, CA: Semiotext(e), 2014), 162.
27 Arlie Russel Hochschild, *Strangers in Their Own Land: Anger and Mourning on The American Right* (New York: The New Press, 2016), 15.

28 *Ibid.*
29 *Ibid.*, 15–16.
30 Boris Vezjak, 'Janša Kordišu: "Vi potrebujete psihiatrično pomoč"', *Mladina*, January 26, 2021, www.mladina.si/204676/jansa-kordisu-vi-potrebujete-psihiatricno-pomoc (accessed September 8, 2022).
31 *Ibid.*, 5.
32 *Ibid.*
33 For Deleuze's engagement with Spinoza, see his *Expressionism in Philosophy: Spinoza*, trans. Martin Joughin (New York: Zone Books, 1992) and *Spinoza: Practical Philosophy*, trans. Robert Hurley (San Francisco, CA: City Lights Books, 1988).
34 Here we should point out one fundamental difference between Deleuze and Guattari and Spinoza – namely, for the latter the domain of the body and that of the mind are seen as parallel to one another (determined by the same series of events, without being related in terms of causality), where the former gives priority to the bodily register.
35 Susanna Paasonen, 'A Midsummer's Bonfire: Affective Intensities of Online Debate', in *Networked Affect*, ed. Ken Hillis, Susanna Paasonen, and Michael Petit (Cambridge: The MIT Press, 2015), 27–42, at 28.
36 The concept of 'stickiness' is developed by Sarah Ahmed in *The Cultural Politics of Emotion* (Edinburgh: Edinburgh University Press, 2004), 90.
37 Paasonen, 'A Midsummer's Bonfire', 32.
38 Spinoza, *Ethics*, 295.
39 *Ibid.*
40 Beth Lord and Alexander Douglas, 'Spinoza and "No Platforming"'.
41 Elsewhere Lord also proposes that ambition drives us to associate with those who, as Spinoza puts it, love what we love, and hate what we hate. This is the case as encounters with people with similar affective dispositions validate our own attitudes, thus maximising positive affective intensities and minimising negative ones. This explains the formation of echo-chambers or filter-bubbles not in terms of algorithmic operations, but in terms of affect. See Beth Lord, 'Disagreement in the Political Philosophy of Spinoza and Rancière', *Proceedings of the Aristotelian Society* 117, no. 1 (2017): 61–80, at 75.
42 'Amber Rudd "No Platformed" by Oxford University Society', BBC News, March 6, 2020, www.bbc.com/news/uk-england-oxfordshire-51768634 (accessed September 8, 2022); 'Oxford University Professor

Condemns Exclusion From Event', BBC News, March 4, 2020, www.bbc.com/news/uk-england-oxfordshire-51737206 (accessed September 8, 2022).

43 Lord and Douglas, 'Spinoza and "No Platforming"'.

44 Paasonen, 'A Midsummer's Bonfire', 33.

45 Lord and Douglas, 'Spinoza and "No Platforming"'.

46 F. Scott Fitzgerald, *The Great Gatsby* (New York: Scribner Books, 2004), 1.

47 Benedictus de Spinoza, *Political Treatise*, in *The Complete Works*, ed. Michael Morgan, trans. Samuel Shirley (Indianapolis, IN: Hackett, 2002), 671–782 at 755.

5

Social networks and serendipitous desire

Emily Rosamond

On the TED Talk stage, an illuminated figure pierces the darkness. Psychotherapist Meg Jay is delivering her lecture, 'Why 30 is Not the New 20'. When starting out as a clinical psychology PhD student, Jay recounts, she was initially relieved that her first client was a woman in her twenties who wanted to talk about 'guy problems' – surely an easy case to handle. Soon, however, she realised that she had not handled it. She had been too swayed by her patient's own narrative, that 'thirty is the new twenty' – that it was okay to kill time in an unfulfilling relationship, to remain undecided about one's career path, and to procrastinate on major life decisions because (so the common wisdom went) all these things happened later in life nowadays. Jay counters the tendency to trivialise one's twenties as if they were part of an extended childhood, urging twentysomethings to make the most of their defining decade.[1] First, she advises, 'forget about having an identity crisis and get some identity capital. By identity capital, I mean do something that adds value to who you are. Do something that's an investment in who you might want to be next.' Second, 'the urban tribe is overrated. Best friends are great for giving rides to the airport, but twentysomethings who huddle together with like-minded peers limit who they know, what they know, how they think, how they speak, and where they work.' Opportunities 'almost always come from outside the inner circle. New things come from what are called our weak ties: our friends of friends of friends.' And finally, 'the time to start picking your family is now'; even though, on average, people settle down in committed relationships later than they used to, the best time to work on your marriage or long-term partnership is before you have one. This advice can profoundly change one's course in life – as it did for Jay's client Emma.

At twenty-five, Emma was in a bad relationship with a boy-friend she lived with because it was cheaper than living alone. She wanted to work in art or museums, but she was not sure, so she continued waiting tables. Jay encouraged Emma to look through the list of contacts in her address book, where she found a former roommate's cousin in another city who worked in a museum; this contact helped her get a job there. Moving cities to take the job gave her a reason to end her unfulfilling relationship. The move set her on a fulfilling career path, and through her new life she found a far more suitable partner, to whom she is now happily married. 'Twentysomethings', Jay opines, 'are like airplanes just leaving LAX, bound for somewhere west. Right after take-off, a slight change in course is the difference between landing in Alaska or Fiji. Likewise, at twenty-one, or twenty-five, or even twenty-nine, one good conversation, one good break, one good TED Talk can have an enormous effect across years, and even generations to come.'[2]

Jay's TED Talk has been viewed over 11 million times online and has 'hit a nerve' with viewers, garnering both high praise and heavy criticism. Critics have questioned whether Jay draws enough attention to class privilege as a key source of opportunity for twentysomethings (since those with more valuable 'weak ties' in their social networks are bound to receive better opportunities), and whether she makes heteronormative assumptions about what adults ought to want. (Jay has defended herself against both charges, arguing that weak ties are important for people of all economic backgrounds, and that her advice holds for anyone wanting a long-term partnership, no matter their sexual orientation.[3]) On TED – the American conferencing and media platform that disseminates research talks to a wide audience with the tagline 'ideas worth spreading' – her talk reaches millions. Yet it also, perhaps unwittingly, contributes to TED's rather sensationalised conception of research impact – its reinforcement of the assumption that research must be inspiring, uplifting, entertaining, and linked to a narrative of personal growth in order to count.[4] But let us think through and with this talk, in all its sensationalism, as a poignant staging of self-actualisation for a wide audience, at a turning point in how social networks are instrumentalised and understood.

Jay's former client Emma was leafing through an address book, filled out by hand; but Jay's talk, delivered in 2013, lands squarely in the social media age, when hand-written address books have largely given way to smartphone contact lists, online friends, and followers. For anyone on social media, desire must navigate relentlessly mapped social networks. Social media provides seemingly endless access to social contacts, and, thus, an abundant (if strange and strangely exhausted) sense of social possibility and potential. Potential dates scroll by, by the dozen; 'friend counts' reach into the hundreds and thousands. *There are so many people to choose from.* On the other hand, in a moment of climate crisis, wage stagnation, increasing wealth inequality, and widespread economic dysfunction, a pervasive sense of diminished potential (at once personal, social, economic, and ecological) prevails. Subjects encounter a world of social networks that invites participation by promising that one can turbo-charge one's contacts. Yet late-neoliberal desire must also reckon with an erosion of the landscape of what-could-be-desired, a world in which many Western subjects know that their life and career prospects will not be as good as their parents' might have been.[5] At this critical juncture, what might narratives of 'social network self-help' tell us about how understandings of desire shift within these new social and ecological parameters for potential? What does 'self-actualisation' – that elusive object of self-help, accessed through social networks – look like in a moment of persistently inflated, yet broadly diminished potentials?

Jay's talk, I argue, articulates an imagery and logic of *life paths*, which is fundamental to how understandings of desire are shifting in this late-neoliberal moment. In a landscape of abundant 'bumps in the road', a semi-flexible imagery of desired life trajectories takes hold. Desire comes to be recoded according to the temporal, narrative, and proprietary category of the life-path: one's own, singular trajectory through the challenges of 'manifesting' one's family, career, or 'best life'. The desire to connect with others and discover potential steers and actualises the life-path. Its residue is 'identity capital', as Jay puts it – investments in what one would like to become next, which have left their mark on the subject. As a much-replayed, theatrical moment of staging self-help for a wide audience, Jay's aviation-inflected life-path imagery – her interest in supporting the actualisation of a meaningful and productive life trajectory – answers to the exhaustion of desire in a moment of widespread social death coinciding with hyped-up capitalisation on 'the social'. Like those who hedge financial portfolios, Jay's addressees are called to actualise their life paths by happy accidents that accrue around who knows what edge of their social networks. The life-path imagery that Jay proffers (which echoes many other depictions of the late-neoliberal life path) unwittingly envisions serendipity itself as something whose value can be expropriated and effectively managed, through social networks. One can self-actualise by harnessing serendipity, that is, by learning to seek out what one wants – and thus become who one desires to become – through what one wasn't looking for. This amounts to a desire for abstract potentiality itself, more than an object of desire as such.

In the realm of the weak tie

Jay's talk highlights the importance of weak social ties: acquaintances or friends of friends at the edges of social networks, who ferry new information and opportunity into our lives. A friend of a friend mentions an upcoming opportunity at a new company, and you get the job; a former roommate's cousin helps you get your foot in the door, in the field you always hoped to work in; an acquaintance invites you to a party and that is where you meet a friend of a friend, with whom you fall in love.

Jay's account extends prior sociological work on weak ties in social networks. Her key point of departure is Mark Granovetter's groundbreaking 1973 article 'The Strength of Weak Ties'. One of the most cited social scientific papers of all time, Granovetter's article explores the differing roles of strong ties (roughly, close friendships) and weak ties (roughly, acquaintanceships) in social networks, and posits social network analysis 'as a tool for linking micro and macro levels of sociological theory'.[6] At the time, it was already known that personal contacts help people find jobs. Those who know someone at a company to which they are applying tend to have far better chances of success than those who respond to a job advertisement 'cold'. Investigating this phenomenon further, Granovetter demonstrated that most job opportunities come from weak ties in social networks, not strong ties – for instance, an 'old college friend or a former workmate or employer, with whom sporadic contact had been maintained'.[7] Most often, such ties were weak to begin with, and reactivated by 'chance meetings or mutual friends'.[8] The wealth of opportunities that come from weak ties, Granovetter posited, was due to the fact that weak ties act as 'bridges' between social networks, and thus tend to add more novel information to our lives than do our closest friends and associates. Weak ties, for Granovetter, are most powerful as sources of job opportunity when they are just strong enough to maintain some power of influence, while also being weak enough to introduce novel information and opportunity.

Granovetter did not overly intend for his research to be used as self-help. Indeed, while acknowledging that his advice might be useful to people to a certain extent, he has criticised widespread attempts to instrumentalise his research as advice, quipping that those who 'go on a course' where they are told to make three new contacts each day are likely to send others running in the opposite direction, since their attempts at networking seem so instrumentalising.[9] Nor could Granovetter have imagined, in 1973, that social media platforms would one day pervasively map social networks in real time. And yet, his kind of thinking on social networks seems to have been generalised in both directions: as a means for tech companies to instrumentalise 'the social' by promising to turbo-charge users' social contacts while boosting platform engagement; and as a mythologised site at which the desire for self-actualisation unfolds. Networked thinking has been extensively operationalised and instrumentalised within many forms of contemporary thought and practice that emerge at the interface between subject and network. For instance, the hugely influential theory of 'nudging' within behavioural economics describes how one can exercise 'libertarian paternalism' by modifying 'choice architectures': allowing subjects to do what they like, but 'nudging' them to take the best option by making it the easiest or default action.[10] 'Social physics' uses big data's 'digital breadcrumbs' to understand how ideas and behaviours spread through social networks.[11] Critical geographer Mark Whitehead and colleagues identify a 'neuroliberal' policy shift, which mobilises 'cognitive strategies, emotions, and precognitive affects as a way of securing preferred forms of social conduct while ostensibly supporting liberal orthodoxies of freedom'.[12]

Such policies are sensitive to 'the *lifespan* dynamics of context, particularly in relation to recognising how particular moments in life (such as moving home, having your first child, or going to college) provide opportunities for behavioural modification'.[13] As Wendy Hui Kyong Chun has argued, networks (which have been endlessly mapped and researched in a wide range of contexts over the past few decades) form a perfect practical and conceptual corollary to neoliberal governance.[14] They preclude the genuinely collective, Chun argues, and make it easier to envision a world in which 'there is no such thing as society' (as Margaret Thatcher infamously put it); instead, there are just network nodes and edges. Networks privilege individuals over communities and map in real time the connections between nodes – the 'YOUs' at the heart of new media, as Chun puts it – while remaining unable to envision a 'we'.[15]

Research on weak ties also accrues its own popular mythology, associated with what we might call the realm of the weak tie. This realm consists of the narratives and desires that form around weak ties, as they come to be seen (in ever-shifting ways) as fecund sites of social and personal possibility. How has the realm of the weak tie shifted in the forty years between Granovetter's 1973 paper and Jay's 2013 TED Talk?

The vitaminisation of coincidence

Jay's talk recasts weak social ties. She portrays them not only as abundant sources of opportunity, but also as constitutive of a life-path imagery. Weak-tie life-path imagery envisions an out-of-tune subject, on the 'wrong path' in life, whose life turns around, leaps forward, thanks to a chance encounter. Sure, perhaps this subject is processing their stumbling blocks, working out, working on thinking positively, working through whatever is holding them back. But what is needed, in order to activate all that good, self-actualising work, is a good coincidence: someone who acts as a gateway to an event, through which the subject's wisdom manifests. Weak-tie life-path imagery 'turbo-charges' the life path with a pinch of luck. In that sense, it is a subjective form that readily reconciles itself to a present marked by the 'slow cancellation of the future'.[16] Facing feeble job prospects, worsening storms, fewer safety nets, and no chance of buying a house, the youngish adult (unless rich) faces a diminishing future. In response to this widespread loss of potential, they must seek the good life by accessing the amped-up social potentials that supposedly thrive in tightly mapped, tracked, instrumentalised networks. The networked subject must subject herself to the fabled 'strength of weak ties' in order to self-actualise, stumbling upon some connection that (with luck) just might produce a valuable turning point in life. Serendipitous encounters with soon-to-be-significant others set life on trajectories: career paths, families, callings. This form of thinking entrains desire towards the canny use of social networks and a form of self-actualisation resilient enough to weather difficult circumstances. It is a vitaminisation of coincidence via social networks: a subtle shift in understanding social potential, such that weak ties come to be seen as a rich source of serendipitous possibility – just as a particular food might be viewed as a rich source of vitamin D. In a sense, attending to the serendipitous edges of social networks becomes akin to 'taking one's vitamins'. It proffers an abstracted conception of 'social nourishment' as that which fuels the flourishing life path – just like eating nutritious foods fuels the body and taking one's vitamins supports good health.

At the same time, Jay's conspicuous airplane analogy – her account of the twentysomething as a plane just taking off – inaugurates the 'life path' as a petropolitical construct.[17] Jay brings in fossil fuel 'through the back door', by analogy only. Yet doing so invites reflection on the relation between short-term nourishment and long-term impoverishment within late-late-capitalist life-path imagery. It evokes what Marx referred to as the metabolic rift: a rift in 'the metabolic interaction between man and the earth' within capitalism. For instance, what capitalist agriculture takes out of the soil, it never returns. Thus, capitalist agriculture progresses 'in the art, not only of robbing the worker, but of robbing the soil; all progress in increasing fertility of the soil for a given time is progress towards ruining the more long-lasting sources of that fertility'.[18] While Marx was once regarded as a thinker unconcerned with ecology, recent scholarship situates his metabolic rift as a key early concept linking capitalism with ecological depletion.[19] Today, such depletions extend far beyond the soil, in many directions: deep into the earth's crust – and deep into the earth's past – via the extraction and consumption of fossil fuels, derived from ancient plant and animal matter; and deep into the social fabric, by reimagining social networks as a site of social media extraction. Fossil fuel consumption, too, temporarily improves lives, but in the long term diminishes the earth's fecund potentials. Silicon Valley empires relentlessly assetise social networks, offering short-term measures that ramp up the 'fecundity' and productivity of the social, while diminishing, as Marx put it, the 'more long-lasting sources of that fertility'. Jay's airplane analogy unintentionally reveals how social networking has entered the metabolic rift, positing that to access the good life in an impoverished landscape, it is necessary to add more nourishment.

The pervasive imagining of weak ties as more or less nourishing reconciles two seemingly incompatible aspects of social network imaginaries in an age of both heavily instrumentalised social networks and diminished social potential. On the one hand, this network imaginary envisions a certain fungibility of social desires. If weak ties are, more or less, generally nourishing, then such nourishment can be derived from many different sources; in the face of one 'missed connection', one might as well find another. On the other hand, there is a precise and delicately calibrated calculus of social nourishments. There are many kinds of social 'vitamin', as it were; different aiders and abetters of social potential, of which each potential connection might be a source. This duality of social network potential in the realm of the weak tie lubricates a certain defensiveness that lurks in the 'social nourishment' narrative, revealing a sense in which its orientation of desire proffers a fungible yet precise 'nutrient-defence' against the widespread diminishment of life potential. While, in general, so the narrative goes, the future might be a wee bit cancelled, *you*, the canny initiate of social networks, can escape this general condition of diminishment, though the saving grace of network-savviness. In the face of severe storms, redundancies, market dips, stagnating wages, wealth inequality, and the still relatively early signs of climate catastrophe (any of which may be more or less immediate to those currently seeking to plot the course of their newly adult lives), subjects learn to steel themselves against any number of storms – and, with them, the pervasive sense that *any particular connection might get cut short* – with a fungible, yet carefully calibrated desire for 'social potential' in its abstract, vitaminised sense.

Vitaminised social networks incite their own form of 'cruel optimism'.[20] They offer subjects a stylised pragmatics of hope that revels in *all one can do with one's new, networked tools*. How users transform hyper-mappable social networks in unimagined ways! In a world of diminishing potential, what unexpected riches they find there! Confronted with a general condition of bumpiness – of more and more bumps in the 'life path' – one consults one's network, as a means of taking off. From abstracted imaginaries of 'social potential' emerges a network astrology of life paths: an alienated reimagining of 'the social' as vast, distributed quasi-psychological advice system; a subject suspended in a changeable constellation of friends and followers, through which they self-actualise by chance encounter. Social networks come to be seen as abstracted maps of 'life path' potential. They become vitaminised sources of serendipitous 'right time, right place' moments when, perhaps, a small exchange might lead to a big change: a life turning point. Rather than having constellations of stars as the imagined authority (as in astrology), these relentlessly fertilised constellations of social ties themselves take on the supplicative quality of stars in the horoscope; you may not know your future but, in a sense, *your network knows it for you*. And so, the subject's paradoxical task is to seek out the serendipitous, to artfully wield the network's power by being available to chance encounters – and able to skilfully cultivate these into opportunities.

Networked opportunisms

The social network and its attendant practices of governmentality inaugurate a strangely supplicative form of networked opportunism, extending the condition that Massimo De Carolis described in 2010 as an emergent opportunism in American culture. De Carolis argues that:

> the desire to make oneself a subject, to acquire full consciousness of one's own identity, has been replaced by the need to insert oneself successfully into social structures, even at the cost of rendering identity fluid, malleable, and elusive.[21]

This new opportunistic subject understands freedom as 'practical power' and aims to 'suppress every detachment, or confuse in a more or less profound way the subject and the environment, and dignify the interaction with the world without which, by definition, practical power cannot exist.'[22] It remains an open question whether the 'autonomous' subject De Carolis envisions as having come prior to the opportunistic one simply embodied the opposite problems: suppressing every attachment; over-estimating one's degree of separateness from their surroundings. Nevertheless, De Carolis usefully registers a shift in the orientation of desire, from the 'autonomous' subject's desire to know itself, separately from circumstance, to the opportunist's desire to find a place from which to take off. Opportunism, finally, is characterised by the unselfconscious 'will to *belong* to one's own world, to move through it like a fish through water'.[23] The opportunist's actions blend into the network's logic. Belonging to the world involves negotiating access to the possible, in a world that offers many chances but scant guarantees that these can be accessed. This, in turn, involves an enmeshment of human action with both the concept of possibility and the idea of a network: 'When human action itself becomes just one possibility among others, and as such always already forms part of the network of interactions in which it operates, it shares that network's rules and modes of being and becomes substantially indistinguishable from it.'[24] The opportunist's desire is to usefully align with available opportunities and continue accumulating abstract potential as such, while avoiding spiralling loss. 'The world', De Carolis writes, 'becomes no more than a supermarket of opportunities empty of all inherent value, yet marked by the fear that any false move may set in motion a vortex of impotence'.[25]

Nostalgia for 'autonomous' subjects and 'inherent value' will get us nowhere. Surely, the 'autonomous' subject is a problematic construction in itself, insofar as it risks repeating a patriarchal disavowal of connectedness to one's social and environmental surroundings – not to mention longstanding global patterns of colonial violence that enable the illusion of autonomy and self-determination in the first place. Nor is it fine-grained enough, I would argue, to call the 'supermarket of opportunities' *empty* of 'all inherent value'. It would be better to say that opportunism seeks to resolve the tension between 'inherent value' and 'fungible value' via the vitaminisation of coincidence. The particularity of opportunities' value becomes akin to that of a vitamin; it is inherent to that particular opportunity, and yet a similar sort of value might also be extracted from others. Nevertheless, what I call the vitaminisation of coincidence builds on De Carolis' account of how opportunism takes on new significance in light of a widespread cultural emphasis on finding one's place in the world. Networked opportunism seeks to unlock potentials proffered by ubiquitous networked tools, affording savvy subjects means to amplify audiences and reputations, to expand temporalities of acquaintanceship, to play with networking at scale.

The network's options and the network's call

Jay's talk evinces an invitation to answer the call of opportunism. She asks the listener to gain a reflexive understanding of her positionality in relation to opportunity and possibility – which is to say, her place within a web of overlapping social networks, which in turn might allow her to produce her own, new networks of families, colleagues, and friends. To master the realm of weak ties – to navigate the flows of social networks and make oneself one of the ones who *can* make something come of these fleeting connections – is a predominant style of hope in an age of compulsive, often automated mapping of social networks. To skilfully ride the waves of social networks involves embodying a paradox: obeying the call to self-actualisation by serendipity. Jay asks the listener to see herself as one who harnesses horizons of potential within social networks, in service of a potential life path: a path that *calls* the subject. The social-networked formulation of the calling, we might say, echoes and extends the Althusserian account of interpellation.[26] Now, in a sense, it is not ideology, but rather the network, itself, that calls – 'Hey, you!' – while the subject hears, turns, and answers, 'Yes, me! I am meant to – made to – answer the network's call.' The idea of the life path calling the subject also builds on Max Weber's treatment of the calling – or the *Beruf* – in *The Protestant Ethic and the Spirit of Capitalism*.[27] Weber famously argued that the Protestant idea of a spiritual calling had become secularised within capitalism, turned into vocational calling. In its networked-opportunistic form, the secularised concept of a 'true calling' is not restricted to one's career. It freely blends career and 'life' goals (a dream job, a nice side project, a good house, a husband and two children) and fashions them into an overall trajectory. The trajectory takes the form not of a calling to a particular vocation, but instead to an abstracted quality of abundant potentiality itself, driving the smooth, fruitful unfolding of a meaningful life path; the abundance of one's half-desired-half-imagined, if cruelly optimistic, life; the skilful avoidance of those snags that many others will, unfortunately, get caught on; and, above all, an abstracted quality of the subject's willingness to hear the network's call, to cultivate the life path's coming-into-being at the edges of a social network.

The networked-opportunistic call understands weak ties as sites of potential luck, where serendipity seeps in, where one finds what one was not looking for, and where any number of relationships, families, and career opportunities could spark from just 'one good conversation, one good break'.[28] Weak ties are mythologised as sites of luck – in which neoliberal 'self-appreciating subjects',[29] seeking to fulfil their personal and professional potential, become 'participants in the culture of chance'.[30] Weak ties emit the scent of variable futures: possible life paths, inflected with a form of social network governance that envisions a set of branching potentials emanating from chance social encounters. One navigates weak ties almost as if to imagine one's future as variable, via everyday acts of hedging – *if I don't find a future path through this weak tie, then perhaps I'll find one through that tie, or that one*. The vitaminised social network thus becomes a hedged portfolio of personal and social potential.[31] An emphasis on 'horizon scanning' for possible futures within one's social networks instantiates a 'politics of optionality' (to borrow Edward LiPuma's term).[32] It enacts at the level of the lifespan what Randy Martin has called a 'social logic of the derivative' – that is, seeing one's life as a compilation of possible moments of uncertain investment (when one might meet a new partner, or find the perfect job opportunity), in which the hope for a lucky, life-changing chance encounter is hedged by social networks (if not a new path via this contact, then perhaps via that one, or that one).[33] One can hedge one's bets for oneself – and perhaps even profit from the vitaminised social network – as if to take back, in however small a portion, just a fraction of the resources extracted from social life by capital under its new regime of 'data colonialism': a condition that Nick Couldry and Ulises Ali Mejías describe as one in which 'social life all over the globe becomes an "open" resource for extraction that is somehow "just there" for capital'.[34]

Networked astrologies

Theodor Adorno once wrote a lengthy content analysis of the *Los Angeles Times* Astrology column. Focusing on the outputs of 1952–53, Adorno unpicked how the astrology column addressed its readers, hailing them as those whose decisions were important enough to matter, while, at the same time, reconciling readers to 'the feeling of being "caught," the impossibility for most people to regard themselves by any stretch of imagination as the masters of their own fate'.[35] The astrology column often advised a 'shrewdly meek attitude' towards higher-ups, which Adorno read as a neo-feudal attitude of 'general reconciliation, particularly of placating opponents, of "playing up" to them'.[36] The astrology column abstracted family relations, while emphasising the role of the friend as the 'messenger of society', enforcing social norms.[37] Occasionally, 'the figure of the stranger, strongly affect-laden' would appear; Adorno thought that strangers 'may play a magical role and may help somehow to overcome suspicion of irrational promises by making their source as irrational as the promises themselves are'.[38] The astrology column proffered an abstract authority of timing – today is a good day to impress a higher-up with your attention to detail; tomorrow is best reserved for increasing personal charm. Ultimately, Adorno read the column as aligned with authoritarian tendencies in American society at the time and symptomatic of 'eras of decline in social systems' more generally.[39] In a moment overshadowed by the atomic and hydrogen bombs, an impending 'mood of doom' prevailed – even (and especially) among those who professed the most optimism.[40] Astrology, Adorno argued, 'takes care of this mood by translating it into a pseudo-rational form, thus somehow localising free-floating anxieties in some definite symbolism', while also giving 'some vague and diffused comfort by making the senseless appear as though it had some hidden and grandiose sense while at the same time corroborating that this sense can neither be sought in the realm of the human nor can properly be grasped by humans'.[41]

Jay's appeal to twentysomethings weaves a different flavour of futurity and promise for a different moment of decline. It speaks the temporality of social media subjectivity: rhythms of vitaminised expectation, potential, and promise set into the background of social media life, where the biopolitical governance of subjects becomes social network governance by life path. And it speaks to a different species of doom. There may well be nuclear threats to come, but unlike Adorno's A- and H-bombs, climate disaster is a slow, at first almost undetectable burn – an irreversible unpicking of prior, taken-for-granted Holocene harmonies. Jay's weak-tie imagery unwittingly adapts some of the 1950s astrology column's interpellating tasks to these new existential threats, emitting a sense that temporary measures to increase fertility and inflate potentials will not work for much longer, and yet, for now, still must be tried. When this coupling of short-term nourishment with long-term diminishment of potential reaches a crisis point, the realm of the weak tie harnesses hopefulness in the rationalisation of social networks, and in their capacity to capitalise on serendipity, to make luck just that little bit luckier, by mapping and making use of social network peripheries. The realm of the weak tie's configuration of *subject-desire-world* symptomatises a sense of separateness and abstraction from the world, a transformation of singular instances into abstracted, fungible, yet tightly calibrated understandings of potential. Yet it is also the shape of a pragmatics of diminished potential: a way of orienting oneself toward a diminished world, using life-path imagery as a means to imaginatively *take off*, while sidestepping questions of collectivity or politics. Now, more than ever, we need conceptions of desire that try to think of collectivity beyond nodes and networks, and to understand that previously abundant, readymade, and disavowedly petropolitical readings of the 'good life' (life partner, family of 2.3 children, big house, fluffy pet, fulfilling career path, nice vacations) are increasingly ill-suited to a moment of ecological, financial, and social catastrophe. Acting, in this moment, without blindly repeating the desires of another era necessitates learning to question the subtle yet crucial role that life-path and network imagery play in reshaping and singularising desire. Such imagery expresses and exacerbates the very metabolic rift, the mitigation of which is perhaps this moment's most crucial demand.

Notes

1 Meg Jay, *The Defining Decade: Why Your Twenties Matter and How to Make the Most of Them Now* (Edinburgh: Canongate Books, 2016).
2 Meg Jay, 'Why 30 Is Not the New 20', TED Talk, www.ted.com/talks/meg_jay_why_30_is_not_the_new_20?language=en (accessed September 2, 2022).
3 Morton Bast, 'From Appalled to Applauding: Reactions to Meg Jay's Controversial Talk about 20-Somethings', TED Blog, May 17, 2013, https://blog.ted.com/from-appalled-to-applauding-reactions-to-meg-jays-controversial-talk-about-20-somethings/ (accessed September 2, 2022).
4 This problem with the TED format has been well diagnosed in Benjamin Bratton's own TED Talk, for example. 'New Perspectives: What's Wrong with TED Talks? Benjamin Bratton at TEDxSanDiego 2013 – Re:Think', TEDx Talks, YouTube, December 14, 2013, www.youtube.com/watch?v=Yo5cKRmJaf0 (accessed September 2, 2022).
5 On increasing wealth inequality and its consequences for neo-liberal subjects, see, for instance, Thomas Piketty, *Capital in the Twenty-First Century*, trans. Arthur Goldhammer (Cambridge, MA: Harvard University Press, 2017); Annie McClanahan, 'Serious Crises', *Boundary 2* 46, no. 1 (2019): 103–32; Lauren Berlant, *Cruel Optimism* (Durham, NC: Duke University Press, 2011).
6 Elliott Green, 'What Are the Most-Cited Publications in the Social Sciences (According to Google Scholar)?', LSE Blog, May 12, 2016, https://blogs.lse.ac.uk/impactofsocialsciences/2016/05/12/what-are-the-most-cited-publications-in-the-social-sciences-according-to-google-scholar/ (accessed September 2, 2022).
7 Mark Granovetter, 'The Strength of Weak Ties', *American Journal of Sociology* 78, no. 6 (1973): 1371
8 *Ibid.*, 1372.
9 '2013 Everett M. Rogers Award Colloquium', USC Annenberg, YouTube, October 1, 2013, www.youtube.com/watch?v=9l9VYXKn6sg (accessed September 2, 2022).

10 Richard Thaler and Cass Sunstein, *Nudge: Improving Decisions about Health, Wealth and Happiness* (London: Penguin, 2009).

11 Alex Pentland, *Social Physics: How Social Networks Can Make Us Smarter* (New York: Penguin Books, 2015).

12 Mark Whitehead, Rhys Jones, Rachel Lilley, Rachel Howell, and Jessica Pykett, 'Neuroliberalism: Cognition, Context, and the Geographical Bounding of Rationality', *Progress in Human Geography* 43, no. 4 (2019): 633.

13 *Ibid.*, 641, emphasis added.

14 Wendy Hui Kyong Chun, 'Networks NOW: Belated Too Early', *Amerikastudien/American Studies* 60, no. 1 (2015): 37–58.

15 Wendy Hui Kyong Chun, *Updating to Remain the Same: Habitual New Media* (Cambridge, MA: The MIT Press, 2017), 1–23. While this argument is compelling, it is worth noting that Granovetter has argued against the idea of 'more or less atomised individuals' in what he terms 'undersocialised' accounts of economic action. Further, Deleuze's late-career emphasis on the 'dividual' subject might offer an alternative frame to Chun's emphasis on the singular/plural 'you' of networks. See Mark Granovetter, 'Economic Action and Social Structure: The Problem of Embeddedness', *American Journal of Sociology* 91, no. 3 (1985): 482; Gilles Deleuze, 'Postscript on the Societies of Control', *October* 59 (Winter 1992): 3–7.

16 Franco Berardi, *After the Future*, ed. Gary Genosko and Nicholas Thoburn (Oakland, CA: AK Press, 2011), 13; Mark Fisher, *Ghosts of My Life: Writings on Depression, Hauntology and Lost Futures* (Winchester: Zero Books, 2014).

17 On petropolitics, petroculture, and energy humanities, see, for instance, Imre Szeman, *On Petrocultures: Globalization, Culture, and Energy* (Morgantown: West Virginia University Press, 2019); Sheena Wilson, Adam Carlson, and Imre Szeman, eds, *Petrocultures: Oil, Politics, Culture* (Montreal: McGill-Queen's University Press, 2017); Imre Szeman and Dominic Boyer, eds, *Energy Humanities: An Anthology* (Baltimore, MD: Johns Hopkins University Press, 2017).

18 Karl Marx, *Capital: A Critique of Political Economy*, vol. 1, trans. Ben Fowkes (London: Penguin, 1976), 638.

19 See John Bellamy Foster, 'Marx's Theory of Metabolic Rift: Classical Foundations for Environmental Sociology', *American Journal of Sociology* 105, no. 2 (1999): 366–405; Mindi Schneider and Philip McMichael, 'Deepening, and Repairing, the Metabolic Rift', *The Journal of Peasant Studies* 37, no. 3 (2010): 461–84,

20 Berlant, *Cruel Optimism*.

21 Massimo De Carolis, 'Toward a Phenomenology of Opportunism', in *Radical Thought in Italy: A Potential Politics*, ed. Paolo Virno and Michael Hardt (Minneapolis: University of Minnesota Press, 2010), 38.
22 *Ibid.*, 39.
23 *Ibid.*
24 *Ibid.*, 48.
25 *Ibid.*, 40–41; I hear, in this, an echo of Lacan's remark in Seminar XX: 'We live in an age of supermarkets, so one must know what one is capable of producing, even by way of being.' Jacques Lacan, *On Feminine Sexuality: The Limits of Love and Knowledge*, trans. Bruce Fink (New York: W.W. Norton & Co., 1999), 98.
26 Louis Althusser, 'Ideology and Ideological State Apparatuses (Notes Towards an Investigation)', in *The Anthropology of the State: A Reader*, ed. Aradhana Sharma and Akhil Gupta (Hoboken, NJ: John Wiley & Sons, 2009), 86–111.
27 Max Weber, *The Protestant Ethic and the Spirit of Capitalism*, trans. Talcott Parsons (Abingdon: Routledge, 2001).
28 Meg Jay, 'Why 30 Is Not the New 20'. On serendipity and its histories, see Allen Edward Foster and David Ellis, 'Serendipity and Its Study', *Journal of Documentation* 70, no. 6 (2014): 1015–38.
29 Michel Feher, 'Self-Appreciation; or, The Aspirations of Human Capital', *Public Culture* 21, no. 1 (2009): 21–41. Feher describes the 'self-appreciating' subjects as those who view themselves in terms of appreciation – both in the sense of being esteemed, and in the sense of the value of their self-investment appreciating.
30 T. J. Jackson Lears, *Something for Nothing: Luck in America* (New York: Penguin, 2004), 10.
31 See Ivan Ascher, *Portfolio Society: On the Capitalist Mode of Prediction* (New York: Zone Books, 2016), 81, 59.
32 Edward LiPuma, *The Social Life of Financial Derivatives: Markets, Risk, and Time* (Durham, NC: Duke University Press, 2017), 352.
33 Randy Martin, *Knowledge Ltd: Toward a Social Logic of the Derivative* (Philadelphia, PA: Temple University Press, 2015).
34 Nick Couldry and Ulises Ali Mejías, 'Data Colonialism: Rethinking Big Data's Relation to the Contemporary Subject', *Television & New Media* 20, no. 4 (2019): 337. See also Nick Couldry and Ulises Ali Mejías, *The Costs of Connection: How Data Is Colonizing Human Life and Appropriating It for Capitalism* (Stanford, CA: Stanford University Press, 2019).

35 Theodor Adorno, 'The Stars Down to Earth: The Los Angeles Times Astrology Column', *Telos* 19 (1974): 83.
36 *Ibid.*, 80.
37 *Ibid.*, 75.
38 *Ibid.*, 76.
39 *Ibid.*, 90.
40 *Ibid.*, 84.
41 *Ibid.*

6

Desiring-infrastructures in the crypto economy

Ludovico Rella

Teenagers want to experiment with sex, and so you either don't enter into the conversation and pretend that they are not going to have sex and they will not experiment, in which case watch out, or otherwise you will embrace what is inevitable, and that means that you will have to have a conversation … I think that regulators are being very naive and simplistic about the fact that digital currency and crypto and DLT and data and cloud are here to stay, these are technologies we need to embrace, to adopt them and to transform because transformation is going to happen.[1]

The quote at the start of this chapter, gathered at one of the many crypto trade expos of the past decade, collapses technological and financial experimentation with sexual experimentation, encapsulating an equation that lies at the heart of the cryptoasset industry: that economic investment in monetary technologies is tantamount to a libidinal investment in technological designs and in the capitalisation they enable. Desire for money, albeit subjectively felt, has a pre-personal and intersubjective origin and target.

Money occupies a central place as an object that embodies the impersonal nature of the economy as such … It is in relation to desire that money most fully assumes its position as embodying the economic in its foreignness to subjectivity.[2]

Furthermore, desire not only emerges intersubjectively, but is also 'embedded in the object itself', that is, in money.[3] Since money is, among other things, an infrastructure, here I would like to emphasise how money infrastructures serve as the 'technological unconscious' of money, registering flows of desire and libidinal investments that 'coexist, but [do] not necessarily coincide' with the materiality of such infrastructures.[4] Desire, then, is folded into the architecture of money infrastructures, such that different architectures articulate and express desire in different forms.

This chapter, then, pries open the desires that shape, maintain in place, or disrupt money infrastructures, revealing how such infrastructures actively change and shape the desires on which they feed. To do this, I draw on existing libidinal political economy scholarship that approaches the economy itself as 'a surface expression of an economy of desire, and the central concepts of capitalism as an expression of libidinal energies – or a specific organisation of flows of desire'.[5] The chapter expands on these ideas by foregrounding a more-than-human propensity to desire. The metaphor of the amoeba protruding its pseudopodia towards its environment, which Freud employed to illustrate the way the ego libidinally invests in the ideas and external objects, serves as a jump-off point for forging a connection with algorithm and software studies' understanding of machinic and algorithmic desires.[6] Desire, according to this view, is no longer a solely human affective force that unfolds *through* and *onto* technologies, machines, and infrastructures, but rather is something also felt *by* infrastructures themselves, based on their active forms and dispositions.

More concretely, the chapter focuses on *cryptoassets*: digital representations of value and means of payments, operating on blockchains. Blockchains, in turn, are distributed, time-stamped, append-only ledgers, simultaneously kept on all the nodes within a decentralised network and updated following a set of rules, instructions, and procedures called a 'consensus algorithm' or 'consensus mechanism'.[7] First introduced with Bitcoin in 2008, blockchains have exploded in terms of both number and market capitalisation, with a current total of 24,194 cryptoassets and a total market size of $1.1 trillion. While until 2018 the growth of this industry was fuelled by utility tokens and interoperability technologies, the second peak seems to have been propelled by an expansion in non-fungible tokens (NFTs). NFTs are used to identify unique digital objects. They are often used in videogames to allow buying and selling of unique items and artefacts or to identify unique real-world items such as artworks. Conversely, utility tokens are 'digital assets designed to be spent within a certain blockchain ecosystem'.[8] Last, interoperability technologies provide payment solutions that enable 'cross-chain' trading and transactions, that is, simultaneous or near-simultaneous payment capability across blockchains and between different cryptoassets.

The chapter is organised around key features of the desiring-infrastructures that characterise the new crypto economy. After using metaphors from the 1840s Railway Mania to expand on the role of desire in technology and money, I identify and map the peculiar articulations of desire that different blockchain architectures perform, focusing in turn on NFTs, utility tokens, and interoperability technologies. I conclude by arguing that the role of desire and speculation complicates the ostensibly disruptive and revolutionary capacity of blockchain technologies, at least if these libidinal flows are left unchanneled and unchecked. Furthermore, I propose that we need, through regulation and collective decisions, to harness desire and enchantment as a collective political tool, rather than leave it to the private sector alone. If desire is always pre-personal, then it is always trans-personal, which is to say collective and political. If the Railway Mania metaphor shows how money, technology, and desire are inherently intertwined, the history of that bubble also shows that the outcomes and consequences of libidinal investments are not predetermined in advance, but rather vary based on open-ended decisions on design, architectures, standards, and financial practices.

The libidinal dispositions of money infrastructures

On September 28, 2016, Andrew Hauser, Executive Director for Banking, Payments, and Financial Resilience at the Bank of England, gave a speech that drew a comparison between payment systems and railways.

> People wanting to travel north out of London by trains are spoiled for choice. Spread along a half-mile stretch of the city's Euston Road are no less than three major stations ... The reasons for such an apparently complex system are of course historic, dating back to the period of intense competition between train lines in Victorian Times ... Given a free hand, it is inconceivable that anyone would design such arrangements from scratch today. Yet tens of millions of passengers use each station every year: business is booming ... The situation in UK payments today is rather similar.[9]

While the comparison between railways and payments is not new, Hauser's speech not only defines payments *as* rails metaphorically, but also foregrounds how libidinal and speculative investments can invest the very materiality and shape of infrastructures. The desires projected onto infrastructures leave marks of themselves on the infrastructures' architectures and affordances, and infrastructures, in turn, remain as a 'technological subconscious', a material trace of those desires. As Brian Larkin puts it, 'Infrastructures ... emerge out of and store within them forms of desire and fantasy and can take on fetish-like aspects that sometimes can be wholly autonomous from their technical function.'[10]

In the case of digital infrastructures like blockchains and payment systems, their libidinal political economy is further complicated by the capacity of software code to exert ostensibly immaterial control over the materiality of infrastructures themselves; code is the performative and self-actualising language par excellence.[11] Software code, then, can take on the same 'fetish-like aspect' mentioned by Larkin. This is how Wendy Hui Kyong Chun sees it: 'As a fetish, source code can provide surprising "deviant" pleasures that do not end where they should ... Code is a medium in the full sense of the word that channels the ghost that we imagine runs the machine.'[12] In other words, digital money infrastructures are inhabited by the desire of those who programme them: 'executability makes code not law, but rather every lawyer's dream of what law should be, automatically enabling and disabling certain actions and functioning at the level of everyday practice'.[13] In a similar fashion, 'blockchain architecture is a bookkeeper's dream – the ability to inspect all transactions and be sure that none have been altered gives ... unprecedented power'.[14]

If code is not law but the lawyer's dream, and if blockchains are not just accounting but the bookkeeper's dream, then cryptoassets are the dream of 'token designers'. It is their dreams that are inscribed in specific distributional and reward schemes, which try to produce specific alignments between users' and tokens' behaviour, removing 'perverse incentives' and reinforcing positive ones.[15] In a way, if blockchain can store records indefinitely and cryptoassets, as we shall see below, are means for universal monetisation, valuation, and capitalisation, then we can see their combination as a kind of 'immortality project'.[16]

However, money infrastructures do not only reflect our own desires back to us; they also change them. Keller Easterling defines *disposition* as 'a relationship between potentials ... a tendency, activity, faculty, or property in either beings or objects – a propensity within a context'.[17] Digital infrastructures therefore possess *libidinal dispositions*, deriving from their design and the context within which they are deployed. These libidinal dispositions point to a 'more-than-human' characteristic of libido that is present from the very onset of psychoanalysis. As Earl Gammon elaborates, Freud used the amoeba and its pseudopodia as a metaphor for the investment of the libidinal drives, in that 'they can be extended to encompass external objects or withdrawn back into the main body of the organism'.[18] Different infrastructures show different propensities to 'protrude' towards specific external (physical or digital) objects, and, in incorporating these objects into their own workings, they alter these objects in specific ways.

Recent studies of algorithms have illustrated the capacity, if not the propensity, of computational apparatuses to desire. Regarding artificial intelligence, the moral philosopher Richard Braithwaite has argued the following.

> The peculiarity of men and animals is that they have the power of adjusting themselves to ... their environment based on their appetites, desires, drives, instincts ... If we want to construct a machine which will vary its attention to things ... it would seem to be necessary to equip the machine with something corresponding to a set of appetites.[19]

Luciana Parisi and M. Beatrice Fazi expand on this more-than-human capacity for desire as they foreground algorithms' capability of enjoyment and fun, understood as 'an affective force that exceeds the formal logic that has nonetheless generated it'.[20] Fun, for algorithms, is the enjoyment of their *'own process of determination'*, that is, the achievement of the *'final purpose* of the computational process'.[21] The libidinal disposition of money infrastructures is that process of determination that orients the enjoyment of algorithms, such as blockchains' and cryptoassets' consensus algorithms.

In what follows, I delve deeper into three related and competing claims of value associated with different aspects of blockchain materialities and the specific modes of enchantment these entail.

NFTs incorporate ever-expanding hosts of digital objects within 'magic circles' of collections and repertoires, endowing them with monetary value that makes them desirable 'as if' they were money. Utility tokens incorporate ecosystems of relations: social networks, digital cultural production and consumption, localised economies centred around shared assets. Finally, interoperability technologies – representing the pinnacle of monetisation – protrude towards money itself and represent the desire for the final satisfaction of all other monetary desires.

Non-fungible tokens and the aura of uniqueness

The first libidinal disposition associated with crypto money infrastructures is provided by NFTs. These are cryptoassets that represent unique tangible or intangible assets. They are non-interchangeable with each other (hence their non-fungibility) and non-interoperable (more on this later). They are also indivisible, meaning that they cannot be divided into smaller sums like cryptocurrencies or fiat money.[22] NFTs are used to produce scarcity by attaching a verifiable signature to a real-world or digital unique object, such as a work of art or a digital artifact like a weapon in a videogame. In 2017, the most famous example of an NFT became CryptoKitties. CryptoKitties is a decentralised video game built on the Ethereum blockchain, where people buy and breed digital cats, each of which has specific aesthetic characteristics. The rarer the appearance of the cat, the more valuable it is.[23] There are currently more than 1.8 million CryptoKitties in circulation and the most expensive cat was sold on September 4, 2018, for the equivalent of $172,625.79.[24] The total turnover of CryptoKitties since the game's inception in November 2017, at 2021 prices for the cryptoasset ETH, has been $207 million so far, and, at the peak of its use, it accounted individually for more than 10% of the total number of transactions on the Ethereum blockchain – a volume so high it created a backlog of non-CryptoKitties transactions.[25] However, since January 2018, CryptoKitties traffic has plummeted by 98%.[26]

Subsequent generations of NFTs leveraged microtransactions in video games to sell unique in-game items like weapons and 'skins' (i.e., changes in appearance of characters and items that do not necessarily change the skills or powers of those characters and items) or even plots of digital land.[27] Another strand took the role of certifying ownership of real-world collectibles, in particular artworks.[28] In this way, what during the first 'Crypto Mania' of 2017–18 was a just market niche in 2020 became the very loco-motive of the cryptoasset market explosion.[29] The total number of NFTs now listed on OpenSea amounts to 8,128, although only 784 of these have an exchange volume higher than 100 ETH (currently worth about $181,000). Just about any piece of digital content seems now capable of being rendered unique and sold as an NFT, from the first-ever tweet to a fake Banksy meme, each of which sold recently for $2.9 million and £244,000 respectively.[30]

NFTs' libidinal disposition channels desire for the digital object as a proxy for the desire for uniqueness by producing cryptoassets as 'singularities', that is, goods and services that are hard to price because their value is multidimensional, incommensurable, and uncertain.[31] This obsession with the uniqueness of the digital object echoes the tension between the aura of authenticity surrounding works of art and the economics of mass reproduction.[32] For Walter Benjamin, in fact, 'the whole sphere of authenticity is outside technical … reproducibility'.[33] The auratic dimension of uniqueness is the libidinal disposition that allows the collector and the work of art to reach out to each other: 'the most profound enchantment for the collector is the locking of individual items within a magic circle in which they are fixed as the final thrill, the thrill of acquisition, passes over them'.[34] However, the mass-reproducibility of objects does not in principle pose insurmountable obstacles to the libido of the collector.

> The collector's self-proclaimed need 'to have them all' describes what is sometimes referred to as extension pack logic by computer gamers, or what Baudrillard called a 'system of objects' … that induces the need in consumers to 'collect 'em all' in order to have the com-plete set.[35]

Digital objects, however, are multiple from the start, hence rendering any collection worthless, in that anyone could amass exact copies of the same objects.[36] NFTs produce an aura of authen-ticity that was never associated with the underlying object to begin with.[37] Whence, then, does the aura of NFTs come? On the one hand, NFT certification performs uniqueness by attaching a certificate of individuality to that which can be endlessly copied, and in so doing it 'locks' the digital object within the 'magic circle' that Benjamin evoked. On the other hand, however, desire for NFTs is more profound, entailing a libidinal investment in the idea of interoperability that will be expanded upon later. If Noam Yuran is correct to argue that 'money is an object desired as money', then we can say that NFTs enable digital objects to enter an economy of desire by enabling such objects to be desired *as if* they were money, and this is achieved precisely by inserting them into an infrastructure of exchange.[38]

Utility tokens and the desiring ecosystem

A second libidinal disposition is represented by utility tokens. A utility token works in three ways. First, it can turn the circulation of a myriad of assets – such as real estate, cars, loyalty points, reputation, and data – into one tradeable product that can generate value through property and exchange. Several platforms can use utility tokens to represent interactions on social networks – such as liking and resharing content that has been posted – and some are designed to offer fractional ownership in shared assets like memory storage.[39] Second, utility tokens can create a digital means of exchange that can be used only in the specific community defined by the app where the utility token operates. Continuing the example outlined earlier, a token monetising likes can be subsequently used as a means of payment within that same social network for either exclusive content or for online marketplace solutions. In addition to these two functions, utility tokens have provided business financing for the start-ups constructing the ecosystem itself. During the 2017–18 explosion of initial coin offerings (ICO), many companies would pre-sell utility tokens to raise the necessary capital to get the company started while also building hype around the project. For example, the distribution strategy of a utility coin for social media content could simultaneously raise capital and, by targeting influencers during the pre-sale of the tokens, aim to create the necessary user base for the subsequent content before the social network takes off. ICOs raised over \$31 billion between January 2016 and

August 2019, surpassing venture capital funding for seed and early-stage companies in 2017.[40]

On example of this monetisation is the blockchain STEEM, which is geared towards creating a rewards economy for digital content creators. In STEEM's white paper, three tokens are outlined. STEEM tokens proper are used by members of a given online community when they create, share, or like content posted on the community under the principle 'One STEEM, one vote'.[41] Steem Power (SP) tokens represent funds committed for periods of thirteen weeks, to incentivise loyalty towards the community and the platform ecosystem. SPs entitle users to a larger vote capacity (i.e., the 'likes' of users with more SPs are weighted by the share of the total supply of SPs), a larger bandwidth (i.e., users with more SPs can perform more transactions per second), and a higher chance to participate in the consensus mechanism that validates new blocks. Last, STEEM dollars (SBD) are designed to be a liquid token whose value is meant to oscillate close to a 1:1 exchange rate with the US dollar, although the white paper does not specify how this peg is maintained. To avoid the 'perverse incentive' for speculative traders to instantly cash out of the system if STEEM tokens surge in value, STEEM can only be redeemed into SBD with a 3.5-day lag. In this way, the system tries to keep together the competing forces of speculation, content monetisation, and eco-system strengthening.

The libidinal disposition of utility tokens invests all the social relations traversing the ecosystem established between platforms and their users, while delivering on the platform's owners' desire for quick revenue streams and control over the company. On the one hand, a crypto token turns the circulation of assets into one tradeable product that can generate value through property and exchange.[42] On the other hand, tokenisation promotes the idea that established and standard valuation frameworks cannot explain the growth of blockchain platforms. A similar dynamic characterised the dot-com bubble. Just as we saw with IPOs in the 1990s, ICOs are now perhaps more significant as performative marketing tools than they are as tools for raising capital.[43] The attention, then, has shifted away from the returns, utility, network reach, and internal security of the proposed technologies and towards the returns and growth of cryptoassets in speculative exchanges.

For utility tokens, however, this connection between the token itself and ICO valuations can be dangerous. If the performance of the token looks more strongly linked to that of the company rather than to the function that the token performs in the ecosystem, these tokens might be considered to be securities. In fact, recent regulatory interventions have reminded token designers that any financial product that is acquired with expectation of profits deriving solely from the actions of a third party is a security, which in turn requires their issuers to be licensed and supervised by market authorities like the Securities Exchange Commission in the USA or the Financial Conduct Authority in the UK.[44] This is certainly one of the 'perverse' effects that a token designer must keep in mind. As one informant put it, 'The challenge for someone wanting to design a utility token is how you make sure it's not a security, and for a security token is how you don't go to jail.'[45]

The platform economy established by utility tokens changes fundamentally the relationship between asset, infrastructure, and ecosystem. Rather than being assets used by participants in the ecosystem through the infrastructures, tokens become a way to *assetise* and, hence, *capitalise* on the interactions themselves. In fact, 'liquidity presumes assets that are knowable by a large group of potential buyers and sellers … The creation of liquidity therefore becomes a problem in how to create generalised impersonal knowledge out of idiosyncratic personal knowledge.'[46] Tokenisation, then, is a new form of assetisation; tokens render possible the 'becoming asset' of just about anything because they are neatly delineated, that is, they have 'clear identification of perimeter, detachability from context, an attributable scope, and definite articulation of the agency that owns the asset'.[47] While NFTs promise artificial scarcity and the preservation of an aura of uniqueness and authenticity for digital singularities, utility tokens produce a symbiotic relationship between incentives, behaviour, and monetisation.

Interoperability and the fantasy of frictionlessness

The third libidinal disposition is interoperability, understood as 'the ability for two different and independent software applications to exchange information without loss of data, semantics, or metadata'.[48] Taking further the payment-railway metaphor put forward in the first section of this chapter, interoperability is the building of railway stations and interchanges that allowed trains to travel on rails built by different companies, and the standardisation of time that made these interchanges possible.[49] In the context of payments and blockchains, it means synchronising payments across blockchains and providing for the seamless exchange of value denominated in different cryptoassets.

Of the three dispositions outlined here, interoperability is the most paradoxical. In fact, interoperability represents the pinnacle of the abstraction of money into pure function, pure exchange. Georg Simmel encapsulated this tendency in the following terms.

> The disconnectedness of what exists as substance contradicts the nature of money as an abstract representation of interaction. Only to the extent that the material element recedes does money become real money, that is a real integration and a point of unification of interacting elements of value.[50]

If money, as we said before, is 'an object desired as money', then interoperability as pure exchange seems to entail the disappearance of money's thingness and, hence, of the centre and target of desire. As a pure means of exchange, in fact, 'desire for money in itself is comprehensively rejected in economic thought'.[51] Cognitive scientists Stephen Lea and Paul Webley echo this concern by arguing that in understanding money as a tool for exchange, 'we do not need a psychology of money at all … we only have to understand the job that money does and the human cognitive system that enables us to use it'.[52] Furthermore, if interoperability is synonymous with standardisation, then a libidinal investment in interoperability is paradoxical because 'one … rather comical reason why standards may be neglected … is that they are boring'.[53]

And yet, interoperability emerged as its own zone of speculative investment between 2017 and 2018, with companies like Ripple and Stellar reaching enormous market capitalisation with the promise of seamless cross-border payments and fiat-crypto interoperability. The case of Ripple exemplifies this push, in that the company emerged as a cross-chain and interbank interoperability company, yet its own cryptoasset managed to climb to the top of the ranking of cryptoassets by market capitalisation and, as another industry insider put it, at one point in 2017 'Ripple was worth more than all but maybe twenty banks in the planet. And that made the phone ring!'[54] Other companies like Polkadot and Cosmos promised 'atomic' cross-chain transactions. Payment protocols like Plasma for Ethereum and Lightning for Bitcoin promised to slash transaction times for relatively slow blockchains to free up latency in exchanges and payments.[55]

As one practitioner in this scene described it:

[p]eople have finally started to realise its importance for the development of the next level of applications that the world needs. When we started in 2014 people were actually making fun of the project saying, 'who even wants this?' and now everyone says this is the biggest issue in blockchain.[56]

The solution, I argue, has to do with the paradox that Yuran identifies in relation to the desire for money as such. In fact, the value of an NFT is based on its uniqueness, which in turn tends to render it 'illiquid' – it is difficult to exchange NFTs with each other and for cash. The value of utility tokens, furthermore, pertains to the network in which they are used, understood as a 'walled garden'. However, both NFTs and utility tokens fold within themselves a desire for liquidity and capitalisation; they are still desired 'as money', although with obstacles on the road to the realisation and actualisation of that desire.

Stefan Thomas, a former Ripple employee and CEO of the interoperable micropayment start-up Coil, describing the interledger protocol (ILP) that was designed for cross-chain and cross-currency payments, compared ILP to the open Internet where multiple networks could coexist and interoperate, while individual platforms, insofar as they remained isolated from each other, were like the now defunct America Online (AOL) network and messaging service.[57]

Interoperability is the condition of possibility for both profitability and competition. It is by virtue of the frictionlessness of transfer *across* chains and across infrastructures that margins and profits can be realised in trading volatile assets against each other. As Lana Swartz has pointed out, 'an act of payment for someone is always an opportunity for arbitrage for someone else'.[58] In this way, interoperability also stages the political and economic tension between the scarcity, utility, and liquidity of assets that mediate ecosystems linked to the realisation of value in speculative exchanges.[59] If money infrastructures 'protrude' towards their surroundings, then each infrastructural design expresses libido by protruding in different directions: NFTs towards digital objects, utility tokens towards social networks, interoperability towards money itself.

Crypto enchantment bubbles

'Not architecture alone but all technology is, at certain stages, evidence of a collective dream.'[60] So wrote Benjamin almost a century ago, and the point still stands. Fascination and enchantment have always traversed both money and technology, and blockchain and cryptocurrency infrastructures are no exception; cryptocurrencies have enhanced rather than questioned or challenged the speculative dynamics of financial capitalism.[61] They perform affective and libidinal investments in myriad ways. As Freud would argue, they 'protrude' towards different things and social relations. NFTs incorporate an ever-expanding array of digital objects within 'magic circles' of collections and repertoires, endowing them with monetary value that makes them desirable 'as if' they were money. Utility tokens incorporate ecosystems of relations: social networks, digital cultural production and consumption, localised economies centred around shared assets. Interoperability technologies, representing the pinnacle of monetisation, protrude towards money itself and represent the desire for the final satisfaction of all other monetary desires.

But if money infrastructures are sites where different libidinal economies play out, then what remains underexplored is the role that regulation can play in channelling and influencing the flows of desire that comprise such economies. Even the technical and ostensibly standard-driven project of interoperability is a deeply political endeavour. Recall once more the Bank of England's analogy between payments and railways.

> Convergence could take a number of different forms ... it could imply a single universal payments system, run on a single platform, and handling all payment types. Or it could mean retaining separate

systems, but with a common 'backbone', including a shared language, operating standards, and access protocols ... That is not the model that has developed for UK retail payments – and such a single dominant infrastructure could well have negative implications for innovation and competition.[62]

Hauser's speech obscures the fact that there is no self-evident basis on which to claim that unfettered competition is the only way to engender efficiency, and there is no value-free idea of what this efficiency would look like. In fact, during the Railway Mania, not all countries reacted in the same way.

> When a railway mania had suddenly appeared in Prussia in early 1844, the government reacted quickly by condemning speculation, banning the sale of options and settlement for differences (or futures), and refusing to sanction new lines. In France, military engineers decided on railway routes, before construction was put out to tender by private companies ... The Belgian state undertook responsibility for the construction and management of the nation's railway system.[63]

Swartz is surely onto something when she says that 'the blockchain is meaningful as an inventory of desire ... It is an engine of alterity: an opportunity to imagine a different world and imagine the mechanics of how that different world might be run'.[64] However, in shaping the interior design of money, we ought not to treat emotions, desires, and affects as alien forces, but instead as intersubjective and political energies. The decision as to where to direct these energies, then, should likewise be politicised.

Notes

1 Field notes, September 26, 2018.
2 Noam Yuran, *What Money Wants: An Economy of Desire* (Stanford, CA: Stanford University Press, 2014), 4.
3 *Ibid.*, 14.
4 I address the infrastructural aspect of money in Ludovico Rella, 'Steps Towards an Ecology of Money Infrastructures: Materiality and Cultures of Ripple', *Journal of Cultural Economy* 13, no. 2 (2020): 236–49, and Ludovico Rella, *Money's Infrastructures: Blockchain Technologies and the Ecologies of the Memory Bank*, PhD thesis (Durham: Durham

University, 2021), http://etheses.dur.ac.uk/13969/ (accessed September 2, 2022). The notion of a 'technological unconscious' is borrowed from Nigel Thrift, 'Remembering the Technological Unconscious by Foregrounding Knowledges of Position', *Environment and Planning D: Society and Space* 22, no. 1 (2004): 175–90. The quote regarding flows of desire is from Gilles Deleuze and Félix Guattari's *Anti-Oedipus: Capitalism and Schizophrenia*, trans. Robert Hurley, Mark Seem, and Helen Lane (Minneapolis: University of Minnesota Press, 1983), 104.

5 Earl Gammon and Ronen Palan, 'Libidinal International Political Economy', in *International Political Economy and Poststructural Politics*, ed. Marieke de Goede (New York: Palgrave Macmillan, 2006), 102.

6 Earl Gammon, 'Narcissism, rage, avocado toast', Chapter 1 in this volume.

7 Ludovico Rella, 'Blockchain', in *International Encyclopedia of Human Geography*, ed. Audrey Kobayashi, 2nd edn (Elsevier, 2020), 351–58.

8 Rebecca Campbell, 'The Ultimate Cryptocurrency Explainer: Bitcoin, Utility Tokens, and Stablecoins', The Next Web, February 13, 2019, https://thenextweb.com/hardfork/2019/02/13/bitcoin-stablecoins-utility-cryptocurrency/ (accessed September 2, 2022).

9 Andrew Hauser, 'A New RTGS Service for the United Kingdom: A Platform 9¾ for Sterling Payments?' Speech at SWIFT's SIBOS conference, Geneva, September 28, 2016.

10 Brian Larkin, 'The Politics and Poetics of Infrastructure', *Annual Review of Anthropology* 42, no. 1 (2013): 329.

11 Alexander Galloway, *Protocol: How Control Exists after Decentralization* (Cambridge, MA: The MIT Press, 2004); Lawrence Lessig, *Code 2.0 and Other Laws of Cyberspace*, 2nd edn (New York: Basic Books, 2006).

12 Wendy Hui Kyong Chun, 'On Sourcery, or Code as Fetish', *Configurations* 16, no. 3 (2008): 300, 310.

13 *Ibid.*, 309.

14 Quinn DuPont, *Cryptocurrencies and Blockchains* (Cambridge: Polity, 2019), 123.

15 Interview, May 29, 2019.

16 Sandy Hager, 'Capital as death denial', Chapter 2 in this volume.

17 Keller Easterling, *Extrastatecraft: The Power of Infrastructure Space* (New York: Verso, 2014), 71.

18 Earl Gammon, 'Narcissism, rage, avocado toast', Chapter 1 in this volume.

19 Quoted in Louise Amoore, *Cloud Ethics: Algorithms and the Attributes of Ourselves and Others* (Durham, NC: Duke University Press, 2020), 56.

20 Luciana Parisi and M. Beatrice Fazi, 'Do Algorithms Have Fun? On Completion, Indeterminacy and Autonomy in Computation', in *Fun and Software: Exploring Pleasure, Paradox, and Pain in Computing*, ed. Olga Goriunova (New York: Bloomsbury, 2014), 110.

21 *Ibid.*, 123, 111, emphasis in original.

22 Ollie Leech, 'What Are NFTs and How Do They Work? – CoinDesk', CoinDesk: Bitcoin, Ethereum, Crypto News and Price Data, January 2, 2021, www.coindesk.com/tech/2021/02/01/what-are-nfts-and-how-do-they-work/ (accessed September 2, 2022).

23 CryptoKitties, 'CryptoKitties: Collect and Breed Digital Cats!', www.cryptokitties.co (accessed September 2, 2022); see Rachel O'Dwyer, 'The Strange Case of Cryptkitties', May 2018, http://rachelodwyer.com/blog.html (accessed September 2, 2022).

24 Kitty Sales, 'Kitty Sales', https://kittysales.herokuapp.com/ (accessed September 2, 2022).

25 BBC News, 'CryptoKitties Cripple Ethereum Blockchain', December 5, 2017, www.bbc.com/news/technology-42237162 (accessed September 2, 2022).

26 Tristan Greene, 'CryptoKitties Sudden Lack of Popularity Is a Bad Omen for Blockchain Businesses', The Next Web, June 20, 2018, https://thenextweb.com/hardfork/2018/06/20/cryptokitties-sudden-lack-of-popularity-is-a-bad-omen-for-blockchain-businesses/ (accessed September 2, 2022).

27 DMarket, 'Buy CS:GO Skins & Items | CS:GO Marketplace | DMarket', https://dmarket.com/ingame-items/item-list/csgo-skins (accessed September 2, 2022); Decentraland, 'Decentraland Builder – World Creation Made Easy', https://decentraland.org (accessed September 2, 2022).

28 Rachel O'Dwyer, 'Outside of Borders', in *State Machines: Reflections and Actions at the Edge of Digital Citizenship, Finance, and Art*, ed. Yiannis Colakides, Marc Garrett, and Inte Gloerich (Amsterdam: Institute of Network Cultures, 2019), 83–93.

29 Brady Dale, 'Non-Believable Tokens: The 7 Strangest Crypto Collectibles Explained', CoinDesk, August 18, 2018, www.coindesk.com/markets/2018/08/18/non-believable-tokens-the-7-strangest-crypto-collectibles-explained/ (accessed September 2, 2022).

30 Justin Harper, 'Jack Dorsey's First Ever Tweet Sells for $2.9m', BBC News, March 23, 2021, www.bbc.com/news/business-56492358 (accessed September 2, 2022); Lanre Bakare, 'Collector Buys Fake

Banksy NFT for £244,000', *The Guardian*, September 1, 2021, www.theguardian.com/technology/2021/sep/01/collector-buys-fake-banksy-nft-for-244000 (accessed September 2, 2022).

31 Lucien Karpik, *Valuing the Unique: The Economics of Singularities* (Princeton, NJ: Princeton University Press, 2010); Sam Dallyn, 'Cryptocurrencies as Market Singularities: The Strange Case of Bitcoin', *Journal of Cultural Economy* 10, no. 5 (2017): 462–73.

32 Yuk Hui, *On the Existence of Digital Objects* (Minneapolis: University of Minnesota Press, 2016).

33 Walter Benjamin, *Illuminations*, ed. Hannah Arendt, trans. Harry Zorn (New York: Random House, 2011), 220.

34 *Ibid.*, 60.

35 Joyce Goggin, 'Affective Marketing and the Kuteness of Kiddles', in *The Aesthetics and Affects of Cuteness*, ed. Joshua Paul Dale, Joyce Goggin, Julia Leyda, Anthony McIntyre, and Diane Negra (London: Routledge, 2017), 223.

36 Hui, *On the Existence of Digital Objects*.

37 Laura Lotti, 'The Art of Tokenization: Blockchain Affordances and the Invention of Future Milieus', *Media Theory* 3, no. 1 (2019): 287–320.

38 Yuran, *What Money Wants*, 8, emphasis in original.

39 Filecoin, 'A Decentralized Storage Network for Humanity's Most Important Information', Filecoin, https://filecoin.io/ (accessed September 2, 2022).

40 Saman Adhami, Giancarlo Giudici, and Stefano Martinazzi, 'Why Do Businesses Go Crypto? An Empirical Analysis of Initial Coin Offerings', *Journal of Economics and Business* 100 (November 2018): 64–75.

41 Steem, 'Steem An Incentivized, Blockchain-Based, Public Content Platform', June 2018, https://steem.com/steem-whitepaper.pdf (accessed September 2, 2022).

42 See Kean Birch, 'What is the Asset Condition?' *European Journal of Sociology* 59, no. 3 (2018): 500–06.

43 Hengyi Feng, Julie Froud, Sukhdev Johal, Colin Haslam, and Karel Williams, 'A New Business Model? The Capital Market and the New Economy', *Economy and Society* 30, no. 4 (2001): 467–503.

44 SEC, 'SEC Charges Ripple and Two Executives with Conducting $1.3 Billion Unregistered Securities Offering', December 22, 2020, www.sec.gov/news/press-release/2020-338 (accessed September 2, 2022).

45 Interview, May 29, 2019.

46 Bruce Carruthers and Arthur Stinchcombe, 'The Social Structure of Liquidity: Flexibility, Markets, and States', *Theory and Society* 28, no. 3 (1999): 356.

47 Fabian Muniesa, Liliana Doganova, Horacio Ortiz, Álvaro Pina-Stranger, Florence Paterson, Alaric Bourgoin, Véra Ehrenstein, Pierre-André Juven, David Pontille, Basak Saraç-Lesavre, and Guillaume Yon, *Capitalization: A Cultural Guide* (Paris: Mines ParisTech, 2017), 129.

48 Robert S. Sutor, 'Software Standards, Openness, and Interoperability', in *Opening Standards the Global Politics of Interoperability*, ed. Laura DeNardis (Cambridge, MA: The MIT Press, 2011), 215.

49 Wolfgang Schivelbusch, *The Railway Journey: The Industrialization of Time and Space in the Nineteenth Century* (Berkeley: University of California Press, 2014); Peter Galison, *Einstein's Clocks and Poincaré's Maps: Empires of Time* (New York: W.W. Norton, 2003).

50 Georg Simmel, *The Philosophy of Money*, trans. David Frisby (Abingdon: Routledge, 2011), 212–13.

51 Yuran, *What Money Wants*, 2.

52 Stephen Lea and Paul Webley, 'Money as Tool, Money as Drug: The Biological Psychology of a Strong Incentive', *Behavioral and Brain Sciences* 29, no. 2 2006): 163.

53 Susan Leigh Star and Martha Lampland, 'Reckoning with Standards', in *Standards and Their Stories*, ed. Martha Lampland and Susan Leigh Star (New York: Cornell University Press, 2009), 11.

54 Interview, April 19, 2019.

55 Lightning Network, 'Lightning Network: Scalable, Instant Bitcoin/Blockchain Transactions', https://lightning.network (accessed September 2, 2022); Joseph Poon and Vitalik Buterin, 'Plasma: Scalable Autonomous Smart Contracts', August 11, 2017, https://plasma.io/plasma-deprecated.pdf (accessed September 2, 2022); Polkadot and Cosmos, 'Polkadot and Cosmos', https://wiki.polkadot.network (accessed September 2, 2022); Cosmos Network, 'Cosmos SDK Documentation | Cosmos SDK', https://docs.cosmos.network (accessed September 2, 2022); Blocknet, 'Blocknet', https://blocknet. co (accessed September 2, 2022); Stefan Thomas and Evan Schwartz, 'A Protocol for Interledger Payments', 2015, https://interledger.org/interledger.pdf (accessed September 2, 2022).

56 Interview, April 19, 2019.

57 Ian Jacobs, 'W3C Interview: Coil on Interledger Protocol and Web Monetization', W3C Blog, September 3, 2019, www.w3.org/blog/2019/09/w3c-interview-coil-on-interledger-protocol-and-web-monetization/ (accessed September 2, 2022).

58 Lana Swartz, 'What Was Bitcoin, What Will It Be? The Techno-Economic Imaginaries of a New Money Technology', *Cultural Studies* 32, no. 4 (2018): 640.

59 Udo Pesch and Georgy Ishmaev, 'Fictions and Frictions: Promises, Transaction Costs and the Innovation of Network Technologies', *Social Studies of Science* 49, no. 2 (2019): 264–77.
60 Walter Benjamin, *The Arcades Project*, ed. Rolf Tiedemann (Cambridge, MA: Belknap Press, 1999), 152.
61 Malcolm Campbell-Verduyn and Marcel Goguen, 'Blockchains, Trust and Action Nets: Extending the Pathologies of Financial Globalization', *Global Networks* 19, no. 3 (2018): 308–28.
62 Hauser, 'A New RTGS Service for the United Kingdom'.
63 Edward Chancellor, *Devil Take the Hindmost: A History of Financial Speculation* (New York: Macmillan, 2000), 148.
64 Lana Swartz, 'Blockchain Dreams: Imagining Techno-Economic Alternatives After Bitcoin', in *Another Economy Is Possible: Culture and Economy in a Time of Crisis*, ed. Manuel Castells (Cambridge: Polity, 2017), 83.

7

Normative unconscious processes and US racial capitalism

Lynne Layton

I grew up in the heyday of 1950s US conformity, consciously rather oblivious to class differences, heteronormativity, and systemic racism, but highly attuned to differences in what was possible for a girl versus a boy to do and to be. Unconsciously, of course, all of the above was doing its psychic work. I became a teenager in the socially turbulent 1960s and went to college from 1967 to 1971. My parents most definitely intended that I go to college, but while there I was supposed to become a teacher or nurse, and, more importantly, find a husband (preferably a doctor). But in college I encountered the beginnings of feminism, racial protest, anti-war protest, and Marxist class analysis. All of that changed my conscious sense of self and my conscious understanding of my relation to others, although, to be sure, the libidinal draw to these protest movements suggest that other unconscious processes were, from the beginning, germinating and resisting those that stemmed from mandates to conform. Unconsciously, however, those early libidinal attachments that encouraged conformity to dominant norms, built from both tabooed and sanctioned identifications and disidentifications, laid the groundwork for later psychic struggles; resistance to those norms laid the groundwork for later activist commitments.

I came to psychoanalysis from another discipline, comparative literature, which was attractive to me because of its resistance to disciplinarity. In graduate school in the 1970s, I was introduced to British cultural studies (under Stuart Hall), other neo-Marxisms that focused on how dominant ideologies are structured and are reproduced unconsciously,[1] and, always, feminism, which of course appealed to me because gender inequality was the most conscious location of my own familial and cultural narcissistic woundings or humiliations. In the 1980s, as a new faculty member in interdisciplinary departments, I engaged with Black and Brown feminisms and, later, gay, lesbian, and queer theory.[2] I began psychology training in 1983 and was immediately appalled by its conceptualisation of an individualistic and decontextualised subject whose ideal developmental trajectory was to overcome dependency by separating from an original embeddedness in relationality. I was drawn to the US relational psychoanalytic school that rose to prominence in the late 1980s because fundamental to this approach is the belief that subjectivity emerges from interactions within relational matrices from the beginnings of life and throughout the life span. Environmental forces are thus thought to be key shapers of psychic life. By the 1990s, I had found a community of relational feminist psychoanalysts who, like myself and all the academic feminists with whom I had been engaged, understood subjectivity as both shaped by and shaping of the social world. As well, this analytic movement valued interdependence, mutuality, and care, against individualistic notions of independence, self-assertion, and competition.

Of course, my feminist psychoanalytic community's focus was not only on conscious processes of shaping or being shaped, but on unconscious processes. My early contribution to this movement was to posit a model of identity formation that suggested that the socio-historically inflected relational experience within which we develop, in particular cultural hierarchies built on binary and differentially valued categories of race, class, gender, and sexuality, encourages us to split off those ways of being, feeling, and desiring that do not meet with social approval and that threaten our sense of being loved, of belonging, of experiencing ourselves as the right kind of human.[3] I only later discovered that Erich Fromm's concept of a 'social unconscious', that which a given socio-economic formation encourages its subjects to repress, had likewise rooted the motivation to conform in a fear of social isolation, ostracism, and non-belonging.[4] Fromm's 'social unconscious' emerges in concert with a social character dominant in a given socio-economic order. As my work had begun by looking at character formations brought into being by cultural taboos on what a girl versus a boy could do, I suggested that unconscious processes develop and manifest differently depending on what is idealised and what is denigrated in a given social location. Different social characters emerge, for example, from the particular ways of being, doing, loving possible for a White middle-class girl versus a White working-class girl – but the two are constituted in relation to each other as well as to other race, class, and gender identity positions. Thus, there are many social characters in a culture, and how they relate to one another is crucial to understanding how the socio-economic order functions.

Influenced by the work of Stuart Hall,[5] I posited what I called a negotiation model of identity development that could account not only for the narcissistic wounds brought about by demands to conform but also for resistance to those hegemonic ideological formations hailing the subject into conformity. I based the capacity to resist in relational and other kinds of experience than those that demand conformity, for example, in an embodied sense of what one feels and desires, even when acting on that experience is not deemed proper by the relational surround, and rooted also in the hope that we all have *some* relationships that offer love, approval, perhaps even excitement for our non-conforming self-expressions. Part of one's singularity, perhaps most of one's singularity, emerges from how one mediates among those relationships that demand conformity and those that do not, how one handles conflict. Yet another possible source of resistance lies in the intersectional nature of identities, that is, the unpredictable effects of one's positionalities within different power hierarchies. Finally, as another counter to psychoanalytic theories centred on the primacy of subjection in subject formation, I asserted that social movements like feminism and Black Power support and galvanise individuals' capacities and desires to resist hegemonic formations.

The work that I went on to do after this was predominantly influenced by the poststructuralist focus on how those hegemonic binary logics of heterosexist, capitalist, and racist systems split and differentially value human capacities and how, given existent power relations, such splits are lived in relation or relationally. My interest shifted from a focus on the capacity to resist subjection to an interest in how the very hierarchical binary splits that caused our psychic pain in the first place are unconsciously reproduced. A primary reason I was drawn to US relational psychoanalytic theory is its core assumption that, in treatment, there are two unconsciouses in the room. By the late 1990s and early 2000s, several of my colleagues in the relational psychoanalytic world (though never as many as I would have wished) had begun describing clinical cases in which racist or classist or sexist unconscious enactments created impasses in treatment (note that enactment is a clinical term and, in the sense in which I am using it, refers to relational scenarios in which we unconsciously repeat traumatic experience that has not been able to be worked through consciously). In some reported cases, a therapist seemed unconsciously to enact the kinds of gendered, raced, and classed splits fostered by dominant ideologies, for example, a male therapist, working with a female patient who had suffered from having been encouraged to split off assertive strivings, might unconsciously reproduce – through interpretations, seductiveness, and other means – dominant cultural gender ideologies that split and differentially value such human capacities as autonomy and connection. These enactments occurred in part because the significance of the social positionality of participants in therapy relationships was utterly disavowed in White and male-dominated clinical theory and practice. I suggested the term 'normative unconscious processes' to describe enactments marked by relational repetition compulsions that sustain dominant power relations.[6] This work then was rooted in understanding the familial and cultural narcissistic wounding that brought these lived split states into being, the tendency by those in power positions consciously and unconsciously to reproduce rather than resist such states, and, thus, on understanding the motivational pull towards the libidinal pleasures of conformity.

Psychoanalysis and the psychic life of neoliberalism

Perhaps the shift in my emphasis away from resistance and on to the reproduction of an unequal status quo had to do with what I next felt drawn to think and write about: neoliberal versions of subjectivity. In the introduction to the section on neoliberalism of my collected papers,[7] I describe the personal experiences I had in the 1980s and 1990s that, in retrospect, were clearly rooted in the kind of subject and relational configurations neoliberalism fostered, for instance, the academic institution where I worked in the 1980s was marked by an individualist ethic of every man for himself; it rewarded competition over cooperation (accomplished in part by creating supposedly merit-based hierarchies that pitted a special 1% against a disposable mass); and it increasingly instituted a surveillance and audit culture. But the desire to understand the psychic effects of neoliberalism also came from my clinical work, for example, experience with patients who railed against themselves for failures that clearly stemmed from changes in larger economic forces that favored deregulation, the privatisation of public goods, downsizing and outsourcing, the precipitous decline of unions and the manufacturing sector, tax cuts, and the decimation of the social safety net. In the White, middle-class and upper-middle-class patients I generally treated, I saw new articulations of gender, race, and class – and new ways of splitting and valuing human capacities – that were key to reproducing neoliberalism. For example, I recognised that in the professional and corporate worlds, the subject position once largely open only to White upper-class men, one that increasingly valued 24/7 work performance and devalued relationships, was now open to women as well. Although 1970s socialist variants of feminism had demanded changes in the workplace (as well as wages for housework), little change had actually occurred, so White middle-class women entering the workforce for the first time had psychically to accommodate to the 24/7 work demand. While some of the women I knew and saw in treatment were conflicted about the psychic costs demanded by the neoliberal workplace,[8] others, mostly those who were raised during the 1980s and 1990s, accommodated more easily, having known no alternative to neoliberal ways of being. An avid fan of popular culture, I noted how mass media, too, were hailing a neoliberal White female, middle-class subject.[9] Some popular television shows of the 1990s and early 2000s, for example, featured female protagonists who worked all the time and were either uninterested in or terrible at being in relationship; intimacy was often devalued altogether as 'weak'. An exception was close relationships with fathers who were often in the same profession. The 'relational' female idealised in postwar White middle-class culture was no longer an ideal.

From White middle- and upper-middle-class clinicians whose clients largely came from the same classes, I frequently heard cases like this one: a college student repeatedly performs brilliantly in one semester only to face suspension in the next semester for not completing her work. In one such case, the student had shown symptoms of a raging eating disorder and substance abuse in that disastrous second semester. Discussions of the case revolved around the therapist's temptation to help the patient complete the work. I argued that the patient's alternating behavior perhaps reflected a struggle between her libidinal attachment to the performance demands of a neoliberal economy, which she acted out in the first semester, and a refusal of those demands that she acted out in the next semester. Perhaps the refusal reflected a libidinal attachment to an alternative and as-yet-unformulated economy. In this case, helping the student complete her work while not interpreting the symptoms as resistance enacts a normative unconscious collusion that fortifies the libidinal attachment to neoliberalism.

Clinical experience also revealed that the development of White middle-class neoliberal subject positions often relies on contemptuously distinguishing and distancing oneself from other race and class positions. A vignette from the sketch comedy series *Portlandia* well illustrates this aspect of the psychic functioning of racial capitalism. In this vignette:

> a pre-school boy, Grover, sits at a kitchen counter as his parents try to engage him in understanding how important it is that he do well at his upcoming private pre-school interview. Holding up a chart that graphs the trajectory that will follow if he successfully gets into the Shining Star Pre-school – and noting that they have trademarked his name – the parents point to the first symbol that will mark his upward mobility: an ivy-league college. Then, asking him if he can spell Ferrari, they point to a picture of the car he will drive if he gets into the pre-school. As a cautionary tale, they then hold up a chart that graphs failure. If he does not get into the pre-school, they tell him, he will have to go to a public school, pictured on the graph as a prison. They spew denigrating comments about the lower-class children he will be subjected to in public school, the dumb and low-class kids he will encounter in community college, and the guns and drugs that will inevitably lead to jail or to a life of shooting birds and squirrels for dinner. The crowning touch of the satire is when the father, following one of his contemptuous comments about the lower classes, tells his child, 'Never judge'.
> Grover knows that he is supposed to like the first graph a lot better than the second one, and yet, with each new close-up of his face, we find him looking increasingly bewildered and depressed.

Still, when his parents ask him to say which graph he prefers, he readily endorses the success graph.[10]

From 2006 on, I became interested in what was going on consciously and unconsciously in large group formations; it was then that I began to recognise that individual and group psychic effects of neoliberalism had derived in part from the destruction of whatever limited form of a social safety net had existed in the US. The neoliberal partnership between government and corporate interests, in creating radical economic inequality, had left not only marginalised populations but most of the US population bereft of any containers of care. The abandonment by government and corporate forces was experienced, in different ways depending on class, as traumatic.[11] Against Thomas Frank's and others' thesis that the White working class were stupidly voting against their own interests, I argued that neither the Democratic nor the Republican Party was representing their economic interest; the neoliberal economic consensus left only cultural matters like abortion rights to be fought over.[12] Drawing on D. W. Winnicott's description of two of the psychic sequelae of unworked-through trauma, retaliation and withdrawal, I suggested that neoliberal policies had fostered two different large-group trauma reactions.[13] Egged on by right-wing media, segments of the White working class were retaliating against all of what, in their view, 'the Sixties' had wrought – feminism, civil rights, gay and lesbian equality, erosion of male authority. Meanwhile, borrowing UK sociologist John Rodger's description of 'amoral familism',[14] I argued that the White middle class' reaction to the wholesale abandonment of the population was to withdraw from public life, to retreat into a world in which the little time available for caring relationships was largely given to family and intimates. Neoliberal relationality was redefining 'empathy' as a state on offer only to those who share 'our' values, or to those sufferers experienced as so distant from us that we could easily disavow our complicity in their sorrows.[15] While I was clear about the racial resentment that was part of the White working-class retaliatory response – which became more virulent, permissible, public, and violent after Trump's election – what I missed was the different but also virulent form of raced violence enacted in the withdrawal of those White people whose portfolios were dramatically expanding – Grover's parents.

These kinds of response to the trauma of governmental aban-donment were versions of social narcissism, at the heart of which is a neoliberal 'group-enforced' denial of dependence, interdepend-ence, and vulnerability operating in both groups.[16] As Scanlon and Adlam describe, neoliberal institutions create vicious circles of sadomasochistic forms of relating.[17] Rizq's description of an institution-wide enactment in a mental health clinic in the UK is an excellent example of how neoliberal institutions hail workers into neoliberal subject positions and encourage neoliberal versions of sadomasochistic relational repetition compulsions.[18] Rizq found herself unconsciously participating in an enactment that began when a patient complained to the administration that she had felt treated as a number during an intake. This led the administration to double down on its already intensified surveillance and audit culture. At first, the clinicians reacted by talking about how their excessive workload made it difficult to provide care for all who needed it (the moment of protest), but, soon thereafter, they turned against the 'unreasonably' complaining patient. When Rizq began unravelling her own role in the enactment, she recognised that, in order to meet the heightened demands of the administration, the clinicians and their supervisors and their supervisors' supervisors had disavowed just how overburdened by excessive regulatory paperwork they already had been. They began, instead, to feel that doing their job well consisted less in offering care, less in doing the relational work for which they had trained, than in completing the paperwork in a timely fashion, submitting to the demands of the surveillance and audit culture.

Rizq's description well illustrates neoliberal instances of what Isabel Menzies and other Tavistock institutional researchers called social defense systems, that is, ways that institutions (in Menzies' study, the nursing profession in a UK hospital), attempting to manage the anxieties provoked by the work task (e.g., anxieties that arose from treating the ill and dying), in fact create oppressive systems that defend against those depressive anxieties.[19] For example, Menzies found that the relationship building aspect of nursing was consistently interrupted by the rote procedures demanded by the social defense system, and that such systems tend to drive away some of the most competent and caring practitioners. Researchers updating the social defences tradition to account better for the

changes wrought by neoliberalism have pointed out that the anxieties attendant to care work, such as depressive anxieties, are much
more manageable for workers than the persecutory sadomasochistic anxieties provoked by the relational abandonment inherent
to the surveillance systems of neoliberal institutions.[20] Again, the
need to belong and find social approval creates, in most cases, libidinal attachments to being deemed a good neoliberal subject. Yet, in
these same cases, refusals based in counter-hegemonic longings are
clearly also present. The weakest but most painful form of resistance appears when workers become symptomatic. In Menzies'
study, people resisted by quitting the institution. The strongest
forms of resistance involve finding ways to fight the system.

The current conjuncture and US racial capitalism

As I noted earlier, I have been influenced since the 1970s by the
work of Stuart Hall.[21] Along with his insistence, following Gramsci,
that counter-hegemonic forces always operate to resist hegemonic
forces, his reworking of Gramsci's concept of 'conjuncture' has
always felt to me to be key to understanding what is going on both
socially and psychically.[22] As recently underlined by Tony Jefferson,
Hall's understanding of 'conjuncture' (which, of course, always
kept a laser focus on racism) committed him to analysing a specific historical moment in all its complexity and including all its
stakeholders.

> Conjuncture refers to what is happening – politically, economically,
> ideologically, culturally – at any given historical moment ... all his-
> torical moments comprise an observable, empirical dimension, that
> which is taking place before our eyes (the conjunctural); and an invis-
> ible, structural dimension, that which is taking place 'behind our
> backs' (the organic). Making sense of the historical moment requires
> that both be given full attention.[23]

My original sources for understanding neoliberalism included
Michel Foucault, David Harvey, Richard Sennett, Wendy Brown,
and other theorists too numerous to mention.[24] Much of this work
focused either on a broad history of neoliberal attacks on state
power (Foucault's analysis of neoliberalism in the US begins with a

discussion of revolts against Roosevelt's New Deal programmes of the 1930s) or on the more recent history of Reagan and Thatcher's dismantling of welfare states in the US and the UK.[25] That work largely focuses on class and on increasing income and political inequality.

I would say, however, that what I had previously recognised as crucial to the neoliberal historical conjuncture and its psychic formations was limited by my class and race positionalities, especially my classed racial positioning as White upper-middle class. Jennifer Silva, Michelle Alexander, and many others gave me some insight into, for example, mass incarceration and the effects of deindustrialisation on the Black working class.[26] As it happens, the patient who told me that her parents had given her the message that she had two life choices – Yale or jail – spoke a powerful classed and raced truth about the contemporary conjuncture in the US. It was only during the Trump presidency, however, when I became involved in election work aimed at protecting what was left of already fragile democratic norms and, at the same time, in a Black-led national grassroots reparations movement, that I began to understand more deeply the connections between the *longue durée* of US racism and the more recent anti-state sentiment that culminated in a popular embrace of neoliberalism, the current form of racial capitalism.[27]

My elections work, the post-election Big Lie and January 6, 2021 insurrection, the increasing legitimacy given to right-wing White supremacists, and the ongoing takeover of the Republican Party by anti-democratic forces sent me to sources that delved into the historical origins of contemporary anti-democratic White supremacist movements. Indeed, it was when I read a statistic, after the 2020 election, that no Democratic presidential candidate had won a majority of the White vote since 1964 that I began to question the missing race and class element in my post-1970s historiography of US neoliberalism. I began to recognise how the originally White upper-class and elite anti-government neoliberal agenda had become articulated with anti-Black racism to culminate in the current conjuncture. As Nancy MacLean argues, neoliberal anti-regulation and anti-tax movements that began in the 1940s had little popular support until the mid-1960s; through most of the 1950s, Eisenhower's agenda, which remained faithful to New Deal principles, had White support.[28] Nonetheless, neo-liberal economists and politicians alike recognised early on that the road to undermining people's trust in government would likely lie in stoking racism. MacLean (and many others) suggests that the school integration agenda of the *Brown v. Board of Education* decision, and Eisenhower's decision to send troops to Arkansas to aid de-segregation efforts, began to galvanise neoliberal right-wing forces, which, in fact, had historically opposed public edu-cation. By invoking states' rights (a classic US way of disguising racist intent), they notched an early success in the late 1950s when one Virginia county in which neoliberal elites held power closed its public schools rather than integrate them. However, the attack on public education and anti-government sentiment only gained wide-spread support after the passage of the 1965 Voting Rights Act. As President Johnson predicted, passage of that Act led the South to 'secede' from the Democratic Party. The successful articulation of racism and anti-government sentiment thus began in the 1970s with Nixon's strategy to turn the South Republican, accelerated with Reagan's dog-whistling racism of the 1980s,[29] and has cres-cendoed in current Republican politics that seem hell-bent on dis-mantling democratic government altogether.

The reparations work I have been doing grounds itself in what many have called 'the afterlives of slavery',[30] that is, the unceasing repetitions in US history, always in new forms, of anti-Black pol-icies and practices: Black codes, convict leasing, Jim Crow, red-lining, police violence, the Southern Strategy, the War on Drugs, and mass incarceration. Carol Anderson chronicles the long his-tory of violent White backlash that follows even the smallest signs of Black strivings towards freedom and repair.[31] Frank Wilderson compellingly argues that no comparison can be made between anti-Black racism and other forms of US racism.[32]

Racial capitalism and institutional enactments of normative unconscious processes

It was while doing the reparations work, reading the above texts, and working together with a multiracial group of psycho-dynamic therapists committed to racial justice that I first became aware (!) that most of the institutions in which I worked and played were almost all White and middle to upper-middle class. I began then to notice how systemic racism operates in most White people unconsciously to reproduce White-centred institutions, how normative unconscious processes operate within institutions. For years I had railed against the dissociation of the psychic from the social in clinical theory and practice, attributing it to the ideological effects of heteropatriarchal capitalism. I now realise that my obliviousness to the role racism plays in that dissociation was my way of contributing unconsciously to the reproduction of my White-centred institutions. Indeed, I imagine that while my place outside psychoanalytic circles had to do with my attempts to bring in the social, my place *inside* had to do with being White.

A key reason why White-centred institutions, including liberal ones, are resistant to change is the persistent disavowal in the US of its racist history, institutionalised, for example, in a whitewashed educational system. When that history is openly discussed within White liberal circles, one quickly witnesses a multitude of collective and unconscious psychological operations go into effect to sustain the disavowal. Bryan Nichols and Medria Connolly describe a doubling down on disavowal when White people seem unable to bear the unconscious guilt they carry for the crime of slavery; Carter J. Carter describes White 'shame management systems' that go immediately into effect when White racist shame is evoked; and my Black colleague Dr Natasha Holmes, in personal communication, refers to these maneuvers collectively as 'White shenanigans'.[33] White unconscious processes that reproduce a racial capitalist order operate individually and collectively, in interpersonal enactments and in policies. For example, returning to *Brown v. Board of Education*, the Supreme Court case of 1954 that made 'separate but equal' schooling illegal, Ann Pellegrini has noted that while at least part of that decision rested on work documenting Black children's internalisation of inferiority (e.g., choosing the White doll as the good doll), the decision to integrate schools never questioned what we might think of as the libidinal attachment to White superiority (and of course left neighborhood segregation intact).[34] In other words, as in many of the currently ubiquitous diversity initiatives, the hidden agenda is the demand to assimilate to White norms.

White people in all class fractions find it difficult to think about racism as systemic, as current backlash movements strongly attest.

In sum, the current conjuncture requires a reckoning with a decades-long anti-democratic movement to tear down government, spearheaded originally by elites radically opposed to any redistribution of wealth and whose vision of what government should do includes only protection of private property through policing and the court system. The movement began winning popular support when it was able to articulate the neoliberal decimation of working-class jobs and union busting with racism. Arlie Hochschild's (2016) Tea Party interviewees (a party formed in backlash to the election of Obama), for example, explained their anti-government views and dislike of liberals by insisting that Black and Brown people were unfairly benefitting from government policies while their pain was ignored.[35]

Mainstream media favours framing the current conjuncture as the result of Trump's cult of personality and/or of disinformation. I see it differently. Trump, who shares the racist anti-government vision, is a more or less useful idiot behind whom lies a vast network of think tanks that have been working for decades to, for example, write model legislation for Republican-dominated state legislatures that share the vision that the (male) White upper-class 'makers' can only maintain their dominance if the 'takers', those populations most in need of federal protection, are disempowered.

One of the deepest threats to this iteration of racial capitalism's success is the popular vote, which Republican legislatures are now actively suppressing while also changing electoral processes to favor Republicans. The Big Lie of a stolen election is just the latest in a series of anti-democratic government racist dog whistles; behind the Big Lie is the even bigger lie that the election was stolen by Black and Brown people. At the same time, however (and certainly related to public displays of racism in all classes), increasing numbers of Black and Brown activists', academics', and journalists' voices are being heard in the public sphere, and they are demanding institutional changes in policing, prison abolition, and in professional, White-dominated organisations. It is that demand, perhaps, that has most clearly unmasked the White liberal middle class' libidinal ties to racial capitalism, a crucial component of the current conjuncture.

I believe that it will be difficult to find a way forward if anti-neoliberal voices are unable to make conscious the way race and class are differently articulated in different White class fractions. While conservative White groups in all classes are defining their 'freedom' as the right, for example, not to have critical race theory – or, for that matter, anything about the history of racism in the US – taught in their children's schools,[36] liberal middle- and upper-class White groups engaged, for example, in diversity initiatives rarely question the superiority of what their organisations offer. Thus, assimilation into White ways of doing things is the price charged for admission. I would argue that liberal institutions cannot change without engaging in the kind of psychological reorientation called for by George Yancy: the cultivation of White 'double consciousness'.[37] In Yancy's view, White people need to develop, first, an awareness that what we say, do, feel, and desire is shaped by a particular racial class order, and, second, an awareness of how what we say, do, feel, and desire is experienced by Black, indigenous, and other people of color (BIPoC). In addition, White people and institutions need to become fully accountable for what Michael Rothberg has described as White subjects' conscious and unconscious implication in sustaining the structures that continuously reproduce a White, heteropatriarchal, neoliberal capitalist order.[38]

After the 2020 election and the multiracial Black Lives Matter protests that followed the murder of George Floyd, I had the fantasy that if Biden's anti-neoliberal agenda would begin to make the everyday lives of the White poor, working, and middle class better, anti-government resistance – and, perhaps, some of the more overt forms of racism that flourished under Trump – would recede. Although, as of 2023, Biden's agenda has been partially implemented (minus the 'care' part of that agenda), I severely underestimated the emotional power of anti-government sentiment in the US. As there were many 'infrastructure weeks' during the Trump presidency but no infrastructure policy, and no return of manufacturing jobs – indeed, no policy besides tax breaks for the wealthy and the installation of a large number of conservative judges – it seems clearer and clearer that racism is a driving force behind the popularity of Republican lies about the legitimacy of the election, the rage about government overreach in calling for lockdowns and mask or vaccine mandates, and the fear that could be stoked, even in BIPoC populations, about Democrats' policies being a socialist attempt to destroy the US. While confronting the pandemic proved to some of us that neoliberal policies dangerously put the population at risk and that big government responses were necessary, to others it proved the very opposite: that big government mandates infringed on their freedom (it is worth noting that protests against state government lockdowns began just as news broke that BIPoC communities were disproportionately victims of the pandemic). At this juncture, it seems clear to me that whatever democracy still exists in the US is at great risk of disappearing.

Notes towards a counter-hegemonic libidinal economy

When I was teaching a class last year on the psychic effects of neoliberalism to a group of psychoanalytic candidates, a woman born in the 1980s asked me if things were ever different. For her, neoliberalism was 'normal', 'common sense'. To return to a Gramscian model always mindful of the existence and potential power of counter-hegemonic forces, I would say that what the hegemonic cultural forces of the current conjuncture suppress are the many currently circulating counter-hegemonic movements that are actively challenging the racial capitalist status quo. I want to conclude, then, with a brief discussion of anti-neoliberal solidarity economy movements and the psychic structures these promote.

The principles that underlie solidarity economy movements centre on a political ontology of radical relationality and radical interdependence, according to which nothing in existence pre-exists the relations that constitute it, that is, solidarity economies promote being in 'right' relationship with self, others, and the planet. These are cooperative multiracial movements based in anti-capitalist, feminist, indigenous, and anti-racist solidarity practices. Solidarity economy movements assert that transformation has to occur at psychological, political, and economic levels – building political power, creating alternatives, and changing consciousness.[39]

Examples of solidarity economies include community land trusts that foster a non-extractive relationship to land, for example, promoting community farming and eliminating toxic waste sites predominantly located in marginalised communities; worker-controlled community-serving businesses; participatory budgets (where budgets are seen as social justice documents); restorative justice practices; barter; democratically run funds that support democratically selected solidarity economy businesses in historically under-resourced areas. These movements challenge neoliberal ideologies of 'no alternative' to capitalism by their very existence; maps showing their locations allow others to connect and engage in new and existing projects. Politically, they model a different way of organising against capitalism from the usual modes figured in labour struggles aiming to secure better conditions of existence within capitalist enterprises (struggles that, notably, are having a resurgence in the US as some power has shifted during the pandemic from owners to workers).

At the end of a 2020 webinar held early in the pandemic and hosted by the Center for Economic Democracy, a Boston organisation promoting anti-capitalist solidarity economy initiatives, young activists spoke about the possibilities for anti-neoliberal transformational change in the wake of the horrors unleashed by Trump's handling of the pandemic, the climate crisis, and the other disasters racial capitalism has wrought. One segment of the webinar was devoted to thinking about how we are all psychically caught up in neoliberalism and how, even in the isolated pandemic worlds in which we were then living, our lives still seemed to be speeding up (e.g., 24/7 zooming). I end on the daunting challenge the webinar posed: what will it take to recognise the many ways in which the current conjuncture of racial capitalism is making all of us sick – and that there *are* existing alternatives?

Notes

1 For example, Louis Althusser, 'Ideology and Ideological State Apparatuses (Notes Towards an Investigation)', in *Lenin and Philosophy and Other Essays*, trans. Ben Brewster (New York: Monthly Review Press, 1971), 127–86.
2 For example, see Combahee River Collective, 'The Combahee River Collective Statement', 1977, http://circuitous.org/scraps/combahee.html (accessed September 8, 2022); Gloria Anzaldúa, *Borderlands/*

La Frontera: The New Mestiza (San Francisco, CA: Spinsters/Aunt Lute, 1987); Judith Butler, *Gender Trouble* (New York: Routledge, 1990); bell hooks, *Black Looks: Race and Representation* (Boston, MA: South End Press, 1992).

3 Lynne Layton, *Who's That Girl? Who's That Boy? Clinical Practice Meets Postmodern Gender Theory* (New York: Routledge, 1998).

4 Erich Fromm, *Escape from Freedom* (New York: Holt, Rinehart and Winston, 1941).

5 Stuart Hall, 'Encoding/Decoding', in *Culture, Media, Language: Working Papers in Cultural Studies, 1972–79*, ed. Stuart Hall, Dorothy Hobson, Andrew Lowe, and Paul Willis (London: Hutchinson, 1980), 128–38.

6 Lynne Layton, 'Cultural Hierarchies, Splitting, and the Heterosexist Unconscious', in *Bringing the Plague: Toward a Postmodern Psychoanalysis*, ed. Susan Fairfield, Lynne Layton, and Carolyn Stack (New York: Other Press, 2002), 195–223.

7 Lynne Layton, *Toward a Social Psychoanalysis: Culture, Character, and Normative Unconscious Processes* ed. Marianna Leavy-Sperounis (London: Routledge, 2020).

8 Lynne Layton, 'Relational No More: Defensive Autonomy in Middle-Class Women', in *The Annual of Psychoanalysis 32: Psychoanalysis and Women*, ed. Jerome Winer, James Anderson, and Christine Kieffer (Hillsdale, NJ: Analytic Press, 2004), 29–42.

9 Lynne Layton, 'Working Nine to Nine: The New Women of Prime Time', *Studies in Gender and Sexuality* 5, no. 3 (2004): 351–69.

10 Reported in Layton, *Toward a Social Psychoanalysis*, 220–21. See Jonathan Krisel, 'Grover', *Portlandia*, Season 2, Episode 4. Aired January 27, 2012.

11 Layton, *Toward a Social Psychoanalysis*, 177–233.

12 Thomas Frank, *What's the Matter with Kansas? How Conservatives Won the Heart of America* (New York: Metropolitan Books, 2004); Lynne Layton, 'Retaliatory Discourse: The Politics of Attack and Withdrawal', *International Journal of Applied Psychoanalytic Studies* 3, no. 2 (2006): 143–55.

13 D. W. Winnicott, *Playing and Reality* (London: Tavistock, 1974).

14 John J. Rodger, 'Social Solidarity, Welfare and Post-Emotionalism', *Journal of Social Policy* 32, no. 3 (2003): 403–21.

15 Lynne Layton, 'Who's Responsible? Our Mutual Implication in Each Other's Suffering', *Psychoanalytic Dialogues* 19, no. 2 (2009): 105–20.

16 C. Fred Alford, 'Winnicott and Trauma', *Psychoanalysis, Culture and Society* 18, no. 3 (2013): 259–76.

17 Christopher Scanlon and John Adlam, 'Reflexive Violence', *Psychoanalysis, Culture & Society* 18, no. 3 (2013): 223–41.
18 Rosemary Rizq, 'Perversion, Neoliberalism and Therapy: The Audit Culture in Mental Health Services', *Psychoanalysis, Culture & Society* 19, no. 2 (2014): 209–18.
19 Isabel Menzies, 'A Case-Study in the Functioning of Social Systems as a Defense Against Anxiety: A Report on a Study of the Nursing Service in a General Hospital', *Human Relations* 13, no. 2 (1960): 95–121.
20 For example, Andrew Cooper and Amanda Lees, 'Spotlit: Defences against Anxiety in Contemporary Human Services Organizations', in *Social Defenses Against Anxiety*, ed. David Armstrong and Michael Rustin (London: Karnac, 2015), 239–55.
21 Stuart Hall and Tony Jefferson, eds, *Resistance Through Rituals: Youth Subcultures in Post-War Britain* (London: Hutchinson, 1978); Stuart Hall, *Policing the Crisis: Mugging, the State and Law and Order* (Basingstoke: Macmillan, 1978).
22 Antonio Gramsci, *Selections from the Prison Notebooks*, ed. Quintin Hoare and Geoffrey Nowell Smith (New York: International Publishers, 1971).
23 Tony Jefferson, *Stuart Hall, Conjunctural Analysis and Cultural Criminology* (Cham: Palgrave Macmillan, 2021), 26–27.
24 Michel Foucault, *The Birth of Biopolitics: Lectures at the Collège de France, 1978–1979*, trans. Graham Burchell (New York: Palgrave Macmillan, 2008); David Harvey, *A Brief History of Neoliberalism* (Oxford: Oxford University Press, 2005); Richard Sennett, *The Culture of the New Capitalism* (New Haven, CT: Yale University Press, 2006); Wendy Brown, *Undoing the Demos: Neoliberalism's Stealth Revolution* (New York: Zone Books, 2015).
25 Harvey, *A Brief History of Neoliberalism*.
26 Jennifer M. Silva, *Coming Up Short: Working-Class Adulthood in an Age of Uncertainty* (Oxford: Oxford University Press, 2013); Michelle Alexander, *The New Jim Crow: Mass Incarceration in the Age of Colorblindness* (New York: The New Press, 2010); Ta-Nehisi Coates, *Between the World and Me* (New York: Spiegel and Grau, 2015); Loïc Wacquant, 'The Penalization of Poverty and the Rise of Neo-Liberalism', *European Journal on Criminal Policy and Research* 9 (2001): 401–12. See also Layton, *Toward a Social Psychoanalysis*, 213–33.
27 See, for example, Robin D. G. Kelley, 'What Did Cedric Robinson Mean by Racial Capitalism?', *Boston Review*, January 12, 2017,

https://bostonreview.net/articles/robin-d-g-kelley-introduction-race-capitalism-justice/ (accessed September 8, 2022).

28 Nancy MacLean, *Democracy in Chains: The Deep History of the Radical Right's Stealth Plan for America* (New York: Penguin, 2017).

29 Ian Haney López, *Dog Whistle Politics: How Coded Racial Appeals Have Reinvented Racism and Wrecked the Middle Class* (Oxford: Oxford University Press, 2015).

30 Christina Sharpe, *In the Wake: On Blackness and Being* (Durham, NC: Duke University Press, 2016).

31 Carol Anderson, *White Rage: The Unspoken Truth of our Racial Divide* (New York: Bloomsbury, 2016).

32 Frank B. Wilderson, *Afropessimism* (New York: W.W. Norton, 2020).

33 Bryan Nichols and Medria Connolly, 'Transforming Ghosts into Ancestors: Un-Silencing the Psychological Case for Reparations to Descendants of American Slavery', Other/Wise, May 14, 2020, https://ifpe.wordpress.com/2020/05/14/transforming-ghosts-into-ancestors-un-silencing-the-psychological-case-for-reparations-to-descendants-of-american-slavery/ (accessed September 8, 2022); Carter J. Carter, *Whiteness and the Columbine High School Attack: A Psychoanalytic Case Portrait* (Doctoral Dissertation: Smith College School for Social Work, 2021).

34 Ann Pellegrini, 'Beyond Woke: Why the Focus on Unconscious Bias Will Not Address Systemic Racism', Online presentation for New Orleans-Birmingham Psychoanalytic Center, USA, April 24, 2021.

35 Arlie Hochschild, *Strangers in Their Own Land: Anger and Mourning on the American Right* (New York: The New Press, 2016).

36 It would be hard to overemphasise the number of knock-down drag-out fights going on currently in the USA over the issue of race and racism in public schools. Diversity initiatives are being eliminated, school board committees are replacing pro-diversity candidates with anti-diversity candidates (initiatives sometimes funded grandly by right-wing forces), and conservative forces in schools and media are apoplectic that the history of US racism and whatever their fantasy is of critical race theory is being taught. For one example, see Lisa Lerer, 'The Issue Riling Up Virginia Voters: What's Taught in the Schools', *The New York Times*, October 13, 2021, A1, A16.

37 George Yancy, *Look, A White! Philosophical Essays on Whiteness* (Philadelphia, PA: Temple University Press, 2012).

38 Michael Rothberg, *The Implicated Subject: Beyond Victims and Perpetrators* (Stanford, CA: Stanford University Press, 2019).

39 See, for example, J. K. Gibson-Graham, *A Postcapitalist Politics* (Minneapolis: University of Minnesota Press, 2006); Ethan Miller, 'Solidarity Economy: Key Concepts and Issues', in *Solidarity Economy I: Building Alternatives for People and Planet: Papers and Reports from Center for Popular Economics*, ed. Emily Kawano, Thomas Neal Masterson, and Jonathan Teller-Elsberg (Amherst, MA: Center for Popular Economics, 2010), 25–41; and Arturo Escobar, *Pluriversal Politics*, trans. David Frye (Durham, NC: Duke University Press, 2020).

8

Enjoying inequality

Japhy Wilson

The signifier ... evacuates enjoyment from the body, but this
evacuation is never fully accomplished; scattered around the desert of
the symbolic Other, there are always some leftovers, oases of enjoyment, so-called 'erogenous zones', fragments still penetrated with
enjoyment – and it is precisely these remnants to which Freudian
drive is tied: it circulates, it pulses around them.[1]

Table for Two International is a social enterprise with a simple
idea for doing business while making the world a better place; for
every meal bought at its participating restaurants, one school meal
is provided to a poor child in sub-Saharan Africa. Toilet Twinning
is a charity with a similar premise, which offers participants the
opportunity to 'twin' their toilet with a latrine in a poor region
of south-east Asia or sub-Saharan Africa. Sir Richard's Condoms
is a condom company that likewise donates one condom to a
'developing' country for each condom purchased. This chapter
explores these three cases of compassionate consumerism and asks
what they can tell us about the ideological content of this everyday
practice, in which the consumer participates in 'development'
through the purchase of a specific product. The three examples
are structurally identical; in each case, there is a one-for-one relation between the product consumed and the product donated. This
representation of equality between the Western consumer and the
non-Western recipient can be accused of legitimating or obscuring
the profound global inequalities that underpin it, and the literature
on ethical consumption tends to critique it in these terms, accusing
it of a disingenuous morality that 'celebrates a culture of global capitalism while sympathising with its victims',[2] and that constitutes a

'therapeutic discourse of the West, a feel-good factor hiding us from how our privilege is produced'.[3]

This chapter argues that this critique does not go far enough. Compassionate consumerism does not merely conceal relations of global inequality beneath a veneer of ethical concern or justify them on the basis of the charitable giving of the privileged. Instead, it invites 'us' (the affluent populations of Western consumer societies) to *enjoy* the relations of inequality that it simultaneously stages and disavows. This argument is developed through an engagement with Slavoj Žižek's critique of ideology, which draws on the work of the psychoanalyst Jacques Lacan. At its deepest level, Žižek argues, ideology functions not as an illusory appearance concealing an external reality, but as a web of social fantasies that structures 'reality' itself in relation to *jouissance*.[4]

Jouissance is commonly translated as 'enjoyment'. But it is a much more complex and ambiguous phenomenon than the 'simple pleasures' denoted by our everyday usage of that term. Lacan's understanding of *jouissance* builds on Sigmund Freud's theory of psychosexual development, which describes how the libido comes to be focused in specific erogenous zones during early childhood. In the *oral* phase, it is focused on the mouth in relation to the mother's breast. In the *anal* phase it is attached to the pleasure derived from the retention and expulsion of faeces. And in the *phallic* phase it is shifted to the genitals.[5] Lacan develops Freud's approach through an emphasis on the symbolic and imaginary structuration of enjoyment. For Lacan, the libido is associated with the traumatic Real of *jouissance*. The child is born into a world unstructured by language and replete with the unmediated *jouissance* of the bodily drives. Through its entry into the symbolic order of language, the child abandons its direct relation to *jouissance*, escaping its overwhelming intensity, but also losing access to its enjoyment. Yet *jouissance* continues to impinge upon the symbolic universe of the subject, with an alien material persistence that is both disturbing and compelling.[6] It is only by appealing to specific fantasies, operating in the Imaginary register, that the subject is able to pacify the traumatic dimension of *jouissance*, and to experience it as enjoyment. In Žižek's words, 'fantasy animates and structures enjoyment, while simultaneously serving as a protective shield against its excess'.[7] This understanding of fantasy differs from the common-sense usage of the term in two important respects. First, fantasies are not dream-like illusions through which we escape from an external reality; they are central to our organisation of the Imaginary and Symbolic coordinates of socially constituted 'reality' through which we keep the Real at bay.[8] Second, fantasies are not merely private affairs; they circulate in our intersubjective systems of language and culture.[9]

This social dimension of fantasy is central to its ideological operation. According to Žižek, all social orders are underpinned by the mobilisation and regulation of *jouissance* through the production and circulation of specific social fantasies. However, whereas other societies have attempted to restrict enjoyment through scarcity and moral sanction, Western consumer capitalism entails 'a passage from a *society of prohibition* to a *society of commanded enjoyment*'.[10] Compassionate consumerism is an integral element of this social order in its current configuration, and its critique must therefore inquire into the ways in which it organises the consumer's relationship to *jouissance*. This dimension is missing from the critical literature on compassionate consumerism, which challenges it on the basis of its obfuscation of the politics of global inequality beneath an appearance of ethical concern. This critique is accurate up to a point. But as Žižek explains, 'The relationship between fantasy and the horror of the Real it conceals is much more ambiguous than it may seem: fantasy conceals the horror, yet at the same time it [invites us to enjoy] what it purports to conceal, its "repressed" point of reference.'[11] In what follows, I argue that compassionate consumerism invites us to participate in a disavowed enjoyment of its own 'repressed point of reference', which is global inequality itself.

The chapter is organised around Freud's three infantile stages of psychosexual development, which I relate to the three cases of compassionate consumerism introduced above. The first section addresses Table for Two International as the oral stage. The second explores Toilet Twinning as the anal stage. And the third examines Sir Richard's Condoms as the phallic stage. In each case, I show how the enjoyment of the libidinal drive is procured through the *staging* of a specific fantasy, and how this enjoyment is central to the ideological function and appeal of the product. Each of these fantasies is framed in ethical terms, as an act of generosity for someone less fortunate, in which both consumer and beneficiary receive an equivalent good. But this ethical dimension is underwritten by an invitation to enjoy the inequality that is simultaneously staged and disavowed. This invitation is of course never made explicit – such fantasies are only operational to the extent that they remain unconscious.[12] Yet it can be read between the lines of each of these campaigns. I conclude with some general notes on the libidinal economy of compassionate consumerism.[13]

The oral stage: Table for Two International

Table for Two International is a social enterprise that aims to address the problems of obesity in the 'developed' world and malnutrition in the 'developing' world by tackling both simultaneously. It serves low-calorie meals in its participating restaurants and sends the calories it has 'saved' to countries in south-east Asia or sub-Saharan Africa in the form of a cash donation, which is used to provide free school meals for impoverished children. At the level of immediate appearances, Table for Two thus represents itself in terms of equality. In the words of one of its executives, 'By participating in the initiative, individuals can help themselves avoid obesity while also helping a child suffering from hunger. You make others healthy by becoming healthy yourself. It's a win-win situation.'[14] The concept is of a 'Customer' and a 'Recipient' sharing their meal at the same table, as expressed in the company slogan: 'At Table for Two, you never dine alone'.[15]

Yet closer attention to its promotional literature reveals a consistent focus on the difference between the two meals in terms of quality and price. The Customer is repeatedly told that while their meal costs US$6.25, only US$0.25 of this price will be spent on the meal of the Recipient. This difference is graphically represented in various images in the promotional literature, in which two cartoon figures face each other across the table. In these images, the Customer's meal is consistently much larger than that of the Recipient. Attention is also placed on the difference between the content of the two meals. Prospective customers are presented with mouth-watering images of the healthy and delicious menu options to be enjoyed in participating restaurants on 'this side of the table', including 'braised chicken couscous' and 'tofu salad with plum sauce'. Meanwhile, images of 'the other side of the table' depict huge cauldrons being stirred over open fires, and long queues of poor Black children clutching their plastic bowls in eager expectation of their humble meal.[16] In contrast to the exciting menu options on our side of the table, we are told that in Uganda, 'the food being served is called *"posho"*, made by boiling maize (or corn) flour in water. It is most commonly cooked to a dough-like consistency and eaten with vegetables. Here, it is served as porridge.'[17]

Table for Two thus presents its Customers with an ethical discourse of equality and generosity, while simultaneously inviting them to enjoy the inequality between their meal and that of the Recipients. Crucially, *it is precisely this staging of inequality that makes the Customer's meal enjoyable.* Our common-sense understanding of enjoyment would suggest that Table for Two operates by offering us the natural pleasure of a good meal along with the opportunity to help someone in need. But there is nothing inherently enjoyable about the act of eating – of shoving objects into our mouths and grinding them into a congealed mass before forcing them down our throats. According to Lacanian theory, it is only by framing the oral drive with a specific fantasy that even our 'favourite food' can be enjoyed.

> Fantasy mediates between the formal symbolic structure and the positivity of the objects we encounter in reality – that is to say, it provides a 'schema' according to which certain positive objects in reality can function as objects of desire ... To put it in somewhat simplified terms: fantasy does not mean that when I desire a strawberry cake and cannot get it in reality, I fantasise about eating it; the problem is, rather: *how do I know that I desire a strawberry cake in the first place?* This is what fantasy tells me.[18]

In the case of Table for Two, the fantasy that tells the Customer that he desires his tofu salad with plum sauce is the imagined inequality between this meal and the boiled maize porridge that will be served to the Recipient. Table for Two encourages its participating restaurants to include 'signage' on their walls and tables, in which this inequality is staged in a variety of ways. Its website provides print-offs and instructions for a variety of 'table tents', which are to be placed on the tables at which people eat their meals. One of these tents stages the gap between the two meals in direct visual terms. On one side of the tent, a healthy White woman smiles radiantly into the camera, while tucking into an exotic gourmet salad. On the other, a ragged brown child crams beans into his mouth with his bare hands.[19] Another table tent presents a graphic representation of the Table for Two concept.[20] The slogan at the top of the tent is a statement of equality and global harmony: 'Order for One. Feed Two. And Help the World Eat Better'. But the imagery below it comprises a complex representation of the inequality between the two meals. The Customer is invited to 'Eat a healthy TFT meal to help yourself and another *less fortunate*' (emphasis added). The people on each side of the table are represented in simple 'stick-figure' form. The Customer sits upright before a large plate of food, gazing across the table at the Recipient, whose head is bowed submissively above a plate containing a much smaller portion. A pie-chart beneath the table graphically represents the Recipient's miniscule twenty-five-cent slice of the 'pie', in contrast to the massive six-dollar chunk that the Customer will consume. And while the Recipient '*receives* a healthy school lunch', the Customer '*enjoys* a healthy meal' (emphasis added). Enjoyment is therefore located entirely on the side of the Customer, and from the perspective of Lacanian theory, it is only through this staging of a surplus enjoyment at the expense of the 'less fortunate' Recipient that he is able to really enjoy his meal.

The anal stage: Toilet Twinning

Toilet Twinning is a UK-based charity that offers people in Europe and North America the opportunity to 'twin' their toilet with a latrine in south-east Asia or sub-Saharan Africa. A donation of £60 to the charity purchases a latrine in one of several countries in these regions for a family that did not have one previously. In return, the donor receives a certificate, featuring a photograph of the latrine in question, and the name and GPS coordinates of its location. By providing latrines to people who lack them, Toilet Twinning aims to reduce diseases related to hygiene and sanitation, leading to increased productivity and school attendance, and thus 'helping to flush away poverty'.[21]

The explicit discourse of Toilet Twinning is one of equality – of the one-for-one relationship between 'our' toilet and theirs. But as in the case of Table for Two, this discourse is underwritten by an implicit staging of the difference between them. This is evident in a poster advertising the charity. The poster features a collage of photographs of poor African families stood in front of inauspicious-looking latrines, accompanied by the phrase 'Take Your Pick'.[22] The phrase is obviously designed to be read in two ways: 'Which family would you like to help?' but also 'Which toilet would you like to use?' The implication would seem to be that you would not like to use any of them, and that something must therefore be done to help the families who are forced to do so. But the images are not of the toilets that the families are to be 'saved' from. Instead, they depict the toilets that these families have been given by Toilet Twinning, as an indication of the kind of latrine that the prospective donor can choose to give to others. In other words, the toilet that 'we' are giving 'them' is framed not only as a toilet that will improve their condition, but also as a toilet that we would not want to use ourselves. In the bottom corner of the poster is the Toilet Twinning logo: a White stick-figure representation of a male reading a newspaper on a Western toilet – the instantly recognisable image of a White Western gentleman at stool. Beneath an explicit message of salvation and equality, the poster therefore stages the inequality between 'our' toilet and the one that 'they' will receive.

Toilet Twinning thus functions ideologically by framing the anal drive with a disavowed fantasy of inequality, which promises to make the donor's bowel movement enjoyable. This is evident in the various products associated with the charity. As already mentioned, every person who twins their toilet receives a certificate with a picture of their twinned latrine. Crucially, this certificate comes with the explicit instruction to display it in the donor's bathroom. The donor's use of their toilet is thus framed by a visual representation of the difference in quality and sophistication between it and the latrine of their imagined Third World counterpart. Donors can also purchase branded toilet paper, with photographs of a selection of twinned latrines printed on each individual sheet, allowing them to extend their enjoyment of inequality to one of the most intimate rituals of personal hygiene. A set of stickers is also offered, which are designed to be placed on various objects in the donor's bathroom. Again, these stickers unambiguously stage the difference between the donor's toilet and the twinned latrine. Each sticker includes the phrase 'Welcome to the Toilet Deluxe', and is designed to be applied to a feature of the Western toilet that is missing from (the Western imaginary of) a Third World latrine: 'Door with lock!', 'Working flush!', 'A seat!', and so on.[23]

The list of businesses that partner with Toilet Twinning includes manufacturers of up-market toilets and bathroom fittings such as Thomas Crapper. This partnership is celebrated with a further staging of the imagined gap between Western opulence and Third World squalor: 'The legendary sanitary-ware company Thomas Crapper has joined [the] global Toilet Twinning movement, linking three of its traditional high-quality loos with three latrines deep in the African bush.'[24] Another business partner is Toilet Yoga, an American company that produces books, apps, and other paraphernalia based on a series of yoga exercises that have been adapted for performance while on the toilet, as a means of facilitating the speedy and pleasurable evacuation of one's bowels. Toilet Yoga donates 10% of profits to Toilet Twinning. In doing so it claims to offer purchasers of its products 'the opportunity to connect with others around the world as you share in the joy of relief and satisfaction'.[25] The transparent insincerity of this tongue-in-cheek gesture of harmony and egalitarianism is rendered even more disingenuous when we consider that Toilet Yoga is designed to be performed on a Western-style lavatory, and would be impossible for the 'African' squatting gratefully over a hole in the ground in their humble new latrine. Here again, the discourse of equality and the enjoyment of inequality are intertwined. In the words of Toilet Yoga, you 'Walk out feeling great'.[26]

Toilet Twinning thus provides a complex fantasy space within which its participants can organise their anal *jouissance* to deliver enjoyment, through the staging of the inequality between their sophisticated toilet experience and the imagined horrors of the Third World latrine. This fantasy space can be evoked by imagining the ideal subject of Toilet Twinning, who has bought all its related products and has dutifully followed its instructions: splayed upon his Western toilet in a contorted yoga pose, surrounded by stickers reminding him of how 'deluxe' his toilet is in relation to the grim latrine of his imagined African counterpart, staring at an image of that very latrine on the certificate lovingly framed and hung upon his toilet door, and with images of a hundred more latrines ready to hand on the toilet paper beside him... at last, the committed Toilet Twinner can really enjoy his shit.

The phallic stage: Sir Richard's Condoms

Sir Richard's Condoms is a California-based social enterprise that specialises in 'ethical' condoms. For every condom that it sells, the company donates one to a 'developing country' in order to combat unwanted pregnancies and sexually transmitted diseases in such countries. Its 'one-for-one' structure is identical to Table for Two and Toilet Twinning. Like Toilet Twinning, it adopts a playful and irreverent approach to its taboo subject matter, in which the conditions of poverty and disease that it purports to address are reduced to opportunities for endless innuendo: 'A pleasure pack with a purpose'; 'Give back while getting it on'; 'Doing good never felt better'; and so on.[27] In the words of *Ethical Johnny*, 'Made with natural latex rubber, Vegan and PETA approved, Sir Richard's also donate one condom to charity for every one they sell. That's pretty hot in anyone's book.'[28]

At the level of its discursive articulation, Sir Richard's is based on the principle of harmony and equality. We are told that it is a '*buy-one give-one* initiative' and that its founders live by the motto that 'the power of business can help bring pleasure and health to the global community'.[29] But as in the cases of Table for Two and Toilet Twinning, this message is underwritten by the mobilisation of a disavowed enjoyment of relations of inequality. Like Table for Two, Sir Richard's Condoms emphasises the difference between the product consumed and the product donated. The consumer can select from a variety of condoms, each of which promises a distinct form of enjoyment, 'including Ultra Thin, Classic Ribbed, Pleasure Dots, and Extra Large'.[30] Needless to say, the recipient of the free condom in the 'developing country' is not offered an equivalent choice. Sites are selected on the basis of high rates of unwanted pregnancy and sexually transmitted diseases such as Haiti, which the company claims 'has seen a spike in pregnancies following the 2009 earthquake ... of 2,391 women in 120 camps, almost 12 percent reported being pregnant',[31] and in contrast to the variety of luxury products offered to the Western consumer, the Third World beneficiaries receive a basic condom with simple instructions 'in the area's language, so the intended population can easily understand'.[32] In other words, while 'our' condoms are designed to enhance our safe enjoyment, 'their' condoms are designed to discipline their irresponsible and sexually incontinent behaviour.

Like Table for Two and Toilet Twinning, Sir Richard's Condoms can be accused of depoliticising development by promising an easy solution to highly complex socio-economic problems, based on the selective provision of a single material input, underpinned by the sensual enjoyment of a specific bodily act. But as in these other cases, the common-sense understanding of the relationship between enjoyment and fantasy should be reversed in order to grasp the way in which ideology is operating here. Just as the enjoyment of eating and defecating is not 'natural' but must be framed by specific fantasies to procure pleasure from the alien materiality of their related drives, so there is nothing inherently enjoyable about sex. The *jouissance* of an orgasm is an overwhelming physical event, which might be experienced as traumatic if it remained unmediated by fantasy:

> Imagine a hypothetical human infant, isolated from all human society. In the unlikely event of its surviving, the manifestation of the erotic drive in its genitalia can be answered by masturbation. But it would be masturbation without any link to arousing imaginings: a purely physical response devoid of fantasy – perhaps not even a very pleasurable act.[33]

The intensely relational dimension of sexual intercourse adds a further traumatic element to the raw *jouissance* of the bodily drives – the abyss of the Other's desire. According to Lacan, 'There is no sexual relationship'.[34] We can only engage with each other sexually to the extent that we succeed in mapping our fantasies onto one another, in order to conceal the existential gulf that exists between us in the Real. In Žižek's words, 'Any contact with a real flesh-and-blood other, any sexual pleasure that we find in touching another human being, is not something evident but something inherently traumatic, and can be sustained only insofar as this other enters the subject's fantasy frame.'[35]

For these reasons, we should understand Sir Richard's Condoms not as using sexual enjoyment to sell a charity product, but as using a charity product to provide the fantasy frame within which sexual enjoyment becomes possible. Sir Richard's Condoms are marketed primarily to heterosexual men. The marketing strategy promises to incite and sustain the purchaser's desire in the moment of the sexual act, and to arouse desire and provide satisfaction in his prospective female partners. In the words of one men's lifestyle website, 'When you're getting it on, you're probably not thinking of much outside of "This is awesome"... Now while you're enjoying yourself... you can be thinking of all the good you are doing as well.'[36] This blasé promise of phallic enjoyment betrays the necessarily phantasmatic dimension of the sexual act. If sex were straightforwardly 'awesome', why would you need to think about anything else? The erotic necessity of the fantasy frame is also evident in a poster campaign for the company: 'For every condom you purchase, one is donated to a developing country, which makes even bad sex, good sex.'[37] The joke addresses sexual anxiety with the reassuring message that the ethical act of the condom's purchase will be sufficient to provide enjoyment, even if the act is not enjoyable in itself. Underpinned by its disavowed staging of the inequality between 'our' enjoyment and that of the Third World Other, this messaging offers the compassionate consumers of Western societies a complex 'fantasy screen which enables [them] to sustain the Real of the sexual act'.[38]

Conclusion: The desire of the Other

This chapter has argued that compassionate consumerism operates ideologically through the production of specific fantasies that mobilise and regulate the traumatic Real of *jouissance* that wells up within the erogenous zones associated with the bodily drives. The appeal of its charitable gestures lies not only in compliance with the ethical injunction to help those less fortunate than ourselves, but also in a disavowed enjoyment of relations of inequality between 'us' and 'them'. In the cases of Table for Two, Toilet Twinning, and Sir Richard's Condoms, the libidinal economy of compassionate consumerism procures enjoyment through the production of fantasies that stage these relations of inequality between the lines of an imaginary ethic of egalitarian harmony. This libidinal economy underpins a post-political consensus between businesses, charities, and individual lifestyle choices that legitimates existing relations of global inequality, and that reduces highly complex problems of poverty and marginalisation to simple issues to be resolved through the purchase of a single input.

The development solutions offered by these organisations are childlike in their simplicity, in keeping with the infantile stages of sexuality to which they correspond. The suggestion that global poverty can be meaningfully addressed through the provision of free school meals, the construction of latrines, or the distribution of condoms, based on the individual purchasing decisions of privileged Western consumers, cannot be taken seriously by anyone who pauses to think about it. At one level, of course, this is precisely the point – representations of the Third World as 'Hell on Earth' function to replace critical thought with an urgent 'ethical' gesture.[39] But the ideology at work here cannot be reduced to the obscuring of actual social relations beneath a veil of charitable giving. The cases I have considered share a determinedly 'light-hearted' and 'ironic' attitude, and those participating in them would probably acknowledge that they are not really going to change anything through their actions. As Žižek has argued in another context, 'All this, of course, is meant in an ironic way; it is "not to be taken literally" – *however it is precisely through such self-distance that postmodern "cynical" ideology functions.*'[40] From this perspective, the orthodox Marxist formulation of ideology as false consciousness does not adequately grasp the operation of ideology in contemporary consumer capitalism, in which people fully understand the lies and absurdities that they are participating in, but carry on regardless. Crucially, however, *they are still in ideology.* The ideological moment has simply shifted from the level of belief to the level of practice.[41] It is not necessary for the compassionate consumer to consciously believe that they are really transforming the world through their trivial actions. It is enough for these actions to be performed. Through its colonisation of the mundane rituals of everyday life – eating, shitting, fucking – compassionate consumerism functions ideologically as an embodied dimension of lived experience without anyone having to actually believe in it.

But despite adopting a 'knowing' and 'ironic' attitude, the ethical consumer remains unaware of their disavowed enjoyment of relations of inequality. 'Inequality' is the repressed signifier of compassionate consumerism. It is never once uttered by any of the social enterprises discussed in this chapter. Yet they all circle ceaselessly around it, implicitly staging the gap between Western opulence and generosity on the one hand, Third World poverty and helplessness on the other, as the fundamental fantasy that sustains the Western consumer's enjoyment of their products. This enjoyment is dependent upon the imagined gaze of the grateful beneficiary. 'At Table for Two, you never dine alone', but are invited to think of yourself eating in the company of the African child you are feeding. Similarly, with Toilet Twinning, you never shit alone; the certificate of the twinned latrine in your bathroom reminds you that you are 'sharing the joy of relief and satisfaction'. But this intersubjectivity must remain at the level of the Imaginary for it to be operative. There is no African child at the other side of the table. And the Toilet Twinning certificates all depict empty latrines. The ethical consumer is alone in their *jouissance*. The imagined proximity of the grateful beneficiary is only a prop to sustain their enjoyment of inequality, and to *exclude* the abyssal gaze of the Third World Other in the fullness of their Real presence. This gaze expresses a desire that cannot be satisfied by a meal, a condom, or a latrine. It is a desire for *equality* that directly threatens the privilege on which the enjoyment of the ethical consumer is premised, and that must be excluded before it can be articulated as a *demand*.[42]

All that is required to shatter the fantasy-space of compassionate consumerism is to *realise* the imaginary position of the Other within it: a Table for Two contributor enjoys his braised chicken couscous, smiling charitably across the table at an African child eating a bowl of cornmeal porridge; a donor to Toilet Twinning enjoys her deluxe Western toilet, grinning generously at a peasant woman squatting over a hole in the ground; an affluent couple enjoy their luxury Sir Richard's condom, leering philanthropically at an AIDS sufferer and his impoverished partner using their last free prophylactic. Suddenly the compassionate consumers see themselves through the eyes of the Other, and glimpse the same expression that Freud detected on the face of the Rat Man when confronted with the Real of his *jouissance*. It is an expression of *'horror at pleasure of his own of which he himself was unaware'*.[43]

Notes

1 Slavoj Žižek, *The Sublime Object of Ideology* (London: Verso, 1989), 123.
2 Patricia Nickel and Angela Eikenberry, 'A Critique of the Discourse of Marketized Philanthropy', *American Behavioural Scientist* 52, no. 7 (2009): 979.
3 Joanne Sharp, Patricia Campbell, and Emma Laurie, 'The Violence of Aid? Giving, Power, and Active Subjects in One World Conservatism', *Third World Quarterly* 31, no. 7 (2010): 1140.
4 Žižek, *Sublime Object of Ideology*, 124–25.
5 The infant then enters a period of 'latency', after which the young adult organises the final, 'genital' phase of his or her psychosexual development. According to Freud, childhood experiences can cause adults to remain fixated on earlier stages of development, the enjoyment of which is repressed, leading to pleasure being taken in apparently unrelated activities, such as the meticulous organisation of the 'anal retentive'. See Jon Stratton, *The Desirable Body: Cultural Fetishism and the Erotics of Consumption* (Manchester: Manchester University Press, 1996).
6 Néstor Braunstein, 'Desire and Jouissance in the Teachings of Lacan', in *The Cambridge Companion to Lacan*, ed. Jean-Michel Rabate (Cambridge: Cambridge University Press, 2003), 102–15; Frédéric Declerq, 'Lacan's Concept of the Real of Jouissance: Clinical Illustrations and Implications', *Psychoanalysis, Culture and Society* 9 (2004): 237–51.
7 Slavoj Žižek, *The Plague of Fantasies* (London: Verso, 2008), xxiv.
8 Žižek, *Sublime Object*, 45.
9 Bruce Fink, *The Lacanian Subject: Between Language and Jouissance* (Princeton, NJ: Princeton University Press, 1995), 12–13; Sean Homer, *Jacques Lacan* (London: Routledge, 2005), 85, 126.
10 Yannis Stavrakakis, *The Lacanian Left: Psychoanalysis, Theory, Politics* (New York: State University of New York Press, 2007), 246, emphasis in original.
11 Žižek, *Plague of Fantasies*, 6.
12 'In order to be operative, fantasy has to remain "implicit", it has to maintain a distance towards the explicit symbolic texture sustained by it, and to function as its inherent transgression.' *Ibid.*, 24.
13 This chapter is based on Japhy Wilson, 'The Joy of Inequality: The Libidinal Economy of Compassionate Consumerism', *International Journal of Žižek Studies* 9, no. 2 (2015): 1–26. It focuses on the promotional material produced by Table for Two, Toilet Twinning, and

Sir Richard's Condoms in the early 2010s. Many of the links cited in the text are no longer operational. While all three organisations continue to operate on the same principles, their promotional material is now more subtle in its staging of inequality. The original quotations and descriptions have been retained here, with updated references and links provided where possible.

14 James Kondo, ' "Table for Two" Initiative Combats Hunger, Obesity', *The Washington Post*, January 27, 2011, http://voices.washingtonpost. com/davos-diary/2011/01/table_for_two.html (accessed May 6, 2022).

15 See, for example, Table for Two, 'Global News Letter Volume 20', www.tablefor2.org/documentdownload.axd?documentresourceid=40 (accessed May 6, 2022).

16 Table for Two, 'Brochure', www.tablefor2.org/documentdownload. axd?documentresourceid=40 (accessed May 3, 2014); Table for Two, 'Implementation Guideline (Restaurants)', www.tablefor2.org/ documentdownload.axd?documentresourceid=26 (accessed May 3, 2014).

17 Table for Two, 'New Footage from Ruhiira, Uganda!', http://tablefor 2usa.wordpress.com/2011/06/30/new-footage-from-ruhiira-uganda/ (accessed May 6, 2022).

18 Žižek, *Plague of Fantasies*, 7, emphasis in original.

19 Table for Two, 'Table Tent 3', www.tablefor2.org/documentdownload. axd?documentresourceid=31 (accessed May 3, 2014).

20 *Ibid*.; Table for Two, 'Table Tent 1', www.tablefor2.org/document download.axd?documentresourceid=38 (accessed May 3, 2014).

21 www.toilettwinning.org/ (accessed May 6, 2022).

22 Toilet Twinning, 'Toilet Twinning A4 Poster', www.annashenassa. com/uploads/4/8/5/2/4852674/toilettwinningposter_1.jpg (accessed May 6, 2022).

23 Toilet Twinning, 'Stickers', www.toilettwinning.org/resources/. The stickers were available at this site when accessed on May 3, 2014. It now contains other similar merchandise.

24 Toilet Twinning, 'Thomas Crapper', www.toilettwinning.org/fun-stuff/loominaries/corporations/thomas-crapper/ (accessed April 2, 2014).

25 Cited in Diana Adams, 'Toilet Yoga: Because Sometimes Shit Doesn't Happen', Bit Rebels, 2021, https://bitrebels.com/lifestyle/toilet-yoga-because-sometimes-shit-doesnt-happen/ (accessed May 6, 2022).

26 The relevant image can be viewed at: www.pinterest.com/pin/ 382102349616282549/ (accessed May 6, 2022).

27 Sir Richard's Condoms, '(RED) Condoms', www.sirrichards.com/red (accessed April 3, 2014).

28 Ethical Johnny, 'Sir Richard's Condoms: Hot or Not?' Condom Diary, July 16, 2013, https://condomdiary.wordpress.com/ (accessed 6 May 2022).

29 Cited in Vera Hadzi-Antich, 'Safe Sex: Delivered', *Women's Health*, December 9, 2011, www.womenshealthmag.com/relationships/a19911172/safe-sex-delivered/ (accessed May 6, 2022).

30 Hadzi-Antich, 'Safe Sex'.

31 Cited in Webwire, 'Sir Richard's Condom Company Announces Inaugural Condom Donation to Haiti', Webwire, February 13, 2012, www.webwire.com/ViewPressRel.asp?aId=152754 (accessed May 6, 2022).

32 About.com Contraception, 'Sir Richard's Company', http://contraception.about.com/od/malecondom/p/Sir-Richards-Company.htm (accessed May 3, 2014).

33 Lionel Bailly, *Lacan* (Oxford: Oneworld, 2009), 140.

34 Žižek, *Plague of Fantasies*, 7.

35 Slavoj Žižek, *How to Read Lacan* (New York: W.W. Norton & Co., 2006), 51.

36 Cool Material, 'Sir Richard's Condom Company', http://coolmaterial.com/gear/sir-richards-condom-company/ (accessed April 5, 2014).

37 This poster could previously be viewed at http://carphotos.cardomain.com/story_images/1/2214/4841/5534920002_large.jpg (accessed May 3, 2014).

38 Žižek, *Plague of Fantasies*, 234.

39 *Ibid.*, 24.

40 *Ibid.*, 81, emphasis in original.

41 Žižek, *Sublime Object of Ideology*, 28–35.

42 At its deepest level, 'fantasy is the screen by means of which the subject avoids the radical opening of the enigma of the Other's desire' (Žižek, *Plague of Fantasies*, 41). Analysis aims 'to generate the tension necessary to separate the subject from its fantasised relation to the Other's desire' (Fink, *Lacanian Subject*, xiii).

43 Freud, quoted in Fink, *Lacanian Subject*, 60, emphasis in original.

9

Despair and hope among young Korean investors

Cheolung Choi

Squid Game was Netflix's most-watched show in 2021. According to *Variety*, 'Squid Game pulled in a staggering 1.65 billion hours of viewing in 28 days following its premiere on September 17. That's equivalent to more than 182,000 years in total.'[1] It adopted a popular genre style that involved its characters battling each other to the death in an elaborate gaming arena, as seen in films such as *Battle Royale* and *The Hunger Games*. But mere familiarity with the *Battle Royale*-format was not the main reason for the huge success of *Squid Game*. The show appealed to an enormous audience because it offered an eminently relatable and vivid depiction of the pains, frustrations, and desires that characterise the libidinal economy of contemporary capitalism. Audiences across the world empathised with the series' conflicted and flawed characters who, like us, must everyday navigate the ruthless landscape of capitalist society. Social inequality, burdensome debt, despair about the future – these aspects of *Squid Game* are all too familiar to people of both developed and developing countries.[2] So too is the show's central dream: that of making a fortune in one stroke.

A dramatic turn at the beginning of the series puts into sharp relief this relation between real life and the Squid Game. Soon after beginning the deadly game, in which more than half of the players lost their lives in the first round, a majority of the survivors voted to stop the game. The game's host consented to this suspension of play, in accordance with the contractual rules, allowing the players to return to their normal lives, though leaving the door open for the competition to restart at a later date. Given the depressing and hopeless conditions of their regular lives, the surviving main

characters all returned to the game, drawn by the possibility of an
enormous ₩45.6-billion prize (approximately US$38.4 million),
despite the high probability of their deaths. Unlike previous *Battle
Royale*-type dramas, the characters were not forced to engage in
the survival games. They voluntarily joined with a clear sense of
purpose. As the character Han Mi-nyeo, who is heavily indebted,
laments, 'there is no hope anywhere. It is just as bad out there as it
is in here, goddamn-it.' Only there is one crucial difference. In *Squid
Game*, there is a glimmer of hope: one of the 456 players is guaran-
teed a huge sum of money if they manage to survive. Many Koreans
sympathise with this grim scenario. As one young freelance office
worker in Seoul was quoted as saying in *The New York Times*,
'I wonder how many people would participate if *Squid Game* was
held in real life.'[3] Empathising with the precarity of the drama's
protagonists, he imagined that many of his peers would risk it all.
The young generation of Koreans, particularly those who see themselves as 'dirty spoons' or 'losers', share the despair experienced by
the Squid Game players, and that is why so many have piled into a
risky, speculative game not entirely dissimilar to the one depicted in
the hit Netflix show: Bitcoin trading.

During the COVID-19 pandemic, young Koreans became more
active in financial investments than ever before. Many began
trading in stock and especially cryptocurrency markets. According
to CoinDesk Korea, as of May 2021, the cumulative number of
cryptocurrency subscribers was 5.87 million, over one-tenth of the
population. The number of new monthly subscribers to the four
major exchanges, which was 160,000 in December 2020, increased
more than tenfold in five months, reaching 1.91 million in May
2021.[4] In the first quarter of 2021, the number of new subscribers
was 1.58 million, with those in their twenties and thirties accounting
for 64% of the total.[5] Koreans in their twenties and thirties are
often referred to as the Sampo generation, derived from *Sampo-
sedae*, roughly translating as 'three giving-up generation'. This is
a generation that has given up on dating, marriage, and childbirth
because of soaring housing costs and a dearth of well-paid jobs. For
them, low barriers to entry and high volatility in cryptocurrency
markets meant one thing: the possibility of high returns. That
is why the Sampo generation have cast their fortunes into risky

financial investment, forsaking the traditional and notorious hard-work culture of older Koreans.

How are we to understand the phenomenon of desperate individuals jumping into dangerous speculation? From the perspective of mainstream economics, they can be understood as energetic entrepreneurs who take measured risks in pursuit of high rewards. They are *homines economici* who make rational investment choices based on their income, expenses, and appetite for risk.[6] Behavioural economics challenges this idea of a fully rational subject, integrating non-economic motives – or 'animal spirits' – into its understanding of seemingly irrational phenomena such as speculative mania and asset price bubbles.[7] But despite its efforts to take seriously concerns excluded by mainstream approaches, such as the fear of missing out (FOMO), behavioural economics nonetheless shares in the latter's methodological individualism, conceiving of the social as a simple aggregation of individual behaviour. It remains normatively committed to promoting instrumentally 'rational' decision-making and overcoming the distortions of non-economic factors. Thus, even for behavioural economics, social context and cultural dimensions – such as those that create the speculative subjectivity seen recently in South Korea – are excluded from analysis.

Governmentality studies do much better in this regard, spotlighting the various social processes and discursive mechanisms by which neoliberal capitalism constitutes the individual as a financial subject. Accordingly, neoliberal rationality does not merely propagate an ideology that exults markets and competition; it also inculcates norms and ethics that are the very basis of subjectivity. Neoliberal rationality works to turn individuals into self-responsible subjects who manage their life risks, that is, to *produce* rational economic actors endowed with financial responsibility and transparency.[8] To this end, a series of institutional, technical, and discursive devices are deployed, such as mutual funds and mobile trading systems that mediate the flow of global finance and the daily practices of individuals.[9] In Korea, as neoliberal financialisation has developed since 2000, individuals have been incorporated into global financial networks and financial rationality has taken root as a new ethic of subjectivity.[10] This emphasis in the literature on the production of subjectivity is much needed.

However, there is a tendency in the governmentality literature to overlook the emotional and unconscious aspects of financial subjectivity, such as the fantasies, beliefs, and desires that form and sustain it. Capitalism has long operated as the dominant social relation, organising society by propagating particular forms of morality, belief, and emotional dynamics, and by promoting certain conceptions of human solidarity in line with the logic of economy.[11] As Martijn Konings argues, the unique socialisation mechanism of modern capitalism is to be found in its 'productive admixtures of hope and disappointment, illusion and disillusionment, trauma, and the prospect of salvation'.[12]

Taking this observation as its starting point, the present chapter seeks to elucidate the economy of desire that motivates young Korean investors and to understand its political implications. Section one explores the socio-economic context that underpins the frenzy of speculation described above, including the processes that fomented neoliberal institutions and discourses in South Korea. Section two discusses the internalisation of neoliberal ideology by young Koreans, drawing on Foucault's analysis of governmentality. Section three analyses the process by which Korean millennials came to view risky financial investments as the only escape from their desperate situation, explaining speculation as a form of *fetishised desire* in which the very cause of despair is inverted as a means of hope.[13] Finally, section four discusses how these unconscious dynamics are manifested in a new existential attitude towards betting on financial uncertainty by young Koreans. Korean millennials see few prospects in following the path of previous generations through struggle, sweat, and saving when neoliberalism has ravaged the socio-economic landscape; their only hope of redemption lies in risky financial investments. The chapter concludes with some reflections on the political implications of this gloomy utopian view.

Neoliberal financialisation in South Korea

South Korea underwent rapid economic development in the late twentieth century, becoming known as the 'miracle on the Han River'. However, this initial phase of high economic growth, which was led by the state and a few large corporations, began to show signs of vulnerability in the early 1990s, eventually culminating in a national default crisis in 1997–98. The Korean government received emergency funds from the International Monetary Fund (IMF) in exchange for a major restructuring of its economic system. The primary elements of this restructuring, led by the US Treasury Department and the IMF, were the shuttering of insolvent companies and the restoration of liquidity to financial institutions, along with the liberalisation of both the labour market and the financial sector.[14]

The IMF's structural adjustment programme entailed the infamous 'shock therapy', which convulsed the economy with harsh austerity policies in order to usher in neoliberal market discipline.[15] Korean society immediately faced recession and mass unemployment, and many workers lost their jobs and their homes. The solution the Korean government proposed for tackling economic recession and its attendant social problems was to 'govern through the financial market'.[16] The government soon began to implement policies that prioritised the interests of financial capital and its owners. In particular, the government expanded household loans to stimulate domestic demand and asset markets. Growth in loans of all kinds – mortgage loans, credit loans, even loan-sharking businesses – was praised as signs that a new wave of 'financial democratisation' was underway, promising access to capital for individuals and households hitherto barred from such funds.[17]

Loans became the only lifeboats for many members of the working class who were facing unemployment and declining incomes. Total household debt, which stood at US$12.4 billion in 1997, exceeded US$948 billion in 2013, reaching US$1.56 trillion in 2021.[18] The household debt-to-disposable income ratio increased from 107% in 2003 to 136% in 2012 and reached 174% in 2021.[19] This increase in household debt was largely due to an increase in mortgage lending to the middle class, as well as an increase in loans for subsistence to the working class and the poor. As loan-shark businesses targeted low-income families, millions defaulted because they could not repay their high-interest loans. These conditions precipitated another local financial crisis in 2003, soon after the national default crisis in 1997–98. Only this time, it was households – not large corporations – that were the epicentre of the financial crisis. In the wake of neoliberal financialisation, Korean society shifted from 'a system in which companies overinvest through excessive borrowing to a system of household excessive consumption through excessive borrowing'.[20]

As financial markets were liberalised and loan regulations for individuals and households were relaxed, Koreans actively took out loans and started investing in financial assets. Many members of the middle class took out mortgages and bought fire-sale assets after the crisis of 1997–98. Individuals who were uncomfortable with direct investments joined mutual funds. Mutual funds were widely advertised as attractive wealth building products that could be as easily subscribed to at a bank as purchasing items at a supermarket. This 'Jae-tech' (financial technology) culture represented a new rationality and ethics of mass investment that settled into Korean society at the time. Previously, the desire to become rich was considered self-centred and greedy; from the 2000s onward, wealth acquisition has been viewed instead as a sound life goal that all should work towards. The Jae-tech discourse preached a new ethic in which the person who constantly generates cash flows through financial knowledge and economic prowess is a promising 'entrepreneur' and 'self-responsible subject'.[21] In this way, the public's perception of financial investment as a risky and immoral, speculative act was transformed into its opposite, and such activity now came to be viewed as a rational and efficient course of economic action.

The term 'Debt-tech', which was also popular at that time, likewise reveals an important shift in the perception of debt. After Korea's neoliberal reforms, debt was no longer viewed as a risk or a source of disgrace, instead being seen as a legitimate investment vehicle and a key instrument for attaining success in life. The middle class took advantage of rising housing prices by purchasing apartments with mortgages and a new desire emerged among Koreans to seek asset growth through financial investment and, ideally, to become a 'building owner'. Many started to check housing and stock market trends daily, to exchange market information with one another, and to venture into speculative investments. Neoliberal financialisation settled into Korean society following the debt crisis, but, somewhat paradoxically, it did so by spreading hope that life could also be improved through debt, by subordinating everyday life to the dynamics of finance.

Human capital and the promise of self-investment

Foucault understood neoliberalism not merely as an economic policy or doctrine, but as a total and practical transformation of the principles, forms, and objects of government. According to him, neoliberalism is a governing principle that involves the 'generalisation of the economic form of the market'.[22] The goal of neoliberalism is to create an order in which mechanisms of competition and enterprise operate at a maximum extent and intensity within a society. Therefore, it is necessary to establish a system of competition, evaluation, and supervision in all social fields, including government organisations, social services, and education, where mechanisms of competition have traditionally not been employed. This new rationality is readily observed in today's neoliberal universities, which operate according to a profit-driven model and evaluate and monitor their faculty according to performance indicators, targets, and league tables.[23]

Neoliberalism transforms both the principle of governing and the object of governing. Its rationality redefines an individual as 'human capital', a subject who creates income streams through investments in their physical and mental capabilities. Efforts are made to blur the distinction between capitalists and workers by viewing both as owners of their own human capital. Michel Feher captures well the essence of this shift. 'Rather than a *possessive* relationship, as that of the free laborer with their labor power', he argues, 'the relationship between the neoliberal subject and his or her human capital should be called *speculative*'.[24] Workers and capitalists alike are entrepreneurs of themselves whose self-development and self-valorisation occurs through speculative investments of time and energy in a range of pursuits.

The notion of an entrepreneurial subject or investor in human capital in this sense was established in Korean society in the name of a popular 'self-improvement' culture during the early and mid-2000s. This culture established the entrepreneurial subject as an individual skilled in financial activities and as one who manages their life responsibly. At that time, the young generation, who were facing economic recession and chronic difficulties in finding employment, deeply internalised this ethic. In the 2000s, those in their twenties faced severe difficulties entering the job market due to the high college enrolment rate (approximately 80%) and the prevailing neoliberal 'jobless growth' policy. In 2010, the unemployment rate of those in their twenties was twice the overall rate and half of hires were for non-regular jobs.[25] As competition in the job market intensified, companies began to demand more qualifications from applicants. During the document screening process, which is the first gateway for employment, several types of 'specs' or qualifications are required. The basic screening includes proof of level of education, grade point average (GPA), and Test of English for International Communication (TOEIC) certificates, but additional qualifications and aptitude tests have been added by many employers. To break through the fierce competition, it is now necessary to possess specialist qualifications, to have extensive intern experience, and to have won employee awards. Adding to this list, many firms now request spreadsheet and database certifications and require applicants to pass a Korean history proficiency test. For coveted jobs in the financial sector, applicants need to invest in attaining costly certifications such as Associate Financial Planner Korea (AFPK), Certified Financial Planner (CFP), or Certified Public Accountant (CPA), which commonly exceed the qualifications needed for the positions sought.

The young generation is overwhelmed by this brutal competition. The popular movie *My Dear Desperado* (2010) widely resonated with young Koreans due to its realistic depiction of the difficulties they face in the job market. The heroine possesses a master's degree and excellent TOEIC scores, but still fails to land a job because her degree comes from a local university rather than a prestigious national one. In the film, the corporate interviewers do not even glance at her resume; instead, they ask her to dance in her interviews and request sexual favours. Her degrading experiences, which mirror those of some applicants in real life, relate the desperate situation and poor social status of young job-seekers in contemporary Korea. Nevertheless, the ideology of neoliberal competition and self-responsibility has been successfully entrenched as the natural order of things. The slogans that have dominated Korean society since the 2000s have been 'survival of the fittest' and 'you have to find your own way in the world'. Sociologist Kim Hong-joong talks of three forms of survival to which Koreans have increasingly been subjected: 'economic survival', attained by winning out in the infinitely competitive market sphere; 'social survival', achieved by securing high-status positions and persevering in the aggressive and showy struggle for recognition by others; and 'physical survival', realised by effectively commercialising one's body.[26]

However, no matter how much has been invested in their 'human capital', many remain unsuccessful in obtaining regular employment. Frustration, anger, and dissatisfaction have increased among young people in the last two decades. But the anger of the 99% who are oppressed and excluded is directed towards their competitors, rather than the top 1%, or against the mechanisms of competition to which they are subjected. The neoliberal ethic of self-responsibility mitigates against popular unrest by instilling the belief that socio-economic suffering owes to one's personal failings. The Sampo generation view their failure to obtain decent jobs as a consequence of their lack of effort and diligence. They self-mockingly call themselves 'losers'. Their frustration is often expressed as harsh aggression and hatred towards themselves and others. One's peers are viewed as opponents to be eliminated rather than companions or fellow travellers upon which to draw for mutual support. They believe that compassion is a sign of weakness and that calls for solidarity are disingenuous in the cut-throat world they inhabit. *Squid Game* captured the essence of this ethos in its main protagonist, Sang-woo, an intelligent and formerly successful businessman, who, despite an affable demeanour, has few scruples in betraying his allies to advance to the end of the competition.

For most young Koreans, the optimistic vision of self-improvement and self-valorisation promoted by neoliberal rationality has been little more than empty rhetoric. The ethic of self-responsibility promotes an aggressive attitude towards one's social peers rather than increasing one's own value. In this way, neoliberal rationality reproduces itself not simply by instilling a calculative and instrumental disposition, but through the anxiety and anger that it induces.

Financial speculation and the lure of Bitcoin

Over the past two decades, the enormous investment that young Koreans have made in themselves as 'human capital' has failed to produce the expected returns. The job market has not rebounded and competition has become even more intense. Intentionally low-interest rates, the deregulation of asset markets, and credit expansion policies have fuelled asset price inflation. Housing prices in Seoul and the metropolitan area have skyrocketed since the 2000s, reaching levels that are unaffordable with normal income and savings. According to Yunhap News, the land price of apartments in Seoul rose by US$12,000 per 3.3 square metres between 2017 and 2020, 7.5 times the increase of US$2,600 over the previous 10 years.[27] The young 'dirty spoons' have come to understand that no matter how much they invest in themselves, they have a vanishingly small hope of any socially upward movement.

Where, then, can they find hope? Investment in human capital offers no guarantee of employment and income growth significantly trails behind climbing asset prices. It is difficult to enter the housing market, and the stock market, with limited volatility, offers modest returns in the near term. One of the few glimmers of hope in recent years has been the growth of Bitcoin. The cryptocurrency's price, which had been on a downward trajectory since its initial peak in 2013, soared from US$218 in 2015 to US$13,850 in 2017, ushering in a new speculative frenzy. Many Koreans quickly joined the global boom, and the country became 'sort of a ground zero for the global bitcoin mania'. According to Bloomberg News, approximately 21% of global Bitcoin transactions in December 2017 were made in South Korea. Coin stories were to be heard on every corner, in cafes and on the streets, and market information was actively exchanged in online communities.[28]

As the Bitcoin market overheated, the government enacted a series of restrictions on cryptocurrency trading, provoking backlash from many young speculators. An anonymous petition against these restrictions was posted on the Blue House's public petition bulletin board, revealing the desperate economic straits of many young Koreans. The petition, garnering more than 200,000 signatures in one month, evoked a distraught plea for the government not to close what many saw as their last remaining route to success.

> I want to ask the government, 'Have you ever given people a happy dream?' ... Thanks to Bitcoin, we can now have a happy dream that we have never had. I might be able to have my own house in this country where houses are exorbitant. I might be able to make a living

while doing something I want to do ... The government says that the regulations are necessary to protect people from risky gambling, but I think that the government is depriving us of our dreams. Please do not take away our hopes and dreams.[29]

The implausible optimism that Korean youth have of striking Bitcoin fortunes correlates with the helplessness and despondency of the Sampo generation. The lure of Bitcoin is that it offers the chance of becoming rich quickly through highly leveraged crypto trading. Especially with the onset of the COVID-19 pandemic in 2020–21, even more young people ventured into trading cryptocurrencies. The rise of new entrants has seen even riskier investments in overseas meme stocks, such as GameStop, and the rise of trading in Bitcoin futures. Futures trading is especially tempting, as one only need bet on the direction of the currency's price, allowing one to make a profit even in a down market, and to obtain high returns by increasing the leverage ratio. Unlike spot trading, leveraged bets bring the risk that one's entire principal can be wiped out in an instant, but it is a risk that many are willing to take in the hope of attaining economic freedom.

Critics regularly warn of the dangers of the crypto craze, emphasising how bitcoin is a fictional asset with no intrinsic value. What they overlook is the way this very quality accounts for the attraction of Bitcoin. The absence of a foundation for its value is what underwrites its rapid volatility. Prices of assets such as real estate, which are still tied to their actual use value, experience limited fluctuations, and are unlikely to produce quick returns. The impossibility of an accurate valuation is a prerequisite for the functioning of financial markets, including Bitcoin. The simple reason that financial assets are traded is that some people value them highly while others value them less so.

Following Ole Bjerg, we can say that the value and price of financial assets belong to the real and symbolic in the Lacanian sense. Lacan sees the reality of human existence as comprised of three intertwined dimensions of subjectivity: the Symbolic, the Real, and the Imaginary. The Symbolic refers to the symbolic order that guides and constrains our consciousness and behaviour, such as occurs through language and law. The Real is defined as that which escapes the symbolic, that which is neither spoken nor written. Thus it is related to the unapproachable, irreducible realm of non-meaning. However, 'although it does not exist, [it] has a series of properties and can produce a series of effects'.[30] The Imaginary is an illusory wholeness to which we cling in order to compensate for our irrevocable separation from the real through our entrance into the symbolic order. Applying these notions to the financial market, price is the product of the social process in which traders symbolise the value of an asset through trading, but this symbolisation never 'discovers' the Real of value. When a stock is traded at a specific price, this price functions as a symbolic representation of the value of the underlying asset and expected future returns. The operation of this symbolisation is not determined by the intrinsic properties of the underlying asset, that is, the Real. In many cases, the price of a financial asset fluctuates according to rumours that have nothing to do with the actual conditions of the underlying assets. The exact calculation of the value of a financial asset is always ambiguous and incomprehensible. We only assess the value retrospectively in terms of price.[31]

The market price generated through every moment of transaction symbolises value. The coordination between these two ontologically inconsistent orders is driven by the operation of the Imaginary, that is, the belief that this discrepancy can be resolved through market analysis and the illusion that one can beat the market. Therefore, value is, in Lacanian terms, like an *objet petit a* in the financial market that drives the subject's desire through lack. For Lacan, the *objet petit a* is 'the unfathomable "something" that makes an ordinary object sublime'.[32] Although this object is 'nothing' in itself, an absence rather than presence, it provokes the subject's desire and, at the same time, becomes a mysterious and unattainable object of the subject's desire. Money itself, for example, is a seemingly straightforward object used as a medium of exchange, but when it becomes an object of desire, it acquires a mysterious property that lures us in with the promise of fulfilling our desires and allaying our fears. It is not dissimilar to when a person becomes an object of desire and their illusory qualities activate one's yearning.[33] In this sense, 'the market is driven by the desire to attain this object, i.e. for the prices in the market to coincide with the true value of the assets traded in the market'.[34]

Although the value and price of Bitcoin cannot fundamentally coincide, this structural impossibility creates a space where desires and fantasies can play out. Young investors obsessively follow cryptocurrency price indices and exchange information about market trends. They seek out stories and narratives that legitimate their investment decisions. They believe that knowledge that arises from such narratives can resolve the discrepancy between value and price, and they derive performative pleasure from their incessant monitoring of the market and from making trades. In this sense, investors gain pleasure from circling the object of their desire and from the endless chase to acquire it. What drives their passion is a fetishised object of money and 'the fantasy of beating the market'.[35] For them, it is the elusive object that will confer them status and freedom from their cruel predicament. Investors commonly say things such as 'the market is not interesting today' (implying low volatility) or 'we need to beat the market'. They see the market as a mysterious order that operates according to its own intrinsic law. Such investors retain the belief, though, in their ability to analyse and predict cryptocurrency prices, to outsmart the market and their competitors.

This speculative way of life, in which leverage is used to pre-empt the future, leads to a life dominated by uncertainty, contingency, and instability. But financial markets thrive on uncertainty and neoliberal rationality asserts that finance is the best means of attaining security. And so, for desperate youth, loan and leverage opportunities seem to promise future safety. The precarious lives of young investors is a consequence of a financialised socio-economic structure, but it is, paradoxically, also in finance where the young find hope for redemption. For the Sampo generation, financial investment has become 'the last narrative of hope, ... [the last] opportunity to realise the attractive ideal of economic freedom'.[36] The very source of their despair is transformed into a bastion of hope. The result is a bad dialectic in which the opposites of despair and hope are united in an inverted form.

From an ascetic work ethic to an investment in uncertainty

During their country's developmental regime from the 1960s to the late 1980s, South Koreans shared a mass utopia of industrial modernity founded on the belief that hard work would lead to a stable, respectable life and happiness.[37] The generation that grew up in the neoliberal era harboured no such expectations. For this later generation, hard work was no guarantee, with the future being one of unbridled uncertainty. But embracing this uncertainty has become the basis of new utopian visions. Nowadays, uncertainty appears in a near mystical light, offering young Koreans what they desperately want, which is an end to their precarity and the attainment of stable lives.

Arjun Appadurai foregrounds the link between uncertainty, subjectivity, and speculation in an analysis of Max Weber's argument in *The Protestant Ethic*.[38] According to Weber, when confronting the uncertainty of salvation, those of the Reformed faith sought assurance of divine election through vocational activity. Because salvation is already foreordained and one's worldly actions cannot influence God's plan in any way, their conduct can offer little more than a sign of election. Calvinists must therefore wager that they themselves have been chosen and strive to reveal God's grace through their worldly endeavours. For them, doing good works is not a means of salvation, but 'a technical means of getting rid ... of the fear of damnation'.[39] In this way, their faithful and ascetic labour is 'a gamble on God's grace'.[40]

According to Lee Seung-cheol, this logic is inverted among the Sampo generation. They can no longer relieve their anxiety about their prospects for salvation through ascetic labour, as was possible for Calvinists. So they seek salvation through finance instead. 'For labourers who are disillusioned by the hopelessness and despair of labour, speculation in uncertain financial markets is suggested as the way of salvation.'[41] Young investors view work life and wage income as safe assets that allow them to make risky and aggressive investments. For them, work is not a valuable activity or a means of guaranteeing life, but merely a means of collecting seed money for future investment. Since hard work will not redeem them, all they can do is gamble in the hope that doing so will reveal that they are one of the elected, one of the few who will escape an almost certain fate of crushing economic misery. Hence, they are no longer entrepreneurs who carefully manage their risk, but gamblers who bet on uncertainty. As Frank Knight long ago stated, only unpredictable uncertainty, not calculable and predictable risk, is a source of profit.[42] This is because, if a risk is predictable, it can be mitigated through insurance or managed as a cost. Young Korean investors may be epistemologically ignorant of this logic, but their actions show unconscious awareness of it. They typically rely on their 'animal spirits' in making investments, chanting the magic spell 'Let us go to the moon' for self-assurance. They test their luck several times a day on twenty-four-hour coin exchanges, hoping for the revelation of their positive fate. Where Calvinists found fleeting satisfaction through ascetic labour, young investors seek it within frenzied speculation.

Kim Soo-hyun, a young anthropologist, published a book after conducting field research in a 'trading room' in 2018–19. Trading rooms are shared offices where full-time individual investors gather to trade in stocks. One investor who Kim interviewed described the virtue of the trading room in terms of its immersion: 'it is so much fun that you lose track of time'. When his investments failed, though, he would become despairing. 'I go into a trance by 3:30 [when the stock market closes]. Afterwards, I regret and reflect. And then, I think to myself, "ah, what am I doing, am I crazy." '[43] But he and the other investors trade again the next day to escape their depression and bewilderment. They constantly oscillate between despair and hope. And it is the sliver of hope that keeps them going back. In this way, speculation staves off utter despondency for a frustrated youth. By immersing themselves in speculation, they turn their eyes away from a painful reality of economic inequality, climate crisis, and the global pandemic. For young Koreans, the belief that they, through stocks and Bitcoin, might be able to reverse their fortunes helps them to tolerate an otherwise hopeless reality. Describing the affective logic at work here, Kim writes, 'If they do not believe, they cannot stand it.'[44]

Would you like to join *Squid Game*?

Bitcoin is regarded as the last dream and hope for many of the Sampo generation in Korea. However, it is not a collective but an individualised dream. Not everyone can win in the secondary market, where only the redistribution, rather than the creation, of value transpires. Even if someone luckily succeeds in escaping the grim reality of neoliberalism, it changes not the structure of

this reality. The utopia to which young people aspire is a politically impotent one. Speculation is fetishised, increasingly serving
as a goal in itself, rather than a means to 'the good life'. But is
it not a daily task of capitalism to individualise and depoliticise
the aspirations of the masses, to keep them enamoured with unob-
tainable objects? If it is, then the cryptocurrency boom should not
be understood as simply the outcome of distributed ledger technology or a niche concern of geeks. The current obsession with
cryptocurrencies is rather the latest iteration of the recurring libidinal dynamics of capitalism, which has long established itself as the
dominant social relation by mobilising our desires to overcome the
very lack that it creates. Cryptocurrency offers a new *objet petit a*
that sustains a 'cruel optimism' that a sense of wholeness might be
attained through money and finance.[45]

In retrospect, it is ironic that Bitcoin was born in the aftermath
of the 2008 financial crisis. A few years ago, it was argued that
Bitcoin and blockchain technology could transfer the control of
money and information from a small powerful elite to the masses.
The opposite, though, has occurred, with Bitcoin becoming a
speculative vehicle and credit loans to traders and transaction
fees offering new sources of revenue for financial institutions. The
Bitcoin market boomed because of macroeconomic conditions –
globally low interest rates and policies of quantitative easing –
rather than because of its technological potential. As the price of
Bitcoin skyrocketed, young investors briefly enjoyed 'sweet dreams'.
However, it is unlikely that these dreams will last. As inflation
deepened, the Bank of Korea raised interest rates in the second
half of 2021 and commercial banks subsequently increased their
lending rates. After the era of expansion, an era of austerity has
dawned, and as the prices of financial assets plummet, those who
are more leveraged suffer harshly.

For financial institutions, crisis always creates opportunity. As
we have seen in recent decades, governments guarantee the privatisation of profits and socialisation of losses on the grounds of some
firms being 'too big to fail'. But how will this play out for young
Korean investors? Will they be included in future bailout plans by
the government? Is their political voice sufficiently loud that the
state and capital cannot refuse coming to their financial rescue?

Will they be able to collectively unite and take political action to transform the structural contradictions and ills of society generated by neoliberal rationality, rather than blaming themselves for their failures? Can their anger at their hopeless conditions and their desire for salvation be turned into a truly liberating passion?

Notes

1 Todd Spangler, 'Squid Game is Decisively Netflix No. 1 Show of all Time with 1.65 Billion Hours Streamed in First Four Weeks, Company Says', *Variety*, November 16, 2021, https://variety.com/2021/digital/news/squid-game-all-time-most-popular-show-netflix-1235113196/ (accessed July 21, 2022).
2 Aja Romano, 'What Squid Game's Fantasies and Harsh Realities Reveal about Korea', Vox, October 6, 2021, www.vox.com/22704474/squid-game-games-korean-references-symbols (accessed July 21, 2022).
3 Jin Yu Young, 'Behind the Global Appeal of "Squid Game", a Country's Economic Unease', *The New York Times*, October 6, 2021, www.nytimes.com/2021/10/06/business/economy/squid-game-netflix-inequality.html (accessed July 21, 2022).
4 CoinDesk Korea, '5.87 Million Users of the Four Major Exchanges, Average Daily Trading Value of 13 Trillion Won', May 28, 2021, www.coindeskkorea.com/news/articleView.html?idxno=73923 (accessed July 21, 2022).
5 CoinDesk Korea, '2.49 Million Registered Four Major Coin Exchanges in the First Quarter', April 21, 2021 www.coindeskkorea.com/news/articleView.html?idxno=73456 (accessed July 21, 2022).
6 Giuseppe Bertola, Richard Disney, and Charles Grant, eds, *The Economics of Consumer Credit* (Cambridge, MA: The MIT Press, 2006), 2.
7 George A. Akerlof and Robert J. Shiller, *Animal Spirits: How Human Psychology Drives the Economy, and Why It Matters For Global Capitalism* (Princeton, NJ: Princeton University Press, 2009).
8 On this subject, see Pierre Dardot and Christian Laval, *The New Way of the World: On Neoliberal Society* (London: Verso, 2014); Michel Feher, 'Self-Appreciation; or, The Aspirations of Human Capital', *Public Culture* 21, no. 1 (2009): 21–41; Randy Martin, *Financialization of Daily Life* (Philadelphia, PA: Temple University

Press, 2002); and Nikolas Rose, *Powers of Freedom: Reframing Political Thought* (Cambridge: Cambridge University Press, 1999).

9 Paul Langley, *The Everyday Life of Global Finance: Saving and Borrowing in Anglo-America* (Oxford: Oxford University Press 2008).

10 Dongjin Seo, *Ca-yu-ŭi ŭi-chi cha-ki-kye-pal-ŭi ŭi-chi* (Paju: Tol-pe-kae, 2009); Cheolung Choi, 'Il-sang-ŭi kŭm-yung-hwa-wa t'u-ki-chŏk salm-ŭi yŏk-sŏl', *Korean Journal of Converging Humanities* 8, no. 3 (2020): 181–209.

11 Albert O. Hirschman, *The Passions and the Interests* (Princeton, NJ: Princeton University Press, 2013); Martijn Konings, *The Emotional Logic of Capitalism: What Progressives Have Missed* (Stanford, CA: Stanford University Press, 2015).

12 Konings, *The Emotional Logic of Capitalism*, 76.

13 Foucault was notoriously resistant to psychoanalysis and critical of Lacan in particular. Many have since commented on the methodological and political complications associated with any encounter between these two figures. See, for example, the discussion in Joan Copjec, ed., *Supposing the Subject* (London: Verso, 1994); Fabio Vighi and Heiko Feldner, *Žižek: Beyond Foucault* (Basingstoke: Palgrave Macmillan, 2007), chapters 8–10; and Ilan Kapoor, *Confronting Desire: Psychoanalysis and International Development* (Ithaca, NY: Cornell University Press, 2020), chapter 2. The present chapter does not propose a synthesis of Lacan and Foucault's respective frameworks or commitments; it rather seeks a way of using them both to help understand South Korea's libidinal economic history.

14 Jang-sup Shin and Ha-joon Chang, *Restructuring Korea Inc.: Financial Crisis, Corporate Reform, and Institutional Transition* (London: Routledge, 2003).

15 Naomi Klein, *The Shock Doctrine: The Rise of Disaster Capitalism* (London: Penguin, 2008).

16 Cheolung Choi, 'P'o-yong-chŏk kŭm-yung-ŭi yŏk-sŏl: pin-kon-san-ŏp-ŭi hyŏng-sŏng-kwa wi-hŏm-ŭi kae-in-hwa', *Social Science Studies* 27, no. 2 (2019): 38–87, at 54.

17 *Ibid.*

18 Economic Statistics System of Bank of Korea, http://ecos.bok.or.kr (accessed July 21, 2022).

19 Bank of Korea, *Financial Stability Report*, October 2013 (Seoul: Bank of Korea, 2013); Bank of Korea, *Financial Stability Report*, December 2021 (Seoul: Bank of Korea, 2021).

20 Jemin Lee, *Oe-hwan-wi-ki-wa kŭ hu-ŭi han-kuk kyŏng-che* (Seoul: Han-ul-a-k'a-te-mi, 2017), 207.

21 Seo, *Ca-yu-ŭi ŭi-chi cha-ki-kye-pal-ŭi ŭi-chi.*
22 Michel Foucault, *The Birth of Biopolitics: Lectures at the Collège de France, 1978–1979* (New York: Palgrave Macmillan, 2008), 243.
23 Wendy Brown, *Undoing the Demos: Neoliberalism's Stealth Revolution* (New York: Zone Books, 2015).
24 Feher, 'Self-Appreciation', 34.
25 Korean Contingent Workers' Center, 'Economically Active Population Census Additional Survey Analysis by Work Type', August 2010.
26 Hongjoong Kim, *Ma-ŭm-ŭi sa-hoe-hak* (Seoul: Mun-hak-tong-ne, 2009).
27 Yunhap News, 'The Rise in Apartment Land Prices in Seoul Under the Current Governments Soared', December 3, 2020, https://n.news.naver.com/mnews/article/001/0012057755?sid=102 (accessed July 21, 2022).
28 Quoted in Seungcheol Lee, 'Magical Capitalism, Gambler Subjects: South Korea's Bitcoin Investment Frenzy', *Cultural Studies* 36, no. 1(2022): 96–119, at 100.
29 Quoted in *ibid.*, 102.
30 Slavoj Žižek, *The Sublime Object of Ideology* (London: Verso, 1989), 184.
31 Ole Bjerg, *Making Money: The Philosophy of Crisis Capitalism* (London: Verso, 2014), 21–24.
32 Slavoj Žižek, *How to Read Lacan* (New York: W.W. Norton & Co., 2006), 66.
33 Noam Yuran, *What Money Wants: An Economy of Desire* (Stanford, CA: Stanford University Press, 2014), 68.
34 Bjerg, *Making Money*, 29.
35 *Ibid.*, 39.
36 Soo-hyun Kim, *Kae-mi-nŭn wae sil-p'ae-e-to pul-ku-ha-ko kye-sok t'u-cha-ha-nŭn-ka?* (Seoul: Min-um-sa, 2021), 336.
37 Susan Buck-Morss, *Dreamworld and Catastrophe: The Passing of Mass Utopia in East and West* (Cambridge, MA: The MIT Press, 2002).
38 Arjun Appadurai, 'The Ghost in the Financial Machine', *Public Culture* 23, no. 3 (2011): 517–39.
39 Max Weber, *Protestant Ethic and the Spirit of Capitalism* (London: Routledge, 2001), 69.
40 Appadurai, 'The Ghost in the Financial Machine', 521.
41 Lee, 'Magical Capitalism, Gambler Subjects', 10.
42 Frank H. Knight, *Risk, Uncertainty and Profit* (Boston, MA: Houghton Mifflin, 1921).

43 Kim, *Kae-mi-nŭn wae sil-p'ae-e-to pul-ku-ha-ko kye-sok t'u-cha-ha-nŭn-ka?*, 303.
44 *Ibid.*, 338.
45 Lauren Berlant, *Cruel Optimism* (Durham, NC: Duke University Press, 2011).

10

Financialising the eschaton

Amin Samman and Stefano Sgambati

'What do you get when you cross an entire generation raised during a never-ending recession with an app that lets you gamble for a shot at never having to worry about rent money ever again?' You get the twenty-first-century equivalent of a bullet to the head of the body financial. Or at least that is the dark fantasy expressed in one of the many memes associated with the GameStop bubble of early 2021. In this case, a silent clip from the 2019 film *Joker* depicting the on-air execution of a talk show host is parody-subtitled to resemble an episode of CNBC's *Mad Money* with Jim Cramer.[1] The conversation stages a clash between two opposing perspectives (young versus old, millennials versus boomers, online retail investors versus professional money managers), and when the Joker delivers his punchline, stock indexes for the world's top exchanges flash losses in red over the blood spattered scene. A grin cracks across his face as the indexes quickly recover. Though on the gorier end of the spectrum, YouTube videos such as this reveal how class warfare today takes shape through a specific form of apocalyptic imagination, characteristic of financial society and built on an underlying libidinal economy of leverage.

Towards the end of January 2021, hundreds of thousands of day traders crowded onto online trading platforms to buy shares and call options of US video game retailer company GameStop (NYSE: GME). These levered-up investments were sending the value of GameStop shares through the roof, which jumped from less than $40 on January 20 to a trading high of $480 only a week later. It soon emerged that the day traders were rallying on a subreddit forum, *r/wallstreetbets* (WSB), and as TV pundits like Cramer struggled to make sense of this twist, the Redditors began to target other 'unloved' stocks shorted by major hedge funds. The share prices of BlackBerry, Nokia, AMC Entertainment, American Airlines, and other companies climbed considerably. The hedge funds suffered losses of about $20 billion. It was a dirty protest at the gates of Wall Street, a form of class warfare waged from below through the very means of contemporary finance. But it was also a washout, as the day of reckoning that financial elites feared was once again postponed, deferred, rolled over. In both respects, the figure of the *eschaton* – the 'end of days' – connects the functioning of financial markets to the fantasies of those who live under their sway, and in this chapter we aim to articulate the contentious politics of financial society in these terms.

Our central claim is that the machinery of finance feeds off apocalyptic thinking on a day-to-day basis. This is not the same as saying that there is a booming market for catastrophe bonds, although of course there is.[2] Rather, the point is that being in debt, whether by a small amount for consumption purposes or a large amount for investment purposes (i.e., leverage) entails an orientation towards a future point in time at which one's debts must be repaid, a final settling of accounts. This is precisely the structure of apocalyptic prophecy in Western religion and Christian eschatology in particular, only now fed through the temporal mechanisms of capitalist money and finance. As Dominic Pettman points out, 'however we describe the object that lies at the end of history ... it inevitably becomes the focus for intense cathexis – the libidinal transference of value'.[3] The *financial eschaton* is no exception. And yet financialisation also contributes to an ongoing transformation in the form and function of eschatology whose significance we have yet to fully grasp, let alone come to terms with. Frank Kermode was among the first to note this broader shift in his 1967 book *The Sense of an Ending*.

It used to be that an apocalyptic vision would tell you when and how the world would end ('the older, sharply predictive apocalypse'). But with the rise of modern systems of knowledge and communication, Kermode argues, 'eschatology is stretched over the whole of history, the End is present at every moment'.[4] Hans Magnus Enzensberger said something similar a decade later, when he declared an end to the finality traditionally associated with the archetype of apocalypse.[5] Prescient though they were, neither could anticipate the extent to which the ascendancy of finance would aggravate this temporal condition. Building on Minskyan accounts of money and finance, we argue that the current financial system operates on the basis of a 'rolling apocalypse', perpetually scheduling and deferring millions of endpoints around which lives and livelihoods are organised.[6] The financialisation of capitalism in this way installs eschatology at the heart of daily life, binding the contemporary subject to the ends of finance through the unending circulation and leveraging of debt. We all live under the shadow of the financial eschaton, no matter how we find ourselves plugged into the financial machine, and the result is a transference onto indebtedness of all the psychological charge previously reserved for the end of history. This has significant consequences for how we think about debt, about financial economies of desire, and about the fantasies that motivate contemporary forms of market activism.

In what follows, we develop this argument through each of these themes in turn. First, we link the creation and accumulation of money to the circulation of unpayable debts and the rolling apocalypse of contemporary finance. Second, we sketch the contours of an associated and highly divisive libidinal economy of leverage, contrasting its signal moods of fear and loathing with the moral economy of guilt typically ascribed to indebtedness. Finally, we return to the case of the GameStop bubble, analysing the duelling forms of financial eschatology that turned the stock market, however fleetingly, into a site of apocalyptic class warfare. We conclude by briefly offering some further reflections on libidinal economy and class war in light of the outcome of the GameStop saga.

Rolling apocalypse of financial society

Conventional Marxist accounts of finance are apocalyptic at the level of their theory or philosophy of history, which is to say that they see the financial eschaton as an event that arrives through the historical development of capitalism. This has been the case for almost a century now, from the early revisionism of Rosa Luxemburg or Rudolf Hilferding through to Robert Brenner, David Harvey, and Giovanni Arrighi.[7] Despite their differences, these and other thinkers working in the Marxist tradition imagine financial markets as a space of overflow for capital accumulated through commodity production. Consequently, financial expansion appears as so much apocalyptic writing on the wall of history, the last resort of a capitalist class desperate to survive but destined to fall. In this way, contemporary narratives of financialisation carry with them strong theological undertones. But once you look at the mechanics of finance, rather than those of production, it becomes clear that apocalyptic thinking occupies a crucial place within the temporal universe of contemporary capitalism too. Unlike those visions of the end that came before it, this new financialised version of the eschaton is inscribed into money itself; it is endogenous to the operations and practices by which money is made. In order to make clear the meaning and significance of this claim, we must begin with the temporal duplicity of money.

It is no secret that money is a means of connecting present and future. On an everyday, individual level, holding money now implies options later. Keynes called this the 'liquidity preference' and he thought it told us something about our fear of the unknown.[8] The novelist Jorge Luis Borges suspected otherwise, describing money as a 'repertory of possible futures' and therefore the very embodiment of future time or future value.[9] Because money can be converted into anything, he reasons, it is an index of our freedom and imagination. 'It can be an evening in the suburbs. It can be the music of Brahms. It can be maps or chess or coffee. It can be the words of Epictetus teaching us to despise gold.'[10] But while money might make it possible for us to pursue dreams that would otherwise be impossible, at the same time, it might also tempt us into seeking nothing more and nothing other than money itself. And so, the call of money reaches us through temporal paradox: money is always as much the embrace of nothing now as it is the promise of something or indeed anything later. Money can only function as 'an object that allows infinite desire' if it conceals this paradox from our view, if it negates itself.[11]

This is why money is so often described in negative terms, as lack, void, or absence. Already in the fourth century BCE, Aristotle was puzzled by the strangeness of currency, deeming it necessary to remind his contemporaries not to idolise money as an absolute end.[12] Even though money seemed to have a life of its own, autonomously reproducing itself through usury and other practices of wealth-getting, it was in people's power 'to change it and make it useless'.[13] Yet we must be careful not to flatten money's history completely. While the Midas complex first identified by Aristotle might be as old as money itself, modern money does not simply negate itself by appearing to have a natural life of its own.[14] Modern money is the very performance of nothing: it is a promise of payment that functions as a means of payment *ad infinitum* – the 'vanishing point' of finance, as Brian Rotman puts it.[15] Unlike ancient coins, which were nothing but pieces of metal, dug from the ground and minted, modern money is a balance-sheet miracle of double-entry bookkeeping. It is created *ex nihilo* by banks as they leverage their positions in other people's debts; in turn, as it is invested and saved, money is entrusted to the banking system and returned to a state of potentiality. During this fleeting, borrowed existence, money works by producing a constant forgetting of where it comes from, by shrouding itself in mystery. After all, 'where something so important [as making money] is involved, a deeper mystery seems only decent'.[16]

And so, money's duplicity plays out through the temporality of our social system and its financial structure, rather than some timeless riddle or cosmic joke. Money today is created and accumulated only through the circulation of unpayable debts, and it is precisely for this reason that anyone who spends some of their time pursuing money – which, let's face it, means almost everyone – ends up attached to a future punctuated by balance sheet events. In this sense, the eschaton is no longer simply a theological concept or even a future event; it is a temporal figure intrinsic to the operations of contemporary financial capitalism. To use a somewhat different terminology, we could say that apocalyptic revelation is the spirit of the new 'asset economy'.[17] But rather than simply *owning* assets, it is *owing* money – and specifically using debt for investment purposes (i.e., leverage) – that gives fullest expression to this. How so?

Well, first of all, the financial eschaton haunts the community of money. The in-built leverage of contemporary finance means that the machinery of money-making could breakdown at any second, and anyone who deals in debt knows deep down how fragile it all is. Meanwhile, this outcome, which would be a catastrophe for many, is routinely denied and repressed in the very act of making money. As we have already suggested, the game of money-making is not really one of counting and settling debts as liabilities, but one of discounting and capitalising debts as assets that accumulate on the portfolios of banks, investors, and money-managers. This is another way of saying that the end or *telos* of modern money is not to functionally enable payments and therefore the final settlement of debts. On the contrary, as Hyman Minsky recognised, the creation and accumulation of money rests on a regime of debt discounting wherein the circulation of money assumes the shape of a spiral of unpayable debts.[18]

Writing shortly after Minsky, Jean Baudrillard explicitly tied this to the fate of apocalyptic thought: 'the debt will never be paid. No debt will ever be paid. The final counts will never take place … There will be no judgment day for this virtual bankruptcy.'[19] He was onto something for sure. The day of reckoning indeed never comes, but that is because it is always deferred or rolled over for the time being. As long as there is money to be made then payments can be deferred, debts can be rolled over, and securities can continue to accumulate on portfolios. In that sense, making money is a means of buying time,[20] and because of this, it reveals not just the impossibility of redemption, but also the harnessing of this very impossibility by the logic of financial economy. The final rendering of accounts between creditors and debtors will always happen tomorrow, never today, and the idea that one day speculative investments might derail the system of debt financing only serves to feed this system with the churn it requires. Spiralling debts, rolling apocalypse.

Libidinal economy of leverage

Understanding the financial economy described above in terms of the desires that traverse and fuel it, which is our intent here, requires that we depart from another cluster of conventions that would have us associate debt with guilt and guilt with a kind of powerlessness. The unlikely source of this dogma is Nietzsche, whose short commentary on debt in *The Genealogy of Morals* became a touchstone for accounts of indebtedness and subjectivity in the wake of the 2008 financial crisis.[21] This in turn has helped to produce an image of the contemporary subject as guilt-ridden and thereby enslaved or controlled, forever shouldering both the economic and existential burden of unpayable debts.[22] In the age of neoliberal finance, we are told, debt is a mechanism by which creditor-elites govern, discipline, and prey on growingly indebted masses. Among the different versions of this argument, Maurizio Lazzarato's is one of the first and certainly the most influential, so we begin here by briefly outlining his account of debt and guilt.

In his 2011 book *The Making of the Indebted Man*, Lazzarato develops a genealogy of debt by reading Nietzsche through Marx then Deleuze and Guattari.[23] From Nietzsche, he borrows the idea that taking on debt entails a promise, duty, or obligation on the part of the debtor to repay at some later point that cannot help but tame or domesticate the character of the debtor; from Deleuze and Guattari's Marx, he takes the idea that this way of governing society has been unleashed on a worldwide scale through financialisation and the shift from finite to infinite debt associated with capitalist credit money. The result is a bleak picture of permanent guilt before unpayable debts.

> We are no longer the inheritors of original sin but rather of the debt of preceding generations. 'Indebted man' is subject to a creditor-debtor power relation accompanying him throughout his life, from birth to death. If in times past we were indebted to the community, to the gods, to our ancestors, we are henceforth indebted to the 'god' Capital.[24]

There is much in Lazzarato's account worth keeping, above all the observation – consistent with those of Minsky and Baudrillard mentioned above – that through the rise of global financial markets, debt acquires a life of its own, distinct to the one it led when still tethered to the logics of industrial production. But if debt 'represents the economic and subjective engine of the modern-day economy', as Lazzarato has suggested, then what are we to make of the community of money that sits atop this economy, the bankers, investors, and money-managers?[25] What is their place within the libidinal economy of debt? Are they too 'accountable to and guilty before capital ... the Great Creditor?'[26]

In a certain respect, yes, they are. Financial elites are reliant on the system of debt financing for their enrichment, so you could say they owe it something, maybe everything. But by the same token, it seems stupid to lump them together with the indebted mass of humanity and ascribe to everyone the self-same moods: guilty obedience, dutiful sacrifice, universal victimhood. At the root of this problem, we think, is a totalising conception of debt that leaves no way of distinguishing between different kinds of debtors and the psychic charge associated with their debts.

Terms like 'generalised debt' or 'universal indebtedness' surely do capture something important about contemporary financial capitalism. 'The fact that we are all debtors, or are becoming ones, means that there are no more real creditors. Every creditor is a debtor to another, in a chain whose first link has been lost.'[27] But the infinite debt that circles the globe today is kept in motion by different kinds of borrowing and different kinds of borrowers. There are those who borrow to buy goods, to pay rent, to fund their studies and make themselves attractive to employers. These are the 99%, the indebted masses for whom indebtedness has become 'a condition in which to invest'.[28] Then there are those who borrow for an altogether different set of investment purposes, to invest in real estate, stocks and bonds, and an array of more complex, structured financial products, many of which are built precisely on the debts of others. These are the 1%, the indebted elites for whom indebtedness is a ticket to power, wealth, and luxury. Indeed, over the past forty years (and especially in the last two decades), the rich and ultra-rich have made most of their gains not by lending to the rest of society (let alone to the poor), but by borrowing money with a view to leveraging their positions in financial and property markets.[29] Rentiers, shareholders, and financial market investors have been able to make high returns only because their asset portfolios have been so levered-up.

All this puts paid to the notion that we are united by our indebtedness. The logic of leverage has created a fractured society of debtors, indeed a new form of class struggle, which cannot be understood through the traditional lens of the creditor–debtor relation analysed by Nietzsche and Lazzarato. Class struggle in the age of financial capitalism is a struggle between debtors *and* debtors, between the greater borrowers and the lesser ones, the indebted rich and the burdened poor. This is straightforwardly a claim about the politics of finance, but it is also a claim about the culture of finance that links back to our earlier commentary on apocalyptic thinking, which we can now better describe in terms of *duelling financial eschatologies*. As we will show in the next section, while access to and control over the means of leverage are the material grounds of this new conflict, the conflict itself is animated by distinct configurations of apocalyptic desire. The seemingly universal experience of *being in debt* is therefore but a screen, beneath which operates not a moralising economy of guilt, but an amoral, libidinal economy of leverage.

Apocalyptic class warfare on the stock market

If contemporary banking works on the basis of a rolling apocalypse inscribed into money itself, then the figure of the financial eschaton divides humanity in two. For a small minority, leverage has proven to be the key to winning at the game of money-making. For them, the apocalypse is something that can be rolled over to the next day, and in fact it *must* be rolled over if there is to be any money made today. But at the same time, these levered-up elites know that their wealth rests on borrowed time, that *they owe*, and that perhaps one day, maybe someday soon, their time will be up. Consequently, they live in fear of the financial eschaton, which represents for them an economic extinction event. Meanwhile, for the great majority, debt is experienced as an unsustainable, unending burden. Unlike the ultra-rich, the impoverished masses do not borrow to invest in housing or other financial assets, but mostly to finance consumption and pay bills for healthcare, education, and so on. After decades of austerity, these people are beginning to see they are being crucified on a cross of debt for 'sins' they have not committed or for which they are at best only marginally responsible. For them, the apocalypse is already here, and the prospect of a generalised financial meltdown, if anything, carries with it a promise of redemption that is currently denied them by the money they must earn now, the money they must pay today not to die insolvent tomorrow. The libidinal economy of leverage has in this way become a site of apocalyptic class warfare, fuelled by duelling forms of financial eschatology. We can see this clearly in the case of *r/wallstreetbets* and the GameStop saga.

WSB is a subreddit forum where disenfranchised Millennials and Gen Zers come together to boast about the next 'stonk' (big financial gain) or 'YOLO' (you only live once) investment – high-risk, high-reward bets on all sorts of securities. The forum rose to prominence in late January 2021, when hundreds of thousands of WSB investors effectively declared war on Wall Street as they started hunting down a few hedge funds that were aggressively shorting GME and other similar stocks. Over the span of a few weeks, the community grew from fewer than 1 million to more than 6 million subscribers, many of whom swarmed zero-commission trading platforms, such as Robinhood, Webull, and E*Trade, to take advantage of their 'infinite leverage' glitch and go long on rapidly appreciating GME stocks.[30] They were immediately stigmatised by mainstream media analysts as a horde of ill-informed meme investors who 'were bored, sitting at home with nothing to do, often no work to attend [to], and few things to spend their extra cash on'.[31] 'This [was] not the sort of democratisation of finance that the finely tailored Davos set discussed over room-temperature sparkling water',[32] but something more dangerous – a cocktail of idiocy, boredom, and resentment at great risk of spilling over into mob rule and meaningless destruction.[33]

Wall Street had good reason to be alarmed because these idiot meme investors were causing a shitstorm in the markets with a play known as a 'gamma squeeze' (explained below). Melvin Capital and other hedge funds had been shorting GME stocks by an impossible 138%, helped by some broker-dealers – most notably Citadel, a leading market-maker in US equities. This was a blatant instance of naked short selling, which is illegal in the USA, but most financial talking heads did not seem at all bothered by that. This was business as usual. What was unusual was that smart money had been outsmarted by self-described 'retards', 'apes', and 'degenerates' who were not following the usual dumb money script and piling into the most obvious stocks. Instead, they were going *against* the herd, placing bets on the basis of price-to-earnings (P/E) ratios, price-to-book (P/B) ratios, and other key business parameters. WSB investors were essentially following principles of 'value investing' or 'contrarian investing' – a type of investment strategy pursued by the likes of Warren Buffet, George Soros, and John Maynard Keynes. And they had got it right.

In September 2019, financial analyst Keith Gill, future WSB community hero and 'legendary degenerate' also known by the name of *u/deepfuckingvalue*, posted on WSB a screenshot of a trade consisting of a roughly $53,000 long position in GME shares – an investment that by January 28, 2021 had generated a gain of nearly $50 million, as more and more day traders joined the squeeze.[34] It was a 'gamestonk', as Elon Musk tweeted. Both hedge funds and their broker-dealers began to feel the heat; they were massively unhedged and started to scramble for shares to cover their potentially unlimited losses. This caused GME share prices to climb even further, adding more fuel to a GameStop rocket that was going 'to the fucking Moon', jumping from less than $40 on January 20 to a trading high of $480 per share on January 27. Such was the power of a gamma squeeze.

Crucially, for this to be effective, WSB investors had to buy and 'hold the line' at any cost. As one anonymous investor put it, '[w]e needed people with diamond hands, not paper hands – meaning that even if the stock dropped by a lot, you still didn't sell. *You never sold.*'[35] By its very nature, this type of strategy forged a sense of solidarity among day traders, leading in turn to a politicisation of the very objective of the gamma squeeze. For a sizeable number of investors ready to lose everything, this was not just about the money anymore – it was about sending a message.

> For all the recessions they caused. For all the jobs and homes people have lost. For all the people that can't pay for college because minimum wage has stagnated while wall street gets rich. For all the retail traders they left holding the bag. For all the times they got bailed out with our tax money while we got nothing.[36]

The financial establishment was caught completely off-guard. It had no idea that its own weapons could be used to profane the temple of high finance, that leverage itself could be used to turn the spectacle of finance into a spectacle about something other than just making money … *while making money!* For once the joke was on Wall Street, as the retards were willing to let everyone burn, including themselves, just to make a statement. By never exiting their GameStop investment – that is, by never closing their accounts and cashing out – they could stop the money game for just a moment, thereby bringing a relatively small financial eschaton down on some hedge funds and their buddies. Hope, anger, revenge, despair, redemption – such details did not matter. What mattered was *the sound of it*, which must have felt like a huge 'fuck you' reverberating off the walls of Citadel and other market-makers. It was not enough to bring down Wall Street (after all, Rome was not burned in a day), but it was sufficient to show that even the money gods can bleed.

Of course, the financial insurgency had to be crushed, no matter what. On January 28, to ensure 'orderly markets', Robinhood restricted purchases of GME shares on its platform. The move was immediately followed by other online trading platforms, which *de facto* closed the gates of leverage to WSB investors. Meanwhile, hedge funds faced no such restrictions as they continued to buy GME shares at a now controlled price. The financial eschaton was forestalled and the price of GameStop shares plummeted. One day later, to add insult to injury, it was revealed that Robinhood had been selling order-flow information to Citadel, the broker-dealer behind Melvin Capital's shorting attempt and a subsequent bailout, as well as to other high-frequency trading firms whose business consists in trading ahead of retail investors. This type of insider trading is known as 'frontrunning' or 'tailgating': an illegal prac-tice of market manipulation that is very common among market-makers – including big banks such as JP Morgan – but which, like naked short selling, is hard to detect. The revelation that Robinhood was 'nothing more than a client-facing subsidiary of Citadel, one which pretends to offer free trades to tens of millions of young, naive traders, but in reality merely allows Citadel Securities to trade ahead and/or against this orderflow', killed morale in the WSB com-munity – #gamestomp.[37] The rest is history. Many retail traders lost everything, a few big asset managers like BlackRock silently raked in billions, while the rest of us got back to living our new normal lives. We owe it to the infamous Michael Burry, immortalised by actor Christian Bale in *The Big Short*, for best capturing the moral of the story in a now deleted tweet.

> The #mainstreetrevolution is a myth. Zero commissions and gamified apps were designed to feed flows to the two most influential WS trading houses. A few HFs got hurt, but if retail is moving toward more trading and away from fundamentals, WS owns that game. #Stonks by design.[38]

Indebted to the end

In its community guidelines, *r/wallstreetbets* states that '[n]obody cares about your political opinions. If it's not about taking advantage of the political to make money, then leave that baggage at home. WSB is not the stage for your lazy political regurgitation, nor will it be used as a propaganda mouthpiece by anybody.'[39] This formal rejection of politics should not surprise us. The story of GameStop expresses a kind of nihilism that comes easy to many these days. But this is not to say that the WSB insurgency was apolitical – far from it. Even Keith Gill, who at the time went on a paper of record to clarify that he 'wasn't a rabble-rouser out to take on the establishment, just someone who believes investors can find value in unloved stocks', today writes in his subreddit profile (*r/deepfuckingvalue*) that 'it was never about the carrot'.[40] What *was* it about, then?

At first glance, Gill and the hundreds of thousands of degenerates that responded to his call to arms were glorifying a culture of extreme leverage and risk in the name of *nothing*. Their insurgency, like other contemporary forms of resistance to global capitalism – from ISIS to Extinction Rebellion – seemed in effect unable to think of any better course of action than self-destruction: YOLO until you die.[41] For some, this type of suicidal anti-politics nevertheless bears a millenarian promise of organising the great unwashed around the use of the enemy's weapons, such that leverage and options trading might one day become a means of collectively profiting from the failures of a perpetually bankrupt financial establishment.[42] Others see little chance of a transformative politics emerging from financial fanaticism. Both views miss a crucial point and this relates to money. As we argued earlier, money is always as much the embrace of nothing now as it is the promise of something or indeed anything later, a paradox that only works to the extent that we continue to play, or endlessly watch others play, the game of money-making. By openly 'gamifying' the game and playing it like the professionals do – guiltlessly – the WSB movement inadvertently uncovered something profound about financial life today. As they burned their pay cheques, they showed how value investing and fundamental analysis are just ways of filling a void at the heart of the financial system, a void that has made everything – including their money and their lives – valueless. And so, to hell with money, they say; everyone gets burned!

Alas, 2021 was not the year they finally immanentised the eschaton.[43] Instead, it was the year we learned that even the eschaton has been financialised. The GameStop saga gave us a glimpse into the abyss, but no Great Awakening followed, and that is because the financial system is fuelled by apocalyptic obsession, it feeds on it, regardless of the duelling forms this can take. Fear on Wall Street, loathing on Main Street – either way, *the game does not stop*. We have described this totalising culture of money-making as a libidinal economy of leverage: a sophisticated debt cult that, like any other cult, is probably not going to end well. We do not venture to guess when it will end, nor what might cause it to end. Maybe it will never end. After all, disenfranchised youths are still chasing the next stonk on WSB and other online forums, as if the sacrifice of those who went 'long on $rope' with GameStop taught them nothing. So the apocalypse keeps rolling, untroubled by the fact that no one really believes there is any deep value to be found at the bottom of the economy. As Nietzsche once said of religious ideas and the Church, we could say today about financial securities, options trading, and zero-commission apps – that all these 'sinister inventions are … merely so many instruments of torture, systems of cruelty' by which the money-manager 'becomes master and remains master'.[44]

Notes

1 'Joker WSB Jim Cramer Meme |r/wallstreetbets Funny Videos| Wall Street Bets Mad Money', WSB Meme Videos, YouTube, April 1, 2021, www.youtube.com/watch?v=N0SJwKkpyRI&ab_channel=You%27reFullofBaloney (accessed September 2, 2022).
2 In March 2021, the Danish Red Cross offered the first such bond for volcanic eruptions. The bond will 'pay-out whenever a volcanic ash plume reaches a certain height and the prevailing wind directs the ash fall towards vulnerable communities'. See 'World's First Catastrophe Bond for Volcanic Eruptions to Raise Disaster Aid', Howden Group, March 22, 2021, www.howdengroup.com/catastrophe-bond-volcanic-eruptions (accessed September 2, 2022).
3 Dominic Pettman, *After the Orgy: Towards a Politics of Exhaustion* (New York: State University of New York Press, 2002), 3.

4 Frank Kermode, *The Sense of an Ending: Studies in the Theory of Fiction* (Oxford: Oxford University Press, 1967), 26.
5 'Finality, which was formerly one of the major attributes of the apocalypse, and one of the reasons for its power of attraction, is no longer vouchsafed us.' Hans Magnus Enzensberger, 'Two Notes on the End of the World', *New Left Review* 110, July–August (1978): 74–80, at 75.
6 The term 'rolling apocalypse' is borrowed from Rosalind Williams, 'The Rolling Apocalypse of Contemporary History', in *Aftermath: The Cultures of the Economic Crisis*, ed. Manuel Castells, João Caraça, and Gustavo Cardoso (Oxford: Oxford University Press, 2012), 17–43.
7 See Giovanni Arrighi, *The Long Twentieth Century: Money, Power, and the Origins of Our Times* (London: Verso, 1994). Arrighi's account in this book has become emblematic of the world-historical weight given by contemporary Marxist thought to the term 'financialisation'. Compare this with, for example, Costas Lapavitsas' *Profiting Without Producing: How Finance Exploits Us All* (London: Verso, 2014) or Wolfgang Streeck's *How Will Capitalism End? Essays on a Failing System* (London: Verso, 2016), each of which upholds both the productivist method and apocalyptic spirit of Arrighi's analysis.
8 According to Keynes, we hold onto money not in order to actualise any of the futures we wish for, but as a 'barometer of the degree of our distrust of our own calculations and conventions concerning the future'. John Maynard Keynes, *The General Theory of Employment, Interest and Money* (London: Macmillan, 1936), 216.
9 Jorge Luis Borges, *A Personal Anthology* (London: Jonathan Cape, 1968), 131.
10 *Ibid.*
11 Noam Yuran, *What Money Wants: An Economy of Desire* (Stanford, CA: Stanford University Press, 2014), 14.
12 Aristotle, *Politics* (Oxford: Oxford University Press, 1998), 26, 1257b10–11.
13 Aristotle, *The Nicomachean Ethics* (Oxford: Oxford University Press, 2009), 89, 1133a30.
14 The Ancient Greek myth of King Midas, whose golden touch meant he could no longer eat, is widely used in both popular economics and psychology to pathologise greed or the desire for money. For a critical discussion of this tendency and an interesting account of the Midas myth too, see Yuran, *What Money Wants*, 13–77 and 181–221.
15 Brian Rotman, *Signifying Nothing: The Semiotics of Zero* (Basingstoke: Macmillan, 1987), 25.

16 John Kenneth Galbraith, *Money: Whence It Came, Where It Went* (Princeton, NJ: Princeton University Press, 2017), 22.

17 Lisa Adkins, Melinda Cooper, and Martijn Konings, *The Asset Economy: Property Ownership and the New Logic of Inequality* (Cambridge: Polity, 2020).

18 Hyman P. Minsky, *Stabilizing an Unstable Economy* (New York: McGraw-Hill, 1986).

19 Jean Baudrillard, 'Global Debt and Parallel Universe', in *Digital Delirium*, ed. Arthur Kroker and Marilouise Kroker (Montreal: New World Perspectives, 1997), 38.

20 This is a central thesis in Stefano Sgambati, 'The Significance of Money: Beyond Ingham's Sociology of Money', *European Journal of Sociology* 56, no. 2 (2015): 307–39.

21 The text in question is an essay called 'Guilt, Bad Conscience, and the Like', in Friedrich Nietzsche, *The Genealogy of Morals*, trans. Horace B. Samuel (Mineola, NY: Dover Publications, 2003), 34–66.

22 See, for example, David Graeber, *Debt: The First 5,000 Years* (New York: Melville House, 2011); Maurizio Lazzarato, *The Making of the Indebted Man: An Essay on the Neoliberal Condition*, trans. Joshua David Jordan (Los Angeles, CA: Semiotext(e), 2012); or Tim Di Muzio and Richard H. Robbins, *An Anthropology of Money: A Critical Introduction* (London: Routledge, 2017).

23 Lazzarato, *The Making of the Indebted Man*, 37–88.

24 *Ibid.*, 32. Lazzarato's remarks here recall Walter Benjamin's in his 1921 fragment on 'Capitalism as Religion'. According to Benjamin, capitalism is a cult with neither theology nor the possibility of atonement, only the endless production of debt and guilt: 'The nature of the religious movement which is capitalism entails endurance right to the end, to the point where God, too, finally takes on the entire burden of guilt, to the point where the universe has been taken over by that despair which is actually its secret hope.' In *Religion as Critique: The Frankfurt School's Critique of Religion*, ed. Eduardo Mendieta (London: Routledge, 2005), 260.

25 Lazzarato, *The Making of the Indebted Man*, 25.

26 *Ibid.*, 7.

27 Roberto Esposito, *Two: The Machine of Political Theology and the Place of Thought,* trans. Zakiya Hanafi (New York: Fordham University Press, 2015), 208.

28 Elettra Stimilli, *Debt and Guilt: A Political Philosophy*, trans. Stefania Porcelli (London: Bloomsbury, 2018), 123. See also Michel Feher, *Rated Agency: Investee Politics in a Speculative Age* (New York: Zone Books, 2018).

29 The supporting data for this claim is provided and discussed at length in Stefano Sgambati, 'Who Owes? Class Struggle, Inequality and the Political Economy of Leverage in the Twenty-First Century', *Finance and Society* 8, no. 1 (2022): 1–21.

30 At the time of writing, June 2022, the community counts 12.3 million subscribers. The infamous leverage glitch is explained in Ben Winck, 'Robinhood Has a "Free Money Cheat" that Allowed One User to Grow $4,000 into $1 Million through Infinite Leverage', *Business Insider*, November 5, 2019, https://markets.businessinsider.com/news/stocks/robinhood-infinite-leverage-free-money-cheat-user-1-million-2019-11-1028661632 (accessed September 2, 2022).

31 Katie Martin, 'Occupy Wall Street Spirit Returns as Traders Upset the Elites', *Financial Times*, January 28, 2021, www.ft.com/content/bcfb2252-f752-4177-a860-07dc66b0b9e8 (accessed September 2, 2022).

32 *Ibid.*

33 The link to Trumpism, White supremacy, and even 'Telegram Nazis' was made by many, including CNN editor-at-large Chris Cillizza. See 'How Trumpism Explains the GameStop Stock Surge', *CNN Politics*, January 27, 2021, https://edition.cnn.com/2021/01/27/politics/gamestop-stock-surge-trumpism/index.html (accessed September 2, 2022).

34 Gill is now listed on Wikipedia as a 'famous contrarian investor', alongside other more famous names like the aforementioned Buffet, Soros, and Keynes. See Wikipedia's entry on 'contrarian investing': https://en.wikipedia.org/wiki/Contrarian_investing (accessed September 2, 2022).

35 Anonymous, 'I Bought Tens of Thousands of Dollars of GameStop Stock. And I Have No Regrets', *The New Republic*, February 1, 2021, https://newrepublic.com/article/161182/bought-tens-thousands-dollars-gamestop-stock-no-regrets (accessed September 2, 2022).

36 Natasha Dailey, 'Some Redditors Say the GameStop Rally is Revenge against Wall Street for the 2008 Collapse', *Business Insider*, January 28, 2021, www.businessinsider.com/some-redditors-say-gamestop-rally-is-revenge-for-2008-collapse-2021-1?op=1 (accessed September 2, 2022).

37 ZeroHedge, 'Exposing the Robinhood Scam: Here's How Much Citadel Paid to Robinhood to Buy Your Orders', ZeroHedge, February 18, 2021, www.zerohedge.com/markets/exposing-robinhood-scam-heres-how-much-citadel-paid-robinhood-buy-your-orders (accessed September 2, 2022).

38 Cassandra (@michaeljburry), February 9, 2021.

39 www.reddit.com/r/wallstreetbets/wiki/contentguide/ (accessed September 2, 2022).

40 Julia-Ambra Verlaine and Gunjan Banerji, 'Keith Gill Drove the GameStop Reddit Mania. He Talked to the *Journal*', *The Wall Street Journal*, January 29, 2021, www.wsj.com/articles/keith-gill-drove-the-gamestop-reddit-mania-he-talked-to-the-journal-11611931696 (accessed September 2, 2022).

41 Sergei Klebnikov and Antoine Gara, '20-Year-Old Robinhood Customer Dies by Suicide after Seeing a $730,000 Negative Balance', *Forbes*, June 17, 2020, www.forbes.com/sites/sergeiklebnikov/2020/06/17/20-year-old-robinhood-customer-dies-by-suicide-after-seeing-a-730000-negative-balance/ (accessed September 2, 2022).

42 See, for instance, Luca, 'Wall Street Bets, Gamestop, and the End of Capitalism', Medium, January 29, 2021, https://luca2.medium.com/wall-street-bets-gamestop-and-the-end-of-capitalism-60469c2d5309

43 We allude here to the famous opening lines of *The Illuminatus! Trilogy*: 'It was the year when they finally immanentized the Eschaton.' Robert Shea and Robert Anton Wilson, 'Illuminatus! Part I: The Eye in the Pyramid', in *The Illuminatus! Trilogy* (London: Raven Books, 1998), 7. Like Gill and the Redditors, Shea and Wilson hoped to bring about some kind of Great Awakening by fomenting chaos and discord.

44 Friedrich Nietzsche, *The Anti-Christ*, trans. H. L. Mencken (New York: Alfred A. Knopf, 1931), 110.

11

Anxiety and self-sabotage in the neoliberal university

Aris Komporozos-Athanasiou and Max Haiven

In the wake of the 2008 financial crisis, Mark Fisher's theorisation of mental and emotional life under the disenchanted conditions of capitalist realism was deeply compelling for scholars.[1] His exploration of the chasm between, on the one hand, the relentless demand on individuals to become successful 'risk-taking' entrepreneurs of the self, and, on the other, the profound unlikelihood of finding success, let alone happiness or fulfilment, became emblematic for university students in the wake of the crisis. This was a generation who had at least some memory of a 'before', a moment of neoliberal optimism. But today a new generation is emerging into adulthood for whom neoliberalism, financialisation, and their anxieties are all they have *ever* known. As this new generation takes the stage, what forms of subjectivity, struggle, survival, and mutual aid are they inventing? And what might their emergence onto the stage imply for social and cultural critics of financialisation and its aftermaths?

In this chapter, we explore new tendencies within society and subjecthood that may be emerging among capitalism's anxious subjects, for whom risk management is no longer a triumphant imperative to embrace one's potential, but more a banal and fated norm. We take as our case study the Anglophone North Atlantic university and its increasingly anxious students. No person working in the university in these contexts can be unaware, anecdotally at least, of the drastic rise in anxiety among students and efforts by university administrators to address this. Media stories, government reports, and academic studies have been sounding the alarm for more than a decade, not shying away from terms like 'epidemic' or 'crisis' to describe the situation.[2]

Unfortunately, the 'epidemic of student anxiety' tends to be framed in three unhelpful ways. First, as the predictable and annoying plight of oversensitive, 'coddled' youngsters who have been so cushioned by liberal educational discourse, permissive parenting, and strident social justice rhetoric they cannot handle the rigors of the world; second, as the result of a generation raised on and addicted to social media platforms; or, third, as simply an individuated biomedical problem to be addressed by therapy or drugs.[3] There is an element of truth to all these explanations, but they fail to account for the anxiety-inducing elements of the overarching system of financialised capitalism that frames universities, parenting and teaching styles, social media and handheld technology, and biopharmaceutical intervention.

In this chapter, we ask a series of speculative questions about the subterranean cultural politics of anxiety in the neoliberal university. What will, or what can, come after the 'financialised subject' that has been the topic of our collective inquiries now for some years? Is it possible that financialised capitalism might inadvertently be generating a countervailing force at the level of subjecthood? And, if so, then what are the prospects that such subjects might recognise their commonality and band together to challenge the conditions of their misery? Would we critical scholars, who have trained ourselves to look to a now-familiar repertoire of protest tactics and rhetoric, be able to recognise their resistance and rebellion if they took unexpected new forms? By posing these questions, we are seeking the contours of a range of emergent political subjecthoods whose imaginings are fundamentally shaped by financialisation, but that also strive to *exceed* it. We focus, specifically, on university students' inchoate practices of resistance to the neoliberal university through anxious disengagement, practices that we suggest might be understood as forms of *sabotage* against an unacceptable future of financialised extraction and anxiety, for which the university strives to prepare them. Our argument is that what appears to be 'self-sabotaging' behaviour can be fruitfully interpreted as a form of nascent rebellion, an expression of collective refusal of the conditions faced by students in universities today.

In previous moments of capitalism, we have seen workers undertake what outside observers have thought of as 'self-defeating' and counter-productive acts of rebellion, including burning plantations, sabotaging machines, and destroying slums.[4] At the same time, as Thorstein Veblen argued powerfully over a century ago, capitalists themselves may also embrace sabotage as a core tactic for beating market competition and ensuring profitability – in the form of, for instance, keeping production 'short of capacity' through withdrawal, retardation, or the 'unemployment of plant and workmen'.[5] This already suggests how the politics of sabotage plays out through discourse: those whose interests are aligned with the reigning order have every reason to suggest that those who are oppressed by and oppose it are short-sighted, vindictive, and self-destructive in their resistance and refusal. Meanwhile, this rhetoric hides those qualities of the system itself. But as Gavin Muller argues, there is a utopian dream and a generative refusal at play in the collective actions of those who break the machines.[6]

In what follows, we consider today's neoliberal university as a key site of the reproduction and expansion of financialisation, especially at the level of subjecthood, and explore whether the 'anxiety epidemic' can be read as, in part, mass refusal or uncoordinated sabotage. We argue that students' anxious forms of resistance, notably their withdrawal and refusal to participate, are akin to other such moments in the history of capitalism, when sabotage was key to both the system's reproduction but also to forms of resistance. In our case, the productive apparatus being sabotaged is the subject itself: the target of value creation and extraction in an age of financialised cognitive capitalism. Without losing sight of the profound consequences that anxiety presents for individual students and institutions alike, we explore the possibilities emerging out of such a reframing of the current 'anxiety epidemic'.

We begin by outlining the way financialisation has raised a generation, now making their way through university, who are profoundly, indeed constitutively, anxious. We then turn to the way capitalism has historically both feared and sought to incorporate sabotage, including the way that finance itself represents a form of capitalist sabotage. Finally, we reframe students as workers within an apparatus of financialised cognitive capitalism and suggest that anxiety can fuel a particular form of sabotage.

The anxious neoliberal university

The plight of anxiety engulfing public-sector universities in the Anglophone North Atlantic and beyond is, by now, a well-documented and widely debated phenomenon.[7] In this context, students, teaching staff, and other denizens are increasingly governed by stress. The university itself is anxious about its place in the world and its ability to maintain a residual attachment to its founding values – the pursuit of knowledge, the cultivation of student capacities, and so on – in the face of rapid market-oriented restructuring and financial discipline.[8]

This anxiety crisis is intimately linked to an ongoing and intensifying student debt crisis. As Caitlin Zaloom has compellingly shown, middle-class families in countries such as the USA are agonising over swelling debt burdens (taking out second mortgages and draining retirement savings), in an escalating struggle to pay for university education, which further jeopardises their already battered financial security.[9] Pervasive indebtment has particularly devastating effects on working-class students, who are faced with vastly unequal paths to future employment while also being compelled to work alongside their studies.[10] There is perennial concern that such rising debts present a risk to their future ability to invest in housing, business enterprise, even their own social reproduction.

These stressors within the university are compounded by wider societal pressures on young people, including the rising cost of housing and increasingly austere and exploitative labour markets. Keir Milburn, for one, locates the political anxieties and tendencies of this generation in the gulf between, on the one hand, being unable to access assets like housing through which elder generations have secured future wealth and livelihood and, on the other, the dawning recognition that their privatised and increasingly debt-fuelled 'investments' in their own human capital are unlikely to be recompensed in future job markets.[11]

Financialised universities preside over a systematic and wholesale transfer of risk and responsibility to students. Yet their function as debt-fuelled 'promise-machines' is all but lost. Following the motto 'sacrifice today and hope for a reward in the (distant) future' simply becomes untenable in the precarious, anxious university, where horizons of possibility and promise fulfilment are foreclosed, out of reach – slowly cancelled, to recall Fisher's memorable phrase. The university becomes the antechamber of the financialised world of work, precariousness, and socio-economic conditions of relentless uncertainty. The politics of debt, however, does not merely point to the foreclosure of possibilities and narrowed future horizons; indebtment can also trigger a different kind of relationship with the present. It can induce forms of sociality and subjectivity that push beyond lenders' technologies of control.[12]

For all these reasons, the university makes for a particularly salient space in which to study the links between indebtment, anxiety, and sabotage. Beyond the familiar 'poverty of student life', there is a widely reported sense of cynicism, hopelessness, or avoidance prevalent among 'Generation Z' that seems wildly out-of-step with the polished optimism with which universities advertise their services as pathways to a 'good life'. It has become commonplace to note the tongue-in-cheek, post-ironic, meme-driven sentiments of this generation, which makes it difficult to track their political orientations on grids calibrated by their elders.[13] These developments call for fresh approaches to understanding the often surprising realignment of political constellations in the present.

What is undeniable is the rapid increase in reported anxiety among students.[14] Anxiety is an ambivalent descriptor because it names a wide spectrum of phenomena: the kind of embodied and episodic hyper-arousal common to all animals; the kind of existential dread that plagues human beings (especially those in disenchanted modern societies); the pervasive feeling of being unable to cope with circumstances; and, in its most extreme forms, a debilitating psychiatric condition that is widely studied, subdivided, and met with a range of therapeutic and pharmacological treatments. Despite this ambiguity, we retain the term and note that no statistics we have found disprove the claim that, in all its manifestations, anxiety is on the rise among almost all university students. In the most conservative sense, students declaring and seeking learning accommodations from their universities for professionally diagnosed anxiety-related disorders has increased nearly everywhere, with profound consequences. In a broader sense, self-reporting of debilitating anxiety among university students on surveys has also increased precipitously, leading many researchers, commentators, clinicians, and administrators to sound the alarm of a massive 'epidemic' on both sides of the North Atlantic.

The least controversial of our claims is simply that we should not insist on separating these disturbing trends from the experience of this generation growing up under, and understanding that they will graduate into, a financialised society whose undergirding libidinal economy is characterised by profound anxiety. The university is itself an institution that resonates with and reproduces the anxious logics of financialisation, and, in so doing, it provides the backdrop for new, more ambivalent practices of resistance and sabotage that are in some ways redrawing the map of university politics.

Techno-powered ambivalence

Students' immersion in the world of digital technologies is often seen as a key contributor to the 'anxiety epidemic' and is typically met by commentators with derision and cynicism. The most regressive of these views accuse anxious students of malingering, using a poorly defined psychiatric complaint to get out of the hard work universities are supposed to demand to fulfil their role as guardians of a 'capitalist meritocracy'.[15] This conservative critique dovetails with popular narratives that frame Gen Zers as a generation of entitled 'snowflakes' obsessed with 'victimhood', wielding a revanchist 'cancel culture' against anyone or anything that would threaten their comfort. Whereas in previous generations those suffering mental ill health found themselves stigmatised, today's youth seem far less reticent to express their diverse experience and needs. Indeed, this generation generates new complex forms of solidarity, mutual aid, and fellow feeling from these shared experiences. And often these forms of collective organising can appear to take the form of retreat, ambivalence, disinterest, disengagement, and withdrawal. Students' use of technology, in particular, teaches us an important lesson about the complexities of resistance and anxiety in our troubled age.

One of the most palpable manifestations of precarity-induced anxiety is compulsive social media use. Just as indebtedness, work and housing insecurity, and a generalised sense of precarity percolate through university life, there is a growing and uneasy immersion of students into the digital technologies of everyday life. Gen Zers are spending more and more time on digital platforms, with smartphone ownership currently ubiquitous among teenagers, and daily usage of social media reaching record levels in young adults of university age. Fisher used the term *depressive hedonia* to refer to the contradictory state in which young people attempt to cope with emotional stress, low self-esteem, loneliness, and exhaustion by constantly looking for pleasure as a form of distraction.[16]

Students' most preferred social media are image and video sharing platforms such as Instagram and TikTok, whose emphasis on the visual intensifies pressures on young users to meet bodily norms of beauty – with especially pernicious effects for women, queer and trans people, and people of colour, whose bodies are often spectacularised and at the same time erased.[17] Meanwhile, the explosive proliferation of mobile dating apps such as Tinder, Bumble, Her, and Hinge on university campuses adds to the veneration of the 'short-lived' experience, with mixed effects on students' social life, as distance and absorption come to coexist in their digital swipes.[18]

However, and importantly for our discussion, we know that these technologies have become not only instruments that trigger high levels of student anxiety but also, increasingly, *a respite from such anxiety*. The digital sphere is not merely a place of systemic cooptation, surveillance, and commodification of experiences, but a more ambivalent space in which, as Susannah Paasonen puts it, 'Frustration and pleasure, dependence and sense of possibility, distraction and attention, boredom, interest, and excitement enmesh, oscillate, enable, and depend on one another.'[19] Geert Lovink theorises the compulsive checking of smartphones as a way of daydreaming: 'Unaware of our brief absence, we enjoy the feeling of being remotely present. We remember what it's like to feel.'[20] Even outside of the digital realm, studies suggest that these technologies also nurse new types of collective belonging 'in real life', often reducing the feeling of loneliness among school leavers entering the university.[21]

However, there may be other possibilities contained in the 'speculative intimacies' enabled by digital dating apps. Studies of gay intimacy, for instance, emphasise the more transformative ways in which dating apps can inhabit sexual fields to pursue 'connection and community building, which is a very different notion of how to create a better and more secure tomorrow than ' "meeting the one"'.[22] Such connectivities are articulated in apps like Grindr (the world's most popular platform for men seeking men), which explicitly shift focus from the importance of lasting commitment and associated claims of a secure future to a more politicised present experience of sex as an act. Politicised experiences of intimacy may engender more radical forms of sociality, such as those that are 'forged through sharing stories of failure to achieve romantic intimacy or pain and melancholia'.[23] Arguably, then, the 'speculative intimacies' pursued by today's Gen Zers cannot be reduced to doom-scrolling escapism; their political potential lies in their puncturing of the false sense of security offered by the neoliberal notion of the 'romantic entrepreneur'.

Writer Roisin Kiberd captures poignantly the contradictory experience of navigating technologically fuelled anxiety in her recent digital auto-fiction novel *The Disconnect*, where she describes her university student life as 'a mockery of adulthood' with 'actions confused, muddled by a quiet desperation' and yet guided by an inescapable, alluring pull.[24] The uncertainty that is actively cultivated by the techno-worlds of social media undoubtedly benefits Silicon Valley because it is greatly monetisable. The student subject constituted under the effect of these contradictory forces is increasingly an anxious one, buffeted by financial demands on its future and immersed in a vertiginous, precarious present. Yet, a more complex picture of student anxiety begins to emerge when we account for the contradictory role of digital technologies in mediating the collective experiences of students. What threads such experiences within the university (and, more broadly, in Gen Zers' daily life) seems to be *a state of ambivalence*: a feeling of being at once enticed *and* concerned by the thrill of the never-ending scroll and the infinite swipe. The questions we want to ask, then, are as follows: what are the implications of such heightened 'attunement' with the present – even if this is a 'screen present' – for dwelling in the uncertainty of the 'here and now'? How exactly does this 'immersive distraction' feed into a sense of 'togetherness' within financialised universities? And what kind of community is being formed in the ebbs and flows of such ambivalence, where doubt, confusion, and pleasure inform the rites of passage into an uncertain shared reality?

The state of collective suspension and ambivalence that we have so far outlined is important because, at its core, it also reflects the increasingly cynical embrace of a more anxious subjectivity. Often, the mainstream picture painted of Gen Zers is one of a passive disillusionment and withdrawal, manifested in a distrustful stance towards liberal democracy (measured, for instance, by low electoral participation in countries such as the USA, where less than 30% voted in the 2018 elections). When not accused of undermining free speech by 'no-platforming' transphobic or racist speakers, Gen Z students are cast as suspicious and dystopian, even 'misanthropic' – cynical doom-scrollers who have become entirely detached from mainstream political reality.[25] Yet by contrast, we suggest that student cynicism can be both more strategic and collective than such views allow; it can be mobilised and directed towards a more tactical embrace of their ambivalent position in the neoliberal university. Elsewhere, we have looked for such attempts to challenge finance on its own turf through the prism of counter-speculation and revenge.[26] Here, we want instead to examine vernacular sociocultural forms that weaponise ambivalent cynicism and confused collective immersion to articulate a politics of sabotage.

Sabotage, resistance, rebellion

The forgoing discussion of young people's ambivalent engagement with digital technology should inspire in us a curiosity for the way resistance, rebellion, and refusal take on confusing and unexpected forms in this moment. We are familiar with the repertoire of student action that includes coordinated acts of protest and an explicit rhetoric of rebellion. However, in an anxious age, we may need to look elsewhere for signs of refusal and resistance. Though far less dramatic, the way students navigate anxious spaces in and around universities can be seen as challenging the universalising narratives of passive acquiescence in the face of neoliberalism's failed promises and foreclosed possibilities. From the Zoom seminar to the online student information service environment, universities are also sites of *anxious solidarities*, formed around unseen and often 'unseeable' struggles that cannot be answered by either the cloak of individual psychology or the discourse of 'anti-politics'. They often unfold in the dark corners of 'speculative technologies' – in Instagram posts and Facebook comment feeds, where students' anxiety reverberates but at the same time also blends with irony, playfulness, and routine expressions of mutual care. Their fuzzy navigations of such technologies create bonds within ephemeral digital spaces, through rituals that are not necessarily a symptom of anxiety but perhaps a way of countering it as a pathologised individual condition.

We have opted to think this turn through the language of sabotage to call up the long history of workers' resistance to exploitation that, from the perspectives of outsiders, can appear counter-productive, self-destructive, ill-considered, or nihilistic. Marx and Engels, for example, saw workers' sabotage as a counter-productive mode of resistance to domination, but one that might also signal the conditions for a potential solidarity from which more elaborate and successful forms of collective resistance might grow.[27] Importantly, as Eric Hobsbawm elucidates, sabotage and other isolated or reactive forms of resistance might be early signs of the revolutionary potential of a seemingly apolitical class hidden in plain sight.[28] Whereas the militancy of skilled craftsmen was widely celebrated by socialists of the nineteenth century, Marx and Engels looked to the seemingly apolitical, apathetic, and uneducated mass industrial worker as the gravedigger produced by industrial capitalism and destined to destroy it.

Setting aside debates on Marx and Engel's historical determinism, we propose taking seriously their encouragement to look to the *actually existing* forms of rebellion, which might at first seem counter-productive, as indicators of a wider trend or a movement yet to come. Specifically, we follow their lead in trying to understand how the recomposition of capitalist exploitation gives rise to new constituencies and new subjects, and how those constituencies and subjects come to know themselves and their power through forms of resistance and rebellion that might, at first, seem insignificant or counter-productive. Students can indeed appear to be sabotaging their education, their lives, and their careers by the forms of ambivalence, withdrawal, and disengagement which, at one extreme, come to express themselves in the language of anxiety. But perhaps this is how a fully financialised generation, who have no memory of a time before and no vision of a time after, rebel against a system and an institution that makes their own subjectivity part of the cycle of capitalist accumulation.[29] *They themselves* are the machine into which they might throw the proverbial *sabot*, and in sabotaging or putting at risk their own productive apparatus, they take their small revenge. As with saboteurs of the past, they might, in the hiatus when the machine stops, discover who else shares their experience and develop new modes of solidarity.

And yet sabotage is no easily defined thing, in part because the meaning of the word is always political. While workers have, in the past, resisted domination through acts of sabotage, the term has also been used to describe a tactic employed by capitalist actors to undermine their rivals, or by warring states to diminish the other's industrial or war-making capacity.[30] Sabotage, in terms of the intentional disruption of a productive process, can describe a wide variety of activities. In the eighteenth and nineteenth centuries, the bourgeois press was keen to frame both working-class saboteurs and foreign agents as dangerous and unscrupulous villains, an impression compounded by war propaganda in the twentieth century.[31] As a result, notions of sabotage and the saboteur are freighted with infamy. Working-class organisers have, at various points, sought to turn the discursive tables, accusing bosses, corporations, or the ruling class as a whole of sabotaging their livelihoods, organisations, and campaigns.

What this short history of the term's ambiguity reveals is that it is possible to see sabotage not as a startling exception to capitalist development, but as an *integral part* of it.[32] We suggest this in three parallel ways. First, capitalism has long maintained its dynamic equilibrium by sabotaging itself, especially through the mechanisms of the financial sector. Second, capitalist dynamism and the concomitant drive to lower costs sabotages the lifeworld of workers. Third, capitalism's constant pattern of self-sabotage persistently places workers in new geographic or communal constellations, undermining established forms of collective action or rendering them obsolete. This, in turn, leads to the renewal of worker sabotage as a typically individuated and uncoordinated means to resist domination. For centuries, capitalism's advocates and its critics have marvelled at its capacity to rapidly reinvent itself as rival capitalist actors compete to gain market share. The American institutional economist Thorstein Veblen suggested that this process was a kind of integral sabotage, especially when it led to irrational and often deeply inhumane impacts, as with the shuttering of whole industries and the loss of investment, or the laying-off of thousands of workers and the economic denudation of whole regions in favour of the hyper-exploitation of other populations or ecologies.[33]

Anastasia Nesvetailova and Ronen Palan have revisited Veblen's observations in connection with the financial sector, arguing that 'financial innovation' can be understood as an ongoing attempt to sabotage pre-existing financial norms, protocols, and regulations in order to take advantage of loopholes that might allow investors to 'beat the market' (of which they are, of course, a part).[34] To this we can add the way the financial sector actively seeks to sabotage government efforts to effectively regulate, tax, or constrain its activities. While Polanyi does not use the term 'sabotage' to describe the way 'the market' undermines the institutions of society and politics, the term would well describe the process by which, in an uncoordinated fashion, the financial sector drives the kinds of deregulation and market-oriented reform characteristic of neoliberalism and financialisation.[35] We might even see the shift from the mass public university to the financialised and neoliberal university as an example of sabotage; we are, on both sides of the North Atlantic, seeing a highly paid managerial class actively seek to sabotage what remains of the public university system built in the postwar period, with its now anachronistic beliefs in equality of access, affordability, a complement of permanent, non-precarious teaching staff, and its commitment to education in the public interest.[36]

If, then, sabotage can be seen as an integral element of capitalism's reproductive cycles, we must also account for the way in which capitalism's generative self-sabotage also undermines workers' lives and their capacity to struggle and form bonds of solidarity, especially within traditional trade union communities. Closer to the topic of this chapter, we might observe this kind of social sabotage at play in the changing lives of faculty and students in the anxious neoliberal university. As we have seen, these changes have been built on the rapid escalation of student debt and the increasing precariousness of faculty, but they have also fundamentally undermined, or sabotaged, the traditional forms of solidarity by which staff and students resisted their conditions.[37] Faculty trade unions, now starkly divided between permanent and temporary or precarious staff (and often isolated from the rest of the labour movement), have largely been unsuccessful at resisting these shifts. Meanwhile, despite a great deal of heat and some light at times, the mass action of students has had little influence on policy in the last decades.[38] Older modes of subjecthood and solidarity that centred on 'the student' as a social subject have been sabotaged by the imperative to become risk-taking entrepreneurs of the self, in constant competition with one another.

When capitalism sabotages society and the capacity of workers and communities to resist, we might anticipate that rebellion increasingly takes the form of counter-sabotage. Marx and Engels disagreed with the vengeful politics of the Blanquists and the 'propaganda of the deed' promoted by anarchists, which saw sabotage as a means to catalyse worker solidarity and to take direct action against the literal and metaphorical gears of oppression.[39] For the authors of the *Communist Manifesto*, the urge to sabotage was understandable, but unstrategic; it might be a satisfying form of vindication, but it could not build a structured movement for change. Isolated acts of sabotage were not nearly enough to catalyse a revolution and often seemed to undermine the saboteur's own wellbeing; the shutdown of a factory for repairs meant no wages, with potentially lethal consequences. Nonetheless, Marx and Engels recognised that the appearance of sabotage often indicated hotspots of class conflict amid capitalism's rapid changes, and anticipated a form of agency that might, one day, take a more promising form.

Self-sabotage within, against, and beyond the university

If students are workers, then theirs is the kind of 'work of the self' anticipated by Foucault in his lectures on neoliberalism, and more fully developed by Italian post-Autonomist thinkers.[40] Central to this tradition is the concept of 'cognitive capitalism', which not only recasts the student as a worker, but also suggests that the university has moved from the margins to the very centre of economy and society.[41] This body of work, much of which orbited the Edu-Factory Collective, sought to address the changing political situation of 'the student' in a moment of class decomposition and recomposition.[42]

Whether or not we accept the argument that students are workers in a new paradigm of cognitive capitalism, a broad range of scholars agree that the relationship between universities and work is changing and the two institutions are in some ways converging.[43] The birth of the now-paradigmatic globalised tech sector in California's elite universities bestowed it, and the 'no-collar' order of work it inspired, with corporate 'campuses', conspicuously casual workspaces and managerial cultures, even dorm-style accommodation, all aimed at exciting workers' creative and collaborative abilities. While these conditions may only exist in delectable form for the most privileged of workers, management consultants throughout the 1990s and 2000s advised even the most conservative clients that a new generation of workers wanted more flexible, casual, and 'creative' spaces reminiscent of universities, and that providing this could see impressive improvements in productivity.[44]

Meanwhile, university became more work-like. For decades, critical education scholars had been noting the 'hidden curriculum' of schooling to train obedient, diligent workers habituated to performing work, getting evaluated, and obeying the rigid extrinsic rhythms of the institution, punctuated by bells.[45] However, as universities came under neoliberal restructuring and began increasingly to compete for enrolment and ratings, they also accelerated efforts to impress potential students, their parents, and industry that they could instill 'job-ready' skills that would improve graduates' job market prospects. In many ways, today's 'hidden curriculum' is actually the debt students are increasingly forced to incur, instilling the hard lesson that one enters the formal workforce desperate for work and, therefore, presumably less likely to risk workplace organising or resistance for fear of losing one's means of debt servicing.[46]

From a strict political-economic perspective, it is hard to acknowledge students as workers. They may indeed 'work', often under coercive and even exploitative conditions, but they are not remunerated, and (allegedly) they 'work' for their own benefit, rather than that of others. But from a broader Marxist perspective, they are certainly a member of the class we used to call the proletariat – they are non-owning producers – though for various historical reasons, they have not yet been permitted to sell their labour time for wages (although, of course, many do, while also studying).[47] While students may not earn wages for their school work, their work at school might be seen as an effort to improve their capacity for future wage earnings. The proposal that students are workers would likely offend many waged workers, who might see students as privileged youth, and also many serious students, who earnestly prize the acquisition of knowledge for its own sake. But there is perhaps enough evidence to allow us to posit the *political* claim that we can fruitfully imagine students as workers, and to note that the insistence we see students as *not* workers is also a political claim, even if it is a banal one.

If, then, students are workers, how might we see their *refusal to work* as a form of rebellion? Our conjecture here is that refusal to work in the edu-factory is a refusal to work on improving oneself, a form of political self-sabotage that is also a form of economic sabotage aimed at the machine of capitalist value extraction. This perspective makes better sense of the often-bemoaned fact that anxious students, in refusing to engage or compete, seem to 'only be hurting themselves'. Self-sabotage can be situated within a longer history of worker self-actualisation and rebellion that occurs in the wake of capitalist sabotage and under conditions where workers are recomposed into new constellations and must, anew, rediscover the grounds for solidarity and the tools of rebellion. In this interregnum, sabotage is, to borrow Martin Luther King's formulation regarding riots, a language of the unheard.

Mass refusal has long been a strategic horizon of working-class movements, based on the understanding that the capitalist system of domination, because it depends on labour power, is particularly vulnerable to the interruption of supply. The general strike may be the highest articulation of this strategy and gave inspiration to many revolutionaries who surmised that in the mass refusal of work, workers would not only manifest their power in the streets but also come to recognise one another and their collective power, leading to a revolutionary moment. In a favourable reading, the sabotage of industrial machinery aimed towards the same ends; even though workers who idled while machines were repaired might lose a precious day's pay, they would have time and space to recognise how vulnerable were their oppressors and exploiters, and how powerful they were when they dedicated their energies to ends other than generating commodities for their boss to sell.

If, then, anxious students are workers struggling to know themselves and recognise their commonality and collectivity, it is possible they are not aware of this ambition. But we should not be too quick to imagine that student-workers are completely unaware of their power, even if they do not necessarily frame it in such stark or Marxist-inspired terms. Recent waves of student activism have increasingly made access to mental health services, and accommodations for students with disabilities, a key demand.[48] Prior to the COVID-19 pandemic, a number of high-profile student occupations and protests in the USA, UK, and Canada all named these as key demands, often linked to broader issues of institutional racism.[49] Meanwhile, almost every university campus we could investigate has some form of peer-support group for suffering students, sometimes formalised and associated with the university, sometimes autonomously coordinated. And we have observed an effervescence of online spaces dedicated to connecting suffering students to offer moral support, advice, and companionship.[50] A great deal of organising is occurring within, against, and beyond financialised universities by afflicted students.

Conclusion

The problem with anxiety is that while it might indeed prompt a refusal of work, it can license a refusal of the work of rebellion and resistance too. On this view, the decline of traditional student militancy may be a sign of students being *too* anxious to rebel. But, as we have argued in this chapter, as class and capitalism are recomposed, the nature of protest is shifting too. After all, this was also the generation that grew up in the shadow of the largest coordinated street demonstrations in world history, against the US-led invasion of Iraq in 2003, utterly failing to achieve any measurable lasting result, and who were in their early adolescence when the Occupy movement flared.

Berardi has argued that for a generation traumatised by the near complete domination of their subjecthood, the prospects of mass revolt are largely foreclosed. A major influence on Fisher, Berardi suggested that, in the years to come, therapy and radical politics would in a sense merge or at least become largely indistinguishable.[51] At first blush, the enthusiasm for today's anxious students to come together and advocate for access to therapy and 'support', and to provide such support to one another, seems to be evidence in favour of Berardi's prediction. On closer inspection, however, this therapeutic turn also manifests a politics of inchoate rebellion and refusal of work that may go beyond the tragic and melancholic modes.

Here, it seems germane to draw on insights generated by the field of critical disability studies, as well as the debates that have occurred in the mad pride and anti-psychiatric movements since the 1960s. Both fields see 'ability' and 'mental health' as discursive and material constructs of capitalist exploitation, entangled with the power structures that form around gender, race, class, and other vectors of oppression.[52] Turning towards such ideas would beg several further questions. Are 'anxious students' disabled subjects? If so, how might they make common cause with other workers and people whose bodies and minds are wounded, oppressed, or excluded by capitalist systems of domination? Towards what common, revolutionary horizon might such alliances travel? How might such a convergence overcome the significant difference in power between students who feel they cannot go to class or complete an assignment, and people who simply are too sick to find an easy place in movements built around the ideal of the 'able-bodied' radical?

Notes

1 Mark Fisher, *Ghosts of My Life: Writings on Depression, Hauntology and Lost Futures* (Winchester: Zero, 2014).

2 See Richard Scheffler, 'Anxiety Disorder on College Campuses: The New Epidemic', Berkeley Institute for Young Americans, April 2019; Henry Xiao, Dever Carney, Soo Jeong Youn, Rebecca Janis, Louis Castonguay, Jeffrey Hayes, and Benjamin Locke, 'Are We in Crisis? National Mental Health and Treatment Trends in College Counseling Centers', *Psychological Services* 14, no. 4 (2017): 407–15; Payton Jones, So Yeon Park, and G. Tyler Lefevor, 'Contemporary College Student Anxiety: The Role of Academic Distress, Financial Stress,

and Support', *Journal of College Counseling* 21, no. 3 (2018): 252–64; Elizabeth Sweet, ' "Like You Failed at Life": Debt, Health and Neoliberal Subjectivity', *Social Science & Medicine* 212 (2018): 86–93.

3 For a summary and critique of these positions, see Max Haiven and Aris Komporozos-Athanasiou, 'An Anxiety Epidemic in the Financialized University: Critical Questions and Unexpected Resistance', *Cultural Politics* 18, no. 2 (2022): 173–93.

4 Evan Calder Williams, 'Manual Override', *The New Inquiry*, March 21, 2016, https://thenewinquiry.com/manual-override/ (accessed September 8, 2022).

5 See Anastasia Nesvetailova and Ronen Palan, 'Sabotage in the Financial System: Lessons from Veblen', *Business Horizons* 56, no. 6 (2013): 723–32.

6 Gavin Mueller, *Breaking Things at Work: The Luddites Are Right About Why You Hate Your Job* (London: Verso, 2021).

7 See note 2 above.

8 Haiven and Komporozos-Athanasiou, 'An Anxiety Epidemic'.

9 Caitlin Zaloom, *Indebted: How Families Make College Work at Any Cost* (Princeton, NJ: Princeton University Press, 2019).

10 The Debt Collective, *Can't Pay, Won't Pay: The Case for Economic Disobedience and Debt Abolition* (Chicago, IL: Haymarket, 2020).

11 Keir Milburn, 'Generation Left after Corbynism: Assets, Age, and the Battle for the Future', *South Atlantic Quarterly* 120, no. 4 (2021): 892–902.

12 The Debt Collective, *Can't Pay, Won't Pay*.

13 See Geert Lovink, *Sad by Design: On Platform Nihilism* (London: Pluto, 2019).

14 See note 2 above.

15 Malcolm Harris, *Kids These Days: Human Capital and the Making of Millennials* (New York: Little, Brown & Co., 2017).

16 Mark Fisher, *Capitalist Realism: Is There No Alternative?* (London: Zero, 2009), 21–22.

17 Sarah Banet-Weiser, *Empowered: Popular Feminism and Popular Misogyny* (Durham, NC: Duke University Press, 2018).

18 Komporozos-Athanasiou, *Speculative Communities*.

19 Susanna Paasonen, *Dependent, Distracted, Bored: Affective Formations in Networked Media* (Cambridge, MA: The MIT Press, 2021), 4.

20 Lovink, *Sad by Design*, 38.

21 Lisa Thomas, Elizabeth Orme, and Finola Kerrigan, 'Student Loneliness: The Role of Social Media Through Life Transitions', *Computers & Education* 146 (2020): 103754.

22 Laurie Essig, *Love, Inc.: Dating Apps, the Big White Wedding, and Chasing the Happily Neverafter* (Berkeley, CA: University of California Press, 2019), 70.
23 Rohit Dasgupta and Debanuj Dasgupta, 'Intimate Subjects and Virtual Spaces: Rethinking Sexuality as a Category for Intimate Ethnographies', *Sexualities* 21, vols 5–6 (2018): 932–50, at 945.
24 Roisin Kiberd, *The Disconnect: A Personal Journey Through the Internet* (London: Profile Books, 2021), 206.
25 Lovink, *Sad by Design*.
26 Aris Komporozos-Athanasiou, *Speculative Communities: Living with Uncertainty in a Financialized World* (Chicago, IL: University of Chicago Press, 2021); Max Haiven, *Revenge Capitalism: The Ghosts of Empire, the Demons of Capital, and the Settling of Unpayable Debts* (London: Pluto Press, 2020).
27 Darin Barney, 'Sabotage', *Krisis: Journal for Contemporary Philosophy* 2 (2018), https://archive.krisis.eu/sabotage/ (accessed September 8, 2022).
28 Eric Hobsbawm, 'The Machine Breakers', *Past & Present* 1, no. 1 (1952): 57–70.
29 Gigi Roggero, *The Production of Living Knowledge: The Crisis of the University and the Transformation of Labor in Europe and North America*, trans. Enda Brophy (Philadelphia, PA: Temple University Press, 2011).
30 Maureen Ambrose, Mark Seabright, and Marshall Schminke, 'Sabotage in the Workplace: The Role of Organizational Injustice', *Organizational Behavior and Human Decision Processes* 89, no. 1 (2002): 947–65.
31 Elizabeth Gurley Flynn, *Sabotage: The Conscious Withdrawal of the Workers' Industrial Efficiency* (Chicago, IL: IWW Publishing Bureau, 1917).
32 Shimshon Bichler and Jonathan Nitzan, 'Growing through Sabotage: Energizing Hierarchical Power', *Working Papers on Capital as Power* 02 (2017): 1–59.
33 Nesvetailova and Palan, 'Sabotage in the Financial System'.
34 *Ibid.*
35 Karl Polanyi, *The Great Transformation: The Political and Economic Origins of Our Time* (Boston, MA: Beacon, 2001).
36 Randy Martin, *Under New Management: Universities, Administrative Labor, and the Professional Turn* (Philadelphia, PA: Temple University Press, 2011).
37 Peter Fleming, *Dark Academia: How Universities Die* (London: Pluto, 2021).

38 Rose Cole and Walter Heinecke, 'Higher Education after Neoliberalism: Student Activism as a Guiding Light', *Policy Futures in Education* 18, no. 1 (2020): 90–116.
39 Williams, 'Manual Override'; Barney, 'Sabotage'.
40 Daniel Zamora and Michael C. Behrent, eds, *Foucault and Neoliberalism* (Cambridge: Polity, 2015); Michael Hardt and Antonio Negri, *Empire* (Cambridge MA: Harvard University Press, 2001); Franco 'Bifo' Berardi, *The Soul at Work: From Alienation to Autonomy*, trans. Giuseppina Mecchia and Francesca Cadel (Los Angeles, CA: Semiotext(e), 2009).
41 See *Wages for Students*, Trilingual Edition (Brooklyn: Common Notions, 2016); Roggero, *The Production of Living Knowledge*.
42 The Edu-Factory Collective, ed., *Toward a Global Autonomous University* (New York: Autonomedia, 2009).
43 Andrew McGettigan, *The Great University Gamble: Money, Markets and the Future of Higher Education* (London: Pluto, 2013); Marc Bousquet, *How the University Works: Higher Education and the Low-Wage Nation* (New York: New York University Press, 2008).
44 Andrew Ross, *No-Collar: The Humane Workplace and Its Hidden Costs* (Philadelphia, PA: Temple University Press, 2004).
45 Henry A. Giroux, *Theory and Resistance in Education: Towards a Pedagogy for the Opposition, Second Edition* (Westport, CT: Praeger, 2001).
46 Jason Thomas Wozniak, 'The Miseducation of the Indebted Student: An Educational Argument for Full Student Debt Abolition', *Academe*, April 1, 2021, www.aaup.org/article/miseducation-indebted-student?fbclid=IwAR2ZAocx-7cxi2-zIVvUwXzrZFy6xlcXNWz0mW708mwVnHTbAIQLdrtWnEI#.YGXZhGgpDjB (accessed September 8, 2022).
47 George Caffentzis, *In Letters of Blood and Fire: Work, Machines, and the Crisis of Capitalism* (Brooklyn, NY: Common Notions, 2013).
48 Akemi Nishida, 'Neoliberal Academia and a Critique from Disability Studies', in *Occupying Disability: Critical Approaches to Community, Justice, and Decolonizing Disability*, ed. Pamela Block, Devva Kasnitz, Akemi Nishida, and Nick Pollard (Dordrecht: Springer, 2016), 145–57; Annemarie Vaccaro and Jasmine A. Mena, 'It's Not Burnout, It's More: Queer College Activists of Color and Mental Health', *Journal of Gay & Lesbian Mental Health* 15, no. 4 (2011): 339–67.
49 Meagan Casalino, 'Students Protest Outside U of O President's Office for Better Mental Health Services', *The Fulcrum*, February 12, 2020, https://thefulcrum.ca/news/students-protest-outside-u-of-o-presidents-office-for-better-mental-health-services/(accessedSeptember

8, 2022); Samira Shackle, 'The Way Universities are Run is Making Us Ill: Inside the Student Mental Health Crisis', *The Guardian*, September 27, 2019, www.theguardian.com/society/2019/sep/27/anxiety-mental-breakdowns-depression-uk-students (accessed September 8, 2022); Sally Weale, 'Students Occupy Goldsmiths in Protest at Institutional Racism', *The Guardian*, March 20, 2019, www.theguardian.com/education/2019/mar/20/students-occupy-goldsmiths-in-protest-at-institutional-racism (accessed September 8, 2022).

50 Haiven and Komporozos-Athanasiou, 'An Anxiety Epidemic'.

51 Franco 'Bifo' Berardi, *The Uprising: On Poetry and Finance* (Los Angeles, CA: Semiotext(e), 2012).

52 See Nishida, 'Neoliberal Academia and a Critique from Disability Studies'; Mike Condra, Mira Dineen, Helen Gills, Anita Jack-Davies, and Eleanor Condra, 'Academic Accommodations for Postsecondary Students with Mental Health Disabilities in Ontario, Canada: A Review of the Literature and Reflections on Emerging Issues', *Journal of Postsecondary Education and Disability* 28, no. 3 (2015): 277–91; Margaret Price, *Mad at School: Rhetorics of Mental Disability and Academic Life* (Ann Arbor: University of Michigan Press, 2011); Tala Khanmalek and heidi andrea restrepo rhodes, 'A Decolonial Feminist Epistemology of the Bed: A Compendium Incomplete of Sick and Disabled Queer Brown Femme Bodies of Knowledge', *Frontiers: A Journal of Women Studies* 41, no. 1 (2020): 35–58.

Conclusion: Click here to end capitalism

Amin Samman

The title of this chapter is a ruse; there will be no big reveal, no five easy steps – all you will find is a string of observations about the libidinal economies of contemporary capitalism. The first of these is that there remains a lot of money to be made. In 2022, the so-called 'greatest party that never happened' continues to roll on. Those around FuckJerry were not the only ones who got rich fanning the flames of Fyre Festival. Billy McFarland's partner and hip-hop mogul Ja Rule was another winner, his reputation boosted no end by the ultimate hustle, and after him came a string of bootleggers on eBay selling counterfeit Fyre Festival merchandise. Even the US government got a piece of the action when in August 2020 – more than three years after the island debacle – it began to auction off 'genuine' merchandise seized from McFarland to compensate the eighty or so elite investors who lost somewhere in the region of $26 million from the failed festival.[1] By auctioning off the merchandise, the US government helped reignite the brand, which in turn prompted Ja Rule to start selling Fyre Festival art as NFTs in March 2021.[2] The story was widely covered, generating a slew of scandalising headlines that once again lured many back to the scene of the crime, seemingly none the wiser.

This says something about the depth of our psychological investment in today's new economy. As potent cultures of desire take shape around the intersection of digital technology and finance, this very site is beginning to take on the qualities of a fantasy, structuring ever more lives around recursive forms of emotional capture and release, while at the same time fuelling a lucrative game of anticipating and capitalising on such cycles. That is why streaming platforms are making so many new shows about 'bad entrepreneurs', from WeWork founders Adam and Rebekah Neumann in Apple TV's *WeCrashed*, to Theranos CEO Elizabeth Holmes in Hulu's *The Dropout*, to wannabe socialite Anna Delvey in the Netflix series *Inventing Anna*.[3] Renegade scammers and gullible audiences are fast becoming hallmarks of the era. We want to be fooled, robbed, swindled – either that or we want to watch it happen to somebody else, which usually amounts to the same thing. The result is a kind of runaway abstraction that applies to money and technology, for sure, but perhaps also to desire itself. Maybe this is the meaning of 'clickbait capitalism' – a libidinal *dis*-economy premised on the ruinous escalation of both economy and desire.[4] What if the libidinal economies of digital and financial capitalism run best when detached from definite aims, ends, objects?

These questions lead us back to the fundamental wager of libidinal economy and its status within contemporary thought. Despite a long history of mutual implication, economics has yet to properly come to terms with the role of desire within everyday life, let alone the role of libidinal dynamics in the social reproduction of capitalism. The present volume has sought to address these questions by drawing on the minor tradition of libidinal political economy and the fullest possible range of perspectives associated with it. That has meant mobilising not only different conceptions of desire and the unconscious, but also different conceptions of economy, money, and capital. If Marx and Freud, then why not Veblen and Bataille, Keynes and Baudrillard, Minsky and Žižek? The book can therefore be understood as an exercise in theoretical pluralism, and there should be no surprise if we come away from it with a certain degree of ambiguity surrounding the psychological coordinates of capitalism. Death, sex, aggression, enjoyment, despair, hope, revenge – the important thing is to put such matters on the table as key questions for economic thought, not to rank them in order of significance or claim for any one the status of ultimate anchor. Similarly, dating apps, social media, cryptocurrencies, NFTs, and meme stocks are not the lynchpins of new digital-financial economies; they are simply the latest institutions to stage, channel, or reconfigure the psychic energies of political and economic life. In other words, libidinal economy – like capitalism – is an evolutionary concept.[5] It is meant to track a moving target, and there is

just no telling how the economies of desire detailed in this volume
will unfold in the decades ahead.

This raises a further set of questions about the politics of
libidinal-economic thinking. Libidinal economy has always
aimed at something beyond scientific knowledge. The initial
Freudian version was geared towards therapeutic ends for individual patients (engaging the unconscious, bringing up repressed
thoughts, working through trauma, and so on). Later versions
associated with critical theory and the French New Left wanted
revolutionary social change – the emancipation of desire, the liberation of desiring-production, the free flow of intensities across
the social body. In either case, the desire of libidinal economy
itself is totalising, offering not just a theory of the subject but also
an account of the social, even a philosophy of history. But what
happens when there is no longer any grand theory to work towards
and no concrete horizon for a corresponding politics of desire?
What then could possibly be the appeal of libidinal economy?

At least two answers present themselves. The first is that all this
returns in the form of new agendas and programmes, that we repeat
the drive to establish a school of thought, a party, or a movement
in a bid to secure theoretical and practical scaffolds for collective
desire. This is the essence of the Freudian-Marxist tradition and
many today, including some of the authors in this volume, engage
libidinal economy on such terms. To them, theory entails a radical
politics of desire that looks to upset the psychosocial reproduction of capitalism at whatever level possible. In some ways, this
is the ultimate fantasy. The second answer is that all this must
go, that libidinal economy must move with the times and soberly
reckon with the ever-more-elaborate mechanisms of psychological
entrapment at work in contemporary social life, even if that means
giving up on ambitions that were central to its establishment as a
mode or style of contemporary thought. This gives us an endless
map charting out new economies of desire, but, of course, all the
tracking and tracing has an allure of its own. There is a pleasure
to be found in dissecting the psychic life of capitalism. And so, in
different ways, both answers raise the same fundamental question
about the desire called libidinal economy: does it lead anywhere, or
is it all just a cheap thrill?

Notes

1 Madison Darbyshire, 'The Fyre Festival Fire Sale', *The Financial Times*, August 4, 2020, www.ft.com/content/a5cf643d-058a-4450-ac81-ba4b8bd34b9c (accessed September 8, 2022).
2 Kabir Jhala, 'Rapper Ja Rule Launches NFT Platform – and is Selling a Painting from Infamous Fyre Festival On It', *The Art Newspaper*, March 17, 2021, www.theartnewspaper.com/2021/03/16/rapper-ja-rule-launches-nft-platformand-is-selling-a-painting-from-infamous-fyre-festival-on-it (accessed September 8, 2022). Tom McCarthy, 'Ja Rule Sells $122,000 Fyre Festival NFT Artwork – With Real Painting Thrown In', *The Guardian*, March 25, 2021, www.theguardian.com/artanddesign/2021/mar/25/ja-rule-nft-fyre-festival-artwork (accessed September 8, 2022).
3 All of these shows were released within months of one another in early 2022. See Naomi Fry, 'The Comforts of "WeCrashed" and the Modern Grifter Series', *The New Yorker*, March 28, 2022, www.newyorker.com/magazine/2022/04/04/the-comforts-of-wecrashed-and-the-modern-grifter-series (accessed September 8, 2022).
4 Bernard Stiegler coined the latter term, libidinal dis-economy, in order to describe the fate of desire under industrial capitalism, but perhaps the point is that this now applies to economic operations too. See Bernard Stiegler, 'Pharmacology of Desire: Drive-Based Capitalism and Libidinal Dis-Economy', *New Formations* 72, Autumn (2011): 150–61.
5 'Capitalism is not a single or static concept. It is an evolutionary concept'. John Commons, *Institutional Economics: Its Place in Political Economy, Volume 2* (New Brunswick, NJ: Transaction Publishers, 1934), 766.

Index

EU authorised representative for GPSR:
Easy Access System Europe, Mustamäe tee 50,
10621 Tallinn, Estonia
gpsr.requests@easproject.com